Treasure
and Intrigue

Treasure
and Intrigue

The Legacy of
Captain Kidd

Graham Harris

A HOUNSLOW BOOK
A MEMBER OF THE DUNDURN GROUP
TORONTO · OXFORD

Publisher: Anthony Hawke
Copy-Editor: Jennifer Bergeron
Design: Jennifer Scott
Printer: University of Toronto Press

National Library of Canada Cataloguing in Publication Data

Harris, Graham, 1937-
   Treasure and intrigue : the legacy of Captain Kidd / Graham Harris.

Includes bibliographical references and index.
ISBN 1-55002-409-4

1. Kidd, William, d. 1701. 2. Pirates--Great Britain--Biography.
3. Pirates--Indian Ocean--History--17th century. I. Title.

G537.K5H37 2002   364.16'4   C2002-902284-3

1   2   3   4   5   06   05   04   03   02

Canadä

THE CANADA COUNCIL | LE CONSEIL DES ARTS
FOR THE ARTS | DU CANADA
SINCE 1957 | DEPUIS 1957

ONTARIO ARTS COUNCIL
CONSEIL DES ARTS DE L'ONTARIO

We acknowledge the support of the **Canada Council for the Arts** and the **Ontario Arts Council** for our publishing program. We also acknowledge the financial support of the **Government of Canada** through the **Book Publishing Industry Development Program** and **The Association for the Export of Canadian Books**, and the **Government of Ontario** through the **Ontario Book Publishers Tax Credit** program.

Care has been taken to trace the ownership of copyright material used in this book. The author and the publisher welcome any information enabling them to rectify any references or credit in subsequent editions.

J. Kirk Howard, President

Printed and bound in Canada.⊛
Printed on recycled paper.
www.dundurn.com

Dundurn Press
8 Market Street
Suite 200
Toronto, Ontario, Canada
M5E 1M6

Dundurn Press
73 Lime Walk
Headington, Oxford,
England
OX3 7AD

Dundurn Press
2250 Military Road
Tonawanda NY
U.S.A. 14150

Captain William Kidd.
Based upon a woodcut made at his trial.

Contents

Acknowledgements

Many individuals have contributed in the preparation of this book by pursuing lines of enquiry and collecting research data. Several institutions have also given their unstinting assistance. Without their support this book would be less comprehensive, and thereby the poorer. The author is equally indebted to the various biographers who have written about Captain Kidd in the past.

Special mention must be made to George Edmunds of Weymouth, England, who gave his permission to quote passages from his own book on Kidd, thereby making available in this volume the benefit of his many years of research. Equally valuable was the energetic pursuit of information by Dennis Gummer of Sheffield, England, who thrust his attention upon numerous librarians at the author's behest.

Heartfelt thanks are extended to my wife Sue, who with her newly acquired computer skills, took on the burden of transcribing rough drafts into readable form.

Others that the author would like to specially thank for their support and assistance are:

John Byrne, London, England
Henk Damhuis, Almere, Netherlands
Les MacPhie, Montreal, P.Q., Canada
Tim Partridge, Johannesburg, South Africa
Diane Plesner, Sutton Coldfield, England
Peter Smith, Kelowna, B.C., Canada
Kyle Wagner, Bedeque, P.E.I., Canada

Adrian Winchester, Imperial College, London, England
British Library, England
Public Records Office, Kew, England
Woburn Abbey, Bedfordshire, England

Foreword

This is a book about piracy, specifically piracy in the Indian Ocean as it relates to the exploits of Captain William Kidd. In the opinion of the author, Kidd was a pirate, a term which most dictionaries define as being a "robber of the high seas," and as a result of his piracy he was hanged. Many who have written about Kidd have portrayed him as a rather pathetic creature, trapped by circumstances and the cunning of powerful lords and politicians who manipulated his weaknesses for their own dubious ends. Some of this may be true, but weakness of character was certainly not one of Kidd's dominant traits. He may have been stupid, trusting, and overawed by his association with their lordships, but pathetic he surely was not by any stretch of the imagination. He stands out head and shoulders above many of a piratical persuasion that either preceded or followed him. His activities in the Indian Ocean between 1697 and 1699 have given us a legacy that has intrigued the general populace for many decades. This book attempts to dispel some of the mist which shrouds his legacy, as this is also a detective story, but unlike its fictional counterpart, it has no neat ending.

The popular image of a pirate of the seventeenth century, or possibly of any century, is of a villainous, swashbuckling rogue, unkempt, dissolute, without moral or scruple, and more often than not, rum-soaked and scurvy. But pirates were not always the bloodthirsty illiterate beasts often depicted. Amongst the pirate fraternity there were found, on occasion, men of a different mold, men of thorough breeding, education, and sheer ability, who contrasted vividly with the popular portrait. These men rose through the ranks, often to take command of the vessels in which they sailed, purely by the merits and skills they displayed to their shipmates. Some of them even held university degrees. Generally, however, the vast bulk of the crews aboard European pirate vessels were men who, for whatever reason, had resorted to the sea in order to gain a livelihood, and hopefully some profit from a "good voyage." The majority of the European pirates were God-fearing men, at least to a degree, and whether they remained so was very much left to fate.

It is the literate minority that sailed among the crews of pirate ships to whom we are deeply indebted for the written record handed down to us. William Dampier stands out head and shoulders above most, and he is deserving of a chapter to himself in this book, having known William Kidd.

Others who have written accounts of their experiences include Esquemeling, Ringrose, Cooke, Funnell, Wafer, Woodes Rogers, and Cowley, the last-named being one of the university graduates mentioned above. He held an M.A. from Cambridge. Even the most celebrated of English schools, Eton, can claim a connection with the pirate fraternity through Harry Simms, who boasted the alias "Gentleman Harry," and has been collectively described as pickpocket, thief, highwayman, and Old Etonian. Simms appears to have had a hankering for illegality and vice from an early age, and this predisposition put him in continual conflict with the law his entire life, which understandably was very short; he was hanged at the age of 31. Regrettably for us he forms no part of this story, having lived and died some years after Kidd was hanged. He would have been a colourful addition to any pirate vessel, as he is to any narrative on the subject.

One pirate, who was described as being of the gentlest disposition in the exercise of his profession, was a Frenchman named Misson, about whom Lord Byron wrote:

He was the mildest-manner'd man
That ever scuttled ship or cut a throat.

Misson was an idealist, he disavowed the darker side of piracy, and declared that his life and those of his men were to be principled.

Not only were they to be brave, but also just and innocent in the cause of liberty. He and his men sailed under a white flag, rather than the customary black or red ensign. They eschewed foul language, drunkenness, unnecessary slaughter, and they kept the Sabbath, although it is not recorded whether they strictly observed the Fourth Commandment. Like Kidd after him, Misson was attracted to Madagascar, where he established a utopia of his own called Libertatia and, it is rumoured, he was instrumental in developing the artificial language known as Esperanto, a hybrid mix of French, English, Dutch, and Portuguese, in order that he and his men, drawn from various nations, could more easily converse amongst themselves. The settlement of Libertatia was short-lived, as it was finally overrun by hostile natives.

At the opposite end of the spectrum were the coarsest and the vilest of pirates, those who wallowed in a frenzy of bloodletting, cruelty, torture, and rapine. It is these lowermost specimens of the piratical brethren that appear to have become fixed uppermost in the minds and imaginations of the public.

William Kidd and his crew cannot be categorized as falling into either of the extremes of the profession. They were definitely not saints, neither were they irredeemable sinners. As felons went at the time, they were just ordinary common-garden folk. They might be considered case-hardened by today's yardstick, but by seventeenth-century standards they were pretty average specimens of seaborne criminology.

Most of the books on piracy suffer from what may be described as a lack of corroborative detail, and this book is no exception. The authors of pirate books are dependent on the written record as given in personal accounts, or as documented in official archives. As a result, certain pirates have captured centre stage because there is more information about their colourful lives, their doings and/or misdoings. William Kidd is one of these, and the names Avery, Teach, Tew, Roberts, Low, and others come readily to mind, many as the result of the first pirate book ever written, which attempted to authenticate piratical biography. This book, titled *A General History of the Robberies and Murders of the Most Notorious Pyrates,* was first published in 1724. A great deal of debate has ensued in modern times regarding the authorship of this classic work. Ostensibly it has been credited to Captain Charles Johnson, a name which is generally accepted to have been a nom-de-plume. A chapter will be devoted to this enigmatic personality whose book has made such an indelible mark upon pirate biography, and who makes an important observation upon Kidd.

Another invaluable source for information on matters piratical is *The Pirates' Who's Who* by Philip Gosse, first published in 1924. Gosse, in his introduction to the book, bemoans the fact that every profession has its own "who's who," including peers, lawyers, the church, medical men, musicians, schoolmasters, stockbrokers, and saints, and argues why not pirates? Why not indeed, and Gosse's work is an essential reference for anyone interested in this subject, or at least in the lives of those pirates who lived and died centuries ago. Twentieth-century pirates, including those who held high position in business, politics, and the law, are naturally excluded!

It should be noted that prior to 1752, the British followed the Old Style dating system, New Year's Day being March 25. The period between January 1 and March 24, therefore, might be in 1700, whereas the rest of the year from March 25 to December 31 would be in 1701. That year would then extend to the following March 24. In the present text all dates have been converted to the current convention. This is mentioned since the reader may encounter Old Style dating in other references and source material.

Introduction

Pieces of the Puzzle

It's the rich wot gets the gravy,
But the poor wot gets the blame.
— Old Music Hall Song

There are ghosts in Wapping, down by the river. They have haunted the water's edge for centuries. On a winter's night their moans can be heard above the whistle of the wind, the slap of the waves, and the clash of stark upturned tree branches. On a summer's night, when misty vapours are drawn upwards from the sluggish Thames into the vapid air, and clouds scud fitfully across a wan moon, you may catch sight of gaunt visages staring from the ephemeral shadows. If you feel a sudden chill, being of a nervous disposition, you are excused, for this is Execution Dock. It was here that many men died, or to be more accurate, were executed by authority in accordance with the ritual decreed for meting out death to pirates: "To be taken from the place where you are, and to be carried to the place from whence you came, and from thence to the place of execution, and there to be hanged by the neck until you are dead. And the Lord have mercy on your soul."

It is a common belief that those who die violent and unshriven deaths are doomed to haunt the places where they died. Execution Dock is no exception. Yes, there are ghosts down by the river!

The most notorious of the pirates to meet his maker, dangling from the hangman's noose at Execution Dock, was Captain William Kidd. He was by no means the boldest or the bravest, and certainly not the most bloodthirsty of those villains who roved the high seas in

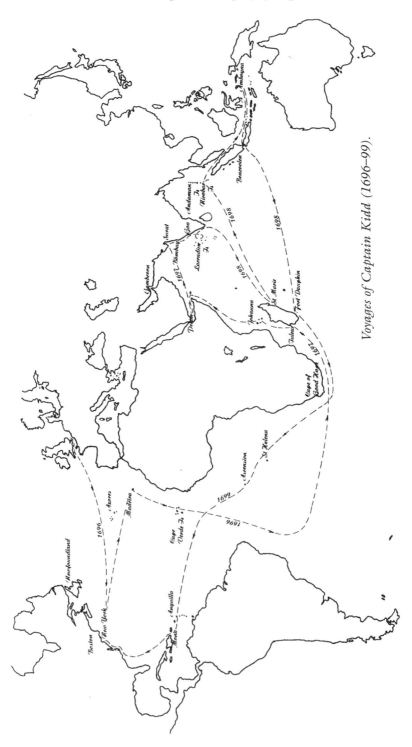

Voyages of Captain Kidd (1696–99).

search of booty. There were numerous others who could excel in these attributes. Strangely enough he garnered little wealth from his exploits in comparison to many of his peers. However, his name has become synonymous with piracy in what has been termed the "Golden Age of Piracy," simply because there exists a written record of his activities, incomplete though that record is. His unique place in the annals of piracy stem from this superficial fact. As a consequence, we know more about him than any other single pirate, or at least we think we do.

Captain Kidd is, unarguably, the best known and perhaps best loved of all the pirates. His deeds have inspired countless books, films, and even plays, all suitably embellished to the extent that much fiction has become interwoven into the fabric of his real life history, with the attendant danger that constant repetition of error perpetuates such error as truth. There are few who can name, with any confidence, a half-dozen or so pirates of the age, but there is scarcely anyone who cannot boast some knowledge, however scant, of Kidd. Despite the profusion of literary and dramatic effort, there are a mere handful of reliable biographies about the man himself. The authors of these works appear content to accept the veracity of the official records in these renderings, a veracity which the present author treats more warily. Most of it is correct of course, indisputably so, but beneath that veneer of officiality there lurks the suspicion that the records hide something else. This book explores those suspicions. It is an attempt to lift the pie crust off the pie to peek at the meat and gravy that lie beneath.

Since Kidd was the most famous, or most infamous if you like, of any of the pirates hanged at Execution Dock, it is appropriate that the local tavern be named after him. There upon the actual gallows site, with the security of a modern police station alongside, stands the Captain Kidd, bearing Kidd's stern visage upon a green sign. The chicken-hearted would do well to quail before that grim countenance, for Kidd did not meet his doom happily. Long after his death, Kidd rose to high position, equalling if not surpassing many a king, queen, duke, or duchess who like him have bequeathed their names to posterity upon the inn signs of Britain.

Courtesy of A. Winchester

Captain Kidd
tavern on Wapping
High Street.

Courtesy of A. Winchester

The sign of the
Captain Kidd.

For the sign of the Captain Kidd hangs high indeed! A warm welcome awaits the visitor chilled by the imagined spectres upon the wafting air. Within its confines the Captain Kidd can serve a warming draught and fine food, and these go far to dispel the imagined horrors of the shades of night.

As may be expected in a tavern carrying his name, the Captain Kidd has on display a number of interesting mementoes of the man. Among these are copies of Kidd's original commission authorizing him to seek out pirates, the articles of recruitment for his crew, and most gruesome of all, the warrant authorizing his execution. Each is worthy of scrutiny, and if so inclined, a visit to nearby Tobacco Dock might be rewarding for those with an interest in the romance of piracy, for there on display are replicas of two pirate vessels, the *Three Sisters* and the *Lark*.

Wapping is steeped in history, though this may not be apparent to the first-time visitor. Modern buildings, apartment blocks, condominiums and the like reflect a more affluent lifestyle than that of yesteryear. Gone are the rambling structures of this riverside community, their disappearance hastened by the pounding it received from German bombing in World War II, and sadly, gone is a great deal of its character, though much remains as its very air is redolent with history. Since man first settled in the Thames valley, Wapping has had its place in that history, which reached its zenith during the Victorian Age, when docks and wharves handled commerce from every corner of the globe. But after refreshment taken at the Captain Kidd, you must try to imagine the sights and sounds that would have met your eyes and ears some 300 years ago when they hanged pirates.

At the end of the seventeenth century Wapping was a close-knit community, the inhabitants of which relied for their livelihood on sea and river traffic, as they had done from the Middle Ages and before. The water's edge was mere tidal flat festooned with the flotsam and jetsam of maritime commerce. Sailing vessels of all sorts were tied up to ramshackle piers and wooden mooring stages, or anchored in the river — huge square-rigged sailing ships, barques, barquentines, brigs, ketches, yawls, hoys, wherries, fishing smacks, and rowboats, and an infinite range of hybrid floating craft that it would be difficult to name with any degree of precision. The river was the lifeline of Wapping's very existence and its reason for being.

The bustle on the river was mirrored by the turmoil on shore. Amidst the dingy dwellings and rickety hovels there was a generous sprinkling of inns and taverns where sailors came and went, wine and ale was drunk, food was cooked and eaten, and women of ill repute plied their trade. In the streets pickpockets, robbers, footpads, and the occasional cutthroat picked out the unwary. Fisherfolk, merchants, chandlers, ironmongers, grocers, hawksters, hucksters, costermongers, cheapjacks, pedlars, and itinerant tradesmen of all kinds pursued the many means by which they could keep body and soul together. Life was colourful, but coarse, hard, and rough. It was also cheap!

From this riverside hamlet men and ships sailed far afield, to the New World, to the Levant, to Africa, and to the Orient. They brought back rum and sugar from the West Indies; tobacco, furs, and fish from America; slaves and gold from Africa; ivory, spices, tea, cotton, silk, and calico from China, Arabia, India, and all the corners of the exotic East, where Europeans struggled for mastery of lands and peoples that held a fatal, but flawed, fascination. London was a major trading centre of the world, and Wapping was one of those many outlets through which the barons of commerce conducted their highly profitable seaborne trade. It was a funnel through which men passed who were hard pressed to make a living on land, and thereby forced to seek a livelihood upon the high seas. They came from far-flung corners of Britain in search of a berth where an honest penny, and often a not-so-honest penny, could be earned safely. They avoided the navy; few took voluntary service where the cat-o'-nine-tails was wielded with impunity to the accompaniment of poor fare and worse pay, with death by shot and ball a constant companion in times of war. It was the merchantmen and the privateers that these men sought, especially the privateers, where despite the adventure and the danger of sailing to foreign lands, there was the chance of returning with a pocket full of gold. Many Wapping men went to places near and far; many went never to return. Some were wrecked upon a distant strand, some lost in tempest, some sunk in battle, and some lost to pirates. Strangely, some of those pirates came from Wapping.

After his arrest, Kidd and members of his crew were incarcerated in the infamous Newgate and Marshalsea prisons. The list of Admiralty prisoners held in these institutions at the time, including Kidd and his men, totalled 153. Most of them were crews from other pirate ships, but in a very short time the tally dwindled to 21 names, retaining Kidd and all his men, who were reserved for special treatment. Of the balance of 132, 10 were executed, some died, and the remainder were tried and acquitted, or released without trial. Justice in her blindfold was swift and final, and the dispassionate observer may be excused for thinking that perhaps the lady ought to have removed her blindfold from time to time to ensure that the decisions of life and death dispensed in her name were indeed just, and not a mere parody. As the lady's eyesight does not seem to have improved over the years, the same sentiments might equally apply today!

This book is not an apologia for Kidd, neither is it a biography of this unfortunate man whose name has gone down in infamy, nor is it a history of piracy in the Indian Ocean, a subject deserving a book of its own, nor yet a history of the East India Company, on which many books have already been written. Instead it is a composite of all these, because the author is convinced that there was more to the conviction and death of Kidd than the desire to see justice done to a pirate, even if this justice was necessary because of the political convulsions that arose from his rash actions.

Kidd, in his own words written before his trial, and repeated before he was carted to the gallows, asserted that he had "lodged goods and treasure to the value of one hundred thousand pounds in the Indies," which he desired the government to have in exchange for his life. His gamble proved futile and his life was not spared. The common interpretation of this is that authority declined to take up his offer and was not prepared to bargain with a convicted felon. A noble motive if there ever was one! But £100,000 was a mighty sum 300 years ago — it still is today for most people, but in those times the total tax revenue of the state was a mere £1.5 million. The treasure that Kidd boasted to have "lodged in the Indies" would have been equivalent to 6 or 7 percent of that largesse. Few inhabitants of Britain, for high and lofty reasons, would voluntarily relinquish 6 or 7 percent of the flood of money pouring into the coffers of Britain's Exchequer today. A fraction of the tax collected on beer alone would satisfy most people!

In the year of Kidd's execution a man with a pound in his pocket was truly well off. It could have represented a month's wages of honest toil. Even a humble penny, weighing almost an ounce, felt as if it would purchase something, and in those days it did. How different the feel of money then to the paltry, valueless coinage of today, whether it be pound or penny! But even now, if you were to declare you had buried £100,000 worth of valuables, stolen or otherwise, you would be met with astonishment and disbelief. Eyebrows would be raised, you would be regarded over the rims of spectacles, food and drink would be suspended in mid-air, and after reality had sunk into the minds of your listeners, suspicion would melt away into interest, and the interest would be profound.

Kidd lived in an age dominated by the pursuit of wealth, an era of insatiable lust, rapine, and avarice. He himself was not unaffected, it is true, but it is unreasonable to expect that the people to whom he wrote, admitting this vast hoard of wealth he had "lodged in the Indies," were not interested. Kidd's life was expendable, no one cared tuppence for it, but the wealth that he had indiscreetly admitted to having cached in the Indies, well that was a different matter entirely. Those familiar with Shakespeare's *Othello* will recognize the following lines spoken by Iago:

Who steals my purse steals trash; 't is something, nothing;
'T was mine, 't is his, and has been slave to thousands;
But he that filches my good name,
Robs me of that which not enriches him,
And makes me poor indeed.

Unfortunately for Kidd, he was not only to be robbed of his "purse" and his "good name," but also his life. That miserable life of his was to be sacrificed upon the altar of greed, greed for the treasure that he had "lodged in the Indies." This book is concerned with that treasure, for it is the meat that lies beneath the pie crust.

The thesis of this book is that Kidd was entirely truthful in his claim of having lodged goods and treasure in the Indies, and that this treasure was coveted by the noblemen to whom he pleaded for his life, gambling upon the fact that in the interests of government, they would spare it in return for the treasure. He made the fatal mistake of believing that these men in their powdered wigs and long robes would put the national interest before their own. We often make the same error today, as Sir Winston Churchill once asked, "Do principles change with dates?" It is believed that the fortune that Kidd left in the Indies was recovered a few years after his hanging, and that some of his crew bartered their own lives in exchange for revealing where the treasure lay, for they had witnessed its concealment.

In the decade leading up to the outbreak of World War II, a number of maps drawn on parchment were discovered. These maps carried the unmistakable signature of Kidd, and some were dated. They were discovered by a wealthy, retired bachelor who pursued the rather eccentric hobby of collecting pirate relics. His name was Hubert Palmer. Since then the maps have become known as the Kidd-Palmer charts. Palmer never attempted to benefit from the possession of these ancient maps, but it is certain that he contemplated a journey to the island he believed was portrayed upon them, an expedition that had to be curtailed because of the outbreak of war. His belief in the validity of these parchment maps cannot be questioned, as he determined their authenticity by taking them to a number of experts, including those at the British Museum, undoubtedly a leader in the authentication of ancient documents and manuscripts.

The existence of the Kidd-Palmer charts came to the attention of the general public in 1935, and since then they have fuelled frenzied speculation regarding the whereabouts of the island depicted on them. As far as anyone knows, no one has identified Kidd's island and recovered treasure from it, though expeditions to far-flung corners of the earth have been mounted. But then it would be natural not to disclose the fact if any treasure had indeed been recovered! Unfortunately, the maps have since disappeared in circumstances as mysterious as their first appearance, so the originals are no longer available. Furthermore, the British Museum, which it is claimed gave expert testimony regarding the validity of the maps in the first instance, has little if anything in its files to suggest it ever played the role for which it is credited.

The Kidd-Palmer charts have been treated in considerable detail by George Edmunds in his book *Kidd — The Search for His Treasure*, and Edmunds has given his permission to include some extracts from his fascinating work, which is the outcome of many years of research. The conclusion reached by the present author, in considering all aspects of the Kidd-Palmer charts, is that they are bogus, or at best some may be replicas. The belief is expressed that they were prepared during the decade about 1924–1934, and that their purpose was to lay a false trail. If people could be convinced that the treasure Kidd claimed to have buried on some distant island was still there, then it could never before have been recovered — right? Stolen goods remain stolen goods, until such time as they are returned to their rightful owners. In the case of the booty that Kidd amassed during his short but colourful career in the Indian Ocean, much had been taken from ships belonging to the Mogul of India. Once recovered, that booty ought to have been restored. But what if it hadn't? What if the proceeds of "fencing" Kidd's treasure after it had been recovered had finished up in the pockets of nobles of the realm? Perhaps some even in the pockets of King William, or in those of Queen Anne, who succeeded him on the throne of England!

At the time the Kidd-Palmer charts began to appear, Anglo-Indian relations were becoming increasingly strained. Since then they have ruptured completely. But in those vital years, with increasing agitation and persistent clamour for Indian independence from Britain, and the lengthening shadows of yet another European war looming upon the horizon, politics (being what it is) may well have cast its own distinctive hue upon sensitive evidence that had come to light in the archives. If, in fact, the evidence unequivocally demonstrated that Kidd's treasure had been recovered, and no attempt made to restore any portion of it to the Mogul, this would explain the preparation of the Kidd-Palmer charts. The conclusion can be drawn that they were forged to protect what may loosely be termed "the nation's interests."

The purpose of this book is to set out a thesis of what might have happened to Kidd's treasure. It is readily admitted that not all the pieces of the puzzle have been found, and that those that have may not fit as well as one may like. For instance, there is much information in the records regarding Kidd's movements as they relate to his voyage to the Indian Ocean with a privateering commission to seek out and destroy pirates, of how he turned pirate himself (though the distinction between privateer and pirate is very fine), his subsequent return to America, his capture, trial, and execution. This in itself is a truly fascinating story, but there are gaps in the narrative. In particular there is a five-month period when, according to the records, he waited at Madagascar for a favourable wind to take his vessel to the Cape. During that period he could have been anywhere in the Indian Ocean, and one contemporary categorically asserts him to have been at Amboyna in the Dutch East Indies. There are many questions to be asked, and many answers to be sought, before the truth will finally out. This book goes only partway to penetrate the intrigue that shrouds the truth of what really happened to the treasure Captain William Kidd vouched to have "lodged in the Indies."

Mention was made earlier of various biographies written about Kidd. Three of these stand out in the mind of the author as being impressive in their content and treatment. The most recent of these is that by Robert C. Ritchie, titled *Captain Kidd and the War against the Pirates* (1986). Ritchie is a professor of history, and his biography forms the central theme to a much wider examination of piracy, and the war waged against it by the British government. It is without doubt the most political in its survey of the effects of piracy in the Indian Ocean, which bedevilled and frustrated the trading strategy of the East India Company. Ritchie avoids any discussion of the intriguing Kidd-Palmer charts, doubtless writing them off as unworthy of serious consideration. He treats with disdain the suggestion that Kidd ever buried anything of value, or even possessed any startling amount of treasure.

The second biography to which the reader's attention is drawn is that by Dunbar Maury Hinrichs, titled *The Fateful Voyage of Captain Kidd* (1955). Hinrichs writes from the aspect of an experienced blue-water sailor. His extremely readable book deals with Kidd's life from a chronological perspective. Many references are reproduced in full as he traces the career and fate of Kidd. Like Ritchie, he shuns any discussion relating to the Kidd-Palmer charts, and scorns the credulity of those believing Kidd's treasure ever existed.

The third, and perhaps the most informal of these biographies, is that by Harold T. Wilkins, titled *Captain Kidd and his Skeleton Island* (1935). Wilkins wrote more romantically and more passionately than either Ritchie or Hinrichs. He actually knew Hubert Palmer, the discoverer of the Kidd-Palmer charts, had seen the charts himself, and as a consequence expresses a firm belief that Kidd did indeed "lodge treasure in the Indies." His book demonstrates the depth of his research and he quotes extensively from many references. Wilkins's style, however, may alarm serious scholars, as he exhibits his emotions on a number of issues, at times in a somewhat abrasive manner. An excerpt from his last paragraph is typical:

> While tortured and tantalized by scoundrel Tory politicians to "rat" on his Whig employers, he [Kidd] resisted to the very end all pressure, most skilfully and artfully applied, to make him "blab" about the part played by his "noble" friends in the affair of the Adventure Galley. The faults of such a man were washed white in the judicial blood bath.

All three biographies are worthy of being taken up by the reader attracted to studying in greater detail the deeds of Kidd and his fellow pirates. Of these three, that by Hinrichs contains the best character assessment of Kidd himself. In summary he paints a picture of Kidd as being no saint, but certainly no irredeemable sinner either. He had many faults, but don't we all! He drank to excess on occasion, lost his temper, and at times swore blasphemously. But with little doubt he was a kind and loving husband and a proud father with many generous traits. Despite the accusation levelled at him of being blasphemous on occasions, he was a pew holder at Trinity Church in New York (in the present Wall Street area), and lent tackle to the church in July 1696 for hoisting stone during its construction. Miraculously, the church was to escape unscathed despite its close proximity to the devastating terrorist attack on the World Trade Center in September 2001. Through his wife Kidd also owned land in that area, which today represents some of the most expensive real estate on earth. They also had a country estate in what is now Harlem.

Without any shadow of doubt, Kidd was far better educated than most of his piratical contemporaries with whom he has been classed. As a seaman and navigator his abilities surpassed most. In fact if he had really wanted to become a pirate he could have easily done so from New York, as the city was a hotbed for piracy, with tacit support from Governor Fletcher and his cronies. For such a career change Kidd had no need to go to the Indian Ocean.

Though Kidd has been stereotyped as a bully, he was without doubt a disciplinarian, as even the most hardy of sea captains can lose patience with a crew of malcontents. It is to Kidd's credit that he accomplished his voyage of adventure into the Indian Ocean and that many of his men stayed loyal to him to the bitter end. Without that underlying acceptance of his leadership, his motley crew would have soon risen up against him, usurped his authority, and commandeered the *Adventure Galley* for their own less laudable purposes.

The opportunity has been taken in this book to deal with Kidd's predations from a slightly different perspective than that of other biographers and writers. Included herein will be found commentaries upon other aspects that will enable the reader to gain a wider perspective of life in the Indian Ocean region at the time when Kidd and his *Adventure Galley* sailed across its vast expanse. Topics such as the riches of the East that beckoned the European traders and pirates in the first place are described, together with some of the depraved actions of the native pirates who infested their own peculiar corners of the region, and the crude instruments of navigation that were all that Kidd had available for sailing in those uncharted waters.

It is now time to lift the crust of the pie and begin to take a peek at the meat and gravy that lie beneath, Kidd's treasure being the "meat" and the intrigue that surrounds it being the "gravy."

Chapter 1

The Hanging of Captain Kidd

All the world's a stage,
And all the men and women merely players:
They have their exits, and their entrances.
— Jaques in *As You Like It* (Shakespeare)

The winter of 1700–01 was drawing to a close. In London, dismal overcast skies were beginning to break up and the sun rose higher in the heavens each day, bringing with it longer intervals of welcome warmth to the inhabitants of the great metropolis. The traces of the Great Fire of 1666 had almost disappeared in the frenzy of rebuilding that had taken place over the intervening years. On the sites of ancient parish churches there had arisen a multitude of new spires and towers that bore the mark of Christopher Wren's fertile genius. Only at the site of the Cathedral of St. Paul's did crowds of workmen, masses of hewn stone, timber, and scaffold testify that the complete eradication of the utter devastation of that evil time still lay in the future. From the Temple in the west, to the Tower in the east, and from the Thames as far north as Moorfields, the City of London had in a few days been gutted of 89 churches and 13,000 homes. But as before the fire, the city was a bustling world of continuous movement, of colour, of noise, and of smell. The numerous spires, towers, and domes that beckoned the populace to prayer were enough to suggest that they were pious to the extreme. And indeed they were, at least on Sundays when men and women rested from serving Mammon and rendered their thanks to Almighty God.

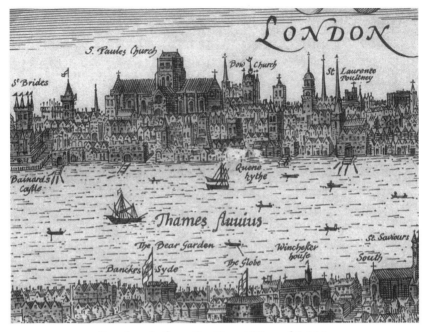

London before the Great Fire of 1666.

On the other six days of the week, the cobbled streets rang with the iron-shod wheels of carts and coaches rattling down the alleyways and narrow crooked passages. The old lines of the streets had been preserved from an age when princes and princesses wended their way on horseback through the city's maze. For centuries the streets had been too narrow to accommodate the passing of wheeled carriages with ease. It was no different as the seventeenth century gave way to usher in the eighteenth. Beneath the solemnity of church bells chiming out the hours with monotonous regularity lay the realm of man, where everyone was busily engaged in the competition for life, if not for the wealth that was its necessary accompaniment. Here, within the city, lay the residences of the rich burghers, not inferior in magnificence to dwellings inhabited by the nobility; here also lay those of the bankers, merchants, shopkeepers, tradesmen, and the humble citizenry which outnumbered all others. Within a stone's throw of a palatial residence could be found hovels and tenements where ragged urchins ran barefoot. Along the narrow, claustrophobic alleyways and streets, goods were exhibited for sale in booths which projected outwards, high above the heads of passersby. These in turn were overhung by upper stories, to such an extent that lovers might touch hands above the multitude below. Into these gloomy canyons little light penetrated, and often less fresh air, as the city's throng ebbed back and forth as if in some vast unwashed tide.

The houses were not numbered. There was no advantage in numbering them for few could read. Shops exhibited gaudy painted signs, which gave a grotesque array of Saracens' Heads, Royal Oaks, Lambs, Bears, Cocks, and other insignia portraying the merchandise on offer. The signs appeared and disappeared as fast as the purveyors' fortunes waxed and waned. A downpour brought a torrent of filth into the gutters from the stalls of butchers and greengrocers. Carriages, heedless of any pedestrian, swept this noxious waste to left and right in their passage. At such times it was the strong and nimble who took the wall as far from the carriage road as possible, and that usually was not very far. The mild, the timid, and the weak were the ones who took the brunt of the splatter of mud and filth. Jonathan Swift aptly portrayed the state of the streets at such times in his poem "A Description of a City Shower":

> Now from all parts the swelling kennels flow,
> And bear their trophies with them as they go:
> Filths of all hues and odours seem to tell
> What streets they sailed from, by the sight and smell.
> … Sweepings from butchers' stalls, dung, guts and blood,
> Drowned puppies, stinking sprats, all drenched in mud,
> Dead cats and turnip tops come tumbling down in flood.

Covent Garden was a noisy, riotous place, where fruit women screamed, carters fought, and where mounds of rotting cabbages and apples were allowed to compost of their own accord. It was not a place for those sensitive to either noise or smell. In Lincoln's Inn Fields the rabble congregated to see bears dance, and mountebanks harangued the mob amidst general commotion and frequent disorder. Beggars were as numerous, and as bellicose, as in any of the worst-governed cities in Europe. Offal, dead cats and dogs, cinders, refuse, and garbage of every description littered the pavements to the disgust of foreigners who were aghast and vocal about the shame of it all. It may have been a great metropolis, but London in 1700–01 was not for the nervous or naive. A stranger, whether from overseas or the country, was soon singled out by con men and women, tumbled into the gutter and robbed, or had his pockets emptied by the multitude of thieves that were as numerous as the flies that plagued the same streets. Thieves and robbers might have plied their trades with impunity, but they were of little consequence compared to the many bands of dissolute young gentlemen, and sometimes of well-bred young women dressed as gentlemen, that swaggered about by night intent on deliberate vandalism and pro-voking mayhem.

Down by the river, below London Bridge, little touched since its completion in 1209, were situated the wharves where merchant vessels brought back to Britain trade goods from the Indies, from America, from the Levant, and from the Orient. Here lay at anchor stately tall ships, their sails furled, disgorging the produce of foreign enterprise, or being loaded with trade goods for fresh ventures far afield. Less impressive were the numerous smaller barques, brigs, and schooners engaged in the same fevered pursuit. The Thames, being the commercial artery of the city, was almost as busy and congested as the streets and alleyways of the city itself.

Beneath a perpetual pall of smoke, the grimy alleyways and other crooked passageways vented forth intriguing odours amidst the general rankness and decay. In the city there were enticing aromas of tobacco, coffee, wine, ale, and rich cooking, but down by the river, nostrils caught a whiff of distant lands, lands where a fortune might be made by the industrious and the daring, whatever his rank and station. The constant clamour that infested the city began at cock-crow and lasted until well after dark and then by swinging lantern or by candlelight gleaming through latticed windows. As the day drew to a close, silence would reluctantly descend, and the watchman would make his rounds accompanying his passage with refrains such as:

Take heed to your clock; beware your lock,
Your fire and your light, and God give you a goodnight,
One o'clock!

For a few brief hours the city would sleep, the king at his palace
in Whitehall; his ministers and the nobles of the land in their man-
sions and great houses; the honest traders, merchants, and citizens
in their humble dwellings; and the homeless wherever they could
find rest for their tired and hungry bodies. Only in the shadows, cast
by a wan and fitful moon, would lurk the footpad and the cutthroat,
intent on capitalizing upon the opportunity of confronting the
unsuspecting late-night reveller, the prostitute homeward bound, or
the naive. One of the newspapers of the day, *The London Post with
Intelligence Foreign and Domestick*, carried the following in its issue
of February 19 to 21, which vividly portrays these dangers:

> Whereas many murders, manslaughters, and other
> great disorders, are frequently committed, and done
> in divers taverns, and other publick houses, within
> this City, and the liberties thereof, by disorderly per-
> sons resorting thereto, and abiding therein, at late
> and unseasonable hours in the night, to the ruin of
> many families. And in such publik houses are often
> harboured housebreakers, robbers, lewd and
> debauched men and women; by reason whereof,
> many thefts, robberies, and other misdemeanors are
> frequently done and committed, to the great distur-
> bance of the peace, contrary to the laws of this
> Kingdom, and to the great dishonour of the govern-
> ment of this City. For preventing of which great evils
> and mischiefs of the future, it is ordered by this
> Court, that all vintners, cauphee sellers, alehouse
> keepers, victuallers, and all others keeping publick
> houses within this City, and the liberties thereof, do
> not from henceforth permit or suffer any person or
> persons, to be, or continue in their respective house

or houses, gaming, tippling, or drinking, after the hour of ten of the clock in the night-time, between Michaelmas and Lady Day; nor after the hour of eleven of the clock in the night-time, between Lady day and Michaelmas; nor on any part of the Lord's Day. And it is further ordered, that all constables, watchmen and others, employed and instructed to keep and preserve the peace and good order of this City, in the night-time do make diligent enquiry after, and due observation and search of all taverns, alehouses, victualling houses, and other publick houses in this City, and the liberties thereof, and give information upon oath from time to time, to the Right Honourable the Lord Mayor, or some other Justice of the Peace of this City, of all persons offending contrary hereunto, to the end that they may be effectually prosecuted, and proceeded against according to law for their so doing, the publick sessions of the peace to be held for this City, as keepers of disorderly houses, as they will answer the contrary at their perils.

signed Ashurst

As dawn broke, the denizens of the night would fade away and the printing presses would begin the clattering ritual of printing the news sheets and fliers that within a few hours would be touted around the streets by urchins intent on earning a few honest coppers. The newspapers of the age bore little resemblance to those of today. They consisted of a single broadsheet with the news printed on both sides. There was none of the gushing sentimentality that we are accustomed to, no sensational headlines or leading articles attempting to mould or direct public opinion or political sentiment, and no live coverage of actual events by roving reporters. The news of the time consisted of statements of fact as received, and reproduced with little, if any, attempt at rephrasing. Apart from

The London Post, there was *The English Post*, *The Flying Post*, *The Post Boy*, and *The Post Man*. They would appear every second or third day, so they were not dailies as we understand the term.

Since the newspapers were one of the means by which the nation's populace could reliably inform itself of news both "foreign and domestick" it scarce needs adding that despite their shortcomings the news they carried was devoured eagerly by the more literate patrons of the innumerable taverns, wine shops, and coffee houses within the city. These establishments were then, unlike today, forums for public debate, where exchanges took place between the intelligentsia on major issues affecting church and state, and from whence issued numerous contributions on matters of politics, religion, and science. One such publication, from which extracts will be given in the next chapter, is titled *A Compleat Collection of Voyages and Travels: Consisting of above Four Hundred of the Most Authentick Writers*, published by John Harris, Fellow of the Royal Society, and printed for Thomas Bennet, at the Half-Moon in St. Paul's Churchyard; John Nicholson, at the Kings Arms in Little Britain; and Daniel Midwinter, at the Rose and Crown in St. Paul's Churchyard, in two volumes (1705). Thanks to the altruism of Bennet, Nicholson, and Midwinter we have access to a unique collection of fascinating accounts of travel in the years leading up to the end of the seventeenth century.

Some excerpts from *The London Post* typify the coverage of what were considered newsworthy events of 1700–01:

> This week two bags of diamonds were entered at the custom-house by the Old East India Company. (February 5)

> This day a proclamation was published for encouraging mariners, seamen and landmen to enter themselves on board His Majesty's ships of war, promising 30 shillings for each able seaman and 25 shillings to each ordinary seaman, or able-bodied landsman. (February 26)

The Tuscan Galley from China has brought over 135 pieces of damask, 146 taffaties, 30 striped satins, 2200 fans, 236 tea tables, 710 ounces of gold, 400 bundles of rattan canes, 5500 pound of copper, 18300 pound of tea, 5200 pound of raw silk, 3200 pound of quick silver, 1500 pound of dragon's blood [a type of gum]; with many rich commodities. (June 19)

In similar vein, *The English Post* reported:

Letters from St John de Acre, a port town of Jerusalem, dated Sept 24, advise that 20,000 Arabians attackt and plundered the caravan in the desert going from Mecca to Damascus, consisting of 5000 mules richly laden, killing the Bassa who accompanied them, with his wives, and a great number of the travellers besides, most of the remainder perishing in the wilderness, the whole loss being computed at 70 tons of gold, but the caravan that went to Egypt escaped. (February 5)

There was coyned last week in the Tower 70,000 pounds in gold and silver. (April 9)

In April 1700 there arrived back in England, following his arrest in Boston nine months earlier, the American arch-pirate, Captain William Kidd. He had been transported in chains to stand trial for his crimes before an English court, as courts in the colonies were denied the entitlement of trying and executing pirates. The British government, being now imbued with a sense of righteousness, no longer needed the skills of privateering adventurers to enhance the nation's interests abroad, nor was it prepared to tolerate any duplicity in condoning piracy through semantics. The trading interests of the East India Company had suffered drastically through the actions of Kidd and others like him, and the government was intent on stamping out piracy once and for all. It can be expected that an announcement of his arrest was made, and that this appeared sooner or later in the newspapers in the same terse manner reflected by the foregoing examples. On April 14 Kidd was brought in chains from HMS *Advice*, anchored in the Thames, for interrogation. After seven hours of cross-examination Kidd was committed to Newgate Prison to await his trial. Fellow members of his crew that had been arrested at the same time were imprisoned in the Marshalsea, the usual place of confinement for Admiralty prisoners.

Newgate stood on the site now occupied by the Central Criminal Court, or Old Bailey, famous for the numerous criminal trials carried out in more recent times with which the British nation has had an almost hypnotic fascination. Its origins stem from the thirteenth century and, after Dick Whittington, who had been Lord Mayor of London a total of four times between 1397 and 1420, died, improvements were made at Newgate as a provision of his will. Dick Whittington, it will be recalled, travelled to London to seek his fortune. Legend tells that he took his cat with him, though this is believed to have little foundation except to make good pantomime. His first attempts to find employment in the city were dogged by misfortune and, turning his back on London, he resolved to return home. Halted by the ringing of Bow Bells, which he took to be a good omen, he retraced his footsteps. He became a successful London cloth merchant, rose to become a sheriff, and finally was elected Lord Mayor. He gave much to charity.

After the Great Fire of 1666, much had been done to rebuild Newgate. Despite this the prison still remained a pestilential hole of disease and vice, and the gaolers who ran it made as much money as they could from their offices. They received no salary and lived off the profits of selling food and drink to the hapless inmates. Young and old, male and female would be herded together during the day, and even at night were not always quartered circumspect-ly. In close and cramped confinement, with little means or oppor-tunity for proper hygiene, and in an atmosphere of stench approaching the point of suffocation, the prisoner of a weak and feeble disposition soon lost an unequal struggle with life. The Great

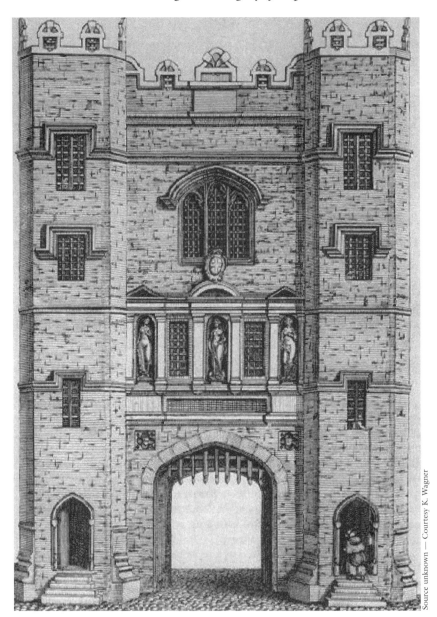

Newgate Prison.

Reaper arrived, more often than not, before the officers of the state came to drag the prisoner to his trial and the fate that would be settled upon him by the judges in their imposing wigs and regalia.

William Kidd was not of a weak and feeble disposition. He was a strong and burly individual and, after having spent his entire life at sea, or in association with it, must be supposed to have been more robust than most of the inmates of Newgate, at least when he was first thrust into this place of perdition. By the winter of 1700–01 even his sturdy vitality was slowly ebbing away. As early as the previous May, after he had been in Newgate a mere month, the keeper had reported him to have a fever and to be suffering great pain. Relatives from Wapping were allowed to see him and he was provided with some clothing and some bedding. A physician was even sent to him as no one in authority wanted to see justice cheated by his untimely death. By December 1700 this desire to keep Kidd alive even extended to permitting him exercise in the fresh air, but under constant guard and on condition that he communicate with no one. It was a terrible situation for a man to find himself in, particularly for one who had been accustomed to the freedom of a quarterdeck, even if it had been somewhat restricted by open sea.

Kidd's actions had been the cause of great disruption to the trade with India, or to put it more correctly, Kidd's actions amounted to the proverbial straw that broke the camel's back to that trade. The directors of the East India Company and their shareholders had received vast increases in dividend payments over the years with a virtually constantly increasing stock price. Though this mighty money-making machine had suffered setbacks in the recent past due to its own greed and misunderstanding of local situations, it also had a new and powerful rival to contend with in the form of the New East India Company, as well as its customary foreign rivals. Anybody who was anybody wanted Kidd out of the way, and preferably hanged in public. Pirates in the Indian Ocean, hitherto considered a private preserve of the East India Company, had not only disrupted trade, especially with the Mogul, but law-abiding merchantmen, interlopers, smugglers, and other undesirables, many of whom were based in the North American colonies, were also seriously affecting the profits of that trade. From the whispers round the boardrooms in the East India Company's offices in Leadenhall Street, to the mutterings of Whitehall, the clamour rose for Kidd's head. The general public liked that too, because a hanging day was a holiday! They could then enjoy the macabre spectacle of a man's life being jerked from him at the end of a rope, toss their greasy caps into the air in general jubilation, and quench their thirsts in gleeful debauchery.

Since the revolution of 1688, there had been a great improvement in the justice system, including the discharge of the death sentence. For that improvement much credit must be given to William III and his ministers. During the preceding reign of James II, torture and beatings were an invariable accompaniment to interrogation. If the crime had a religious connection then the felon could be lashed from Newgate to Tyburn. The flogging was invariably carried out with the utmost brutality as the unfortunate was whipped around the streets. The gory spectacle was intended to strike fear and dread into the multitude. It usually succeeded. In that it might have been effective, but it also led to a coarsening of attitudes, and life was coarse enough already.

In the spring, Kidd was taken from Newgate prison, where he had been confined for almost 13 months, to his trial. It was May 8, 1701. The ordeal was over the following day. In those two days he was tried and convicted on charges of both murder and piracy. The fairness of his trial has been examined, probed, and questioned by other authors, and this fairness, if there was any by today's standards, is of little concern to this book. However, it is fortunate for Kidd that he had been apprehended in a kindlier era than that which prevailed during the reign of James. He was not beaten or tortured in order to extract a confession, though he would have faced the prospect of false testimonies made against him, the twisting and distortion of the evidence, and other questionable legal practices adopted by the authorities in order to obtain a conviction. It is also, perhaps, fortunate that his crime had no religious connotation, unless stealing money worshipped by the rich could be considered such an offence. He had no legal representative to help defend him from the verbal traps and ensnarements that were placed in his path by smooth-tongued lawyers and their clerks, men who couldn't sail a boat on a bathtub, let alone across half the world. The burly prisoner, more accustomed to facing the vagaries of nature in his cockleshell of a ship, would have been plainly out of his element.

Three men, all sea captains, took the time and the trouble to attend Kidd's trial and appear on his behalf. All had known him years before in the West Indies, where Kidd had undertaken various privateering ventures for the British. They were Captain Heweson, Captain Bond, and Captain Humphreys. All gave favourable character references for Kidd, actions in themselves which may well have jeopardized their future careers or prosperity. Heweson even went as far as to say that he had met Kidd on the streets of London before he set out in the *Adventure Galley*, and that Kidd had told him he was "going a-cruising to suppress pirates." The captains' efforts, however, proved useless and Kidd's execution was set for Friday, May 23, a mere 14 days later. King William declined to grant clemency to the man whom he had once described as "trusty and well-beloved."

The London Post reported these happenings with its customary terseness:

> We hear that on the 8th of next month a Sessions of Admiralty will be held at the Old Bayly for trying of several pyrates, and it is thought that Captain Kidd will come to tryal. (April 28)

> Yesterday 10 men of Capt Kidd's crew were removed from Marshalsea to Newgate, in order to take their tryal on the 8th inst at a Sessions of the Admiralty, at the Old Bayly when the Capt is also to come upon his tryal, as likewise Capt Culliford who surrrendered upon the King's proclamation. One Hickman, and another who are not of Kidd's crew and also Capt Roch, formerly mentioned. (May 5)

> This day there was a Court of Admiralty held at the Old Bayly; the Honourable George Oxenden Doctor of Law Judge; when Capt Kidd, John Eldrige, Hugh Parrot, Nicholas Churchill, James How, Gabriel Loff, Darby Mullins, Richard Barlicorn, William Jenkins,

Robert Lamley, Edward Davis, and one Owens were indicted and tryed for piracy, Capt Kidd was found guilty of piracy, robbery and murder; Owen was acquitted upon the King's proclamation, he having surrendered himself upon the same, Barlicorn being Kidd's servant, Jenkins being the mate's apprentice, and Lamley the cook's apprentice, were all acquitted, and the rest found guilty; but about 8 this night, fresh indictments were brought against all of them, and about 9 the Court was busy arraigning of Capt Culliford and several others. (May 8)

Yesterday Captain Kidd, with the other pyrates of his gang, were tried by a Court of Admiralty in the Old Bayly, and Kidd after a long trial was found guilty upon 4 indictments of murder and piracy. Seven other pirates were also convicted and 3 acquitted, after which the Court adjourned for a short time, and then proceeded to the trial of some other pirates. (May 9)

The Flying Post reported the events just as phlegmatically:

Last night the Sessions of Admiralty ended at the Old Baily, when 9 persons received sentence of death, viz Capt Kidd, Rob Hickman, James How, John Aldridge, Gab Luff, William Jenkins and three others. Capt Culliford, Rob Lumly, Edward Davis, Robert Barlicorn were acquitted; and Capt Roch was cleared. (May 9)

We hear that Capt Kidd, Darby Mullins, and John Eldridge, three of the pirates condemned at the Old Baily, have received orders to prepare for death. The other 6 are reprieved. We hear, that two of the French pirates, condemned sometime ago, are likewise ordered to prepare for death. (May 13)

There was only one sector of the London community in which the order for the execution of Kidd might have been received with less enthusiasm than elsewhere. This was in the hamlet of Wapping, downriver from London Bridge. Here it was that Kidd had made his home for the few months after arriving from New York in the latter half of 1695. In this riverside community he had relatives, which though distant had given him a welcoming home. Amongst these were Mr. Blackthorne, an uncle, who was a fishmonger by trade, and a Mrs. Hawkins, a relative of his wife.

The chaplain and Ordinary of Newgate during Kidd's imprisonment was Paul Lorrain, a rather sanctimonious prig, who some 20 years earlier had been a copyist to Samuel Pepys, the Secretary to the Admiralty. Arthur Bryant, in his book *Samuel Pepys: The Years of Peril*, describes Lorrain as "a Huguenot and greatly addicted to piety." When with Pepys, he had held aspirations of taking holy orders, which he later succeeded in obtaining. Lorrain added to his meagre stipend by interviewing the more notorious of the prison's inmates and writing juicy titbits about them for what we would today describe as the "gutter press." Here in print they would be devoured and relished by the lower-class citizenry, at least those who could read, whose appetite for such has changed little to the present day.

It was Lorrain's responsibility as a member of the church to obtain the appropriate confession from a condemned man before he was led off to his untimely fate. Usually Lorrain had little difficulty in extracting the requisite confession, as the great majority of his clients were intent upon entering the next world with a clean conscience. However, with Kidd he encountered a stubborn resistance in the condemned man, who refused to acknowledge that he had committed any crime whatsoever. On the day of his execution the chaplain visited Kidd's cell, and twice later that day had him brought into his chapel in an attempt to extract the wanted confession. "I was afraid the hardness of Captain Kidd's heart was unmelted," he recalled later. "I therefore applied myself with particular exhortations." At the last, Kidd seemed to assent to a degree of repentance by stating that he "truly forgave all the world." This is not exactly the same as acknowledging the crimes for which he had been found guilty and pleading with the Almighty for forgiveness of his sins in the afterlife. Lorrain was satisfied to some degree, however, as within the hour Kidd was marched off to his doom.

Sometime after Kidd left Lorrain's chapel, some benevolent individual slipped him a bottle of liquor, and when Kidd emerged through the prison gates he was reeling drunk and oblivious to the howling of the mob gathering to accompany him, and those other unfortunates who were to be dispatched alongside, on the march down to Execution Dock. To the convicted felons chained upon the cart it was a funeral cortège with themselves (not yet departed) the central attraction. To the mob it was a procession to be followed with merriment and baiting of the "stars" of the show.

One of the men who was to be hanged alongside Kidd was Darby Mullins, an Irishman from Londonderry. Mullins had joined Kidd at New York for the voyage of the *Adventure Galley*. He had been with Kidd, therefore, the entire duration — through all the adventures and the adversities. Though many of his fellow crew members had been found guilty of the same crimes as himself at the trial, they had been reprieved, while Mullins had not. His loyalty to Kidd thus extended to the scaffold.

Darby Mullins had been dealt an unenviable hand by Lady Luck. He had been kidnapped in Ireland and shipped off to Jamaica, where he was sold into slavery. The press gangs of the navy were one thing, but to have oneself seized by profiteers, transported, and sold as a slave was the height of ignominious shame. Despite this humiliating situation Mullins patiently served out his four years on the plantations, thereby buying his freedom, and thereafter worked at odd jobs around Port Royal. His situation was not unique.

The practice was widespread of kidnapping healthy young males in Europe and selling them into slavery in the American colonies. Though the famous Dutch pirate Esquemeling (1645–1707) entered voluntarily into the service of the French West India Company, he was sold by the company, since he represented one of their "assets." He was the author of the classic work on seventeenth-century piracy entitled *The Buccaneers of America*, first published in Amsterdam in 1678 as *De Americaensche Zeerovers* and since translated into numerous languages. Esquemeling was resold a second time to a surgeon for 70 pieces-of-eight. After a year of service, he was offered his liberty for the sum of 100 pieces-of-eight, which represented a tidy profit for his master. He promised to pay the debt for his release, but whether he ever did is not recorded. However, Esquemeling does say this about the evils which befell not only himself and Darby Mullins, but countless others:

> In this country [Tortuga] the planters have but very few slaves, for want of which they themselves, and some servants they have, are constrained to do all the drudgery. These servants commonly oblige and bind themselves unto their masters for the space of three years. But their masters, forsaking all conscience and justice, oftentimes traffic with their bodies as with horses at a fair; selling them to other masters, even just as they sell negroes brought from the coast of Guinea. Yea, to advance this trade, some persons there are who go purposely to France [the same happens in England and other countries], and, travelling through the cities, towns, and villages, endeavour to pick up young men or boys, whom they transport, by making them great promises. These, being once allured and conveyed into the islands I speak of, they force to work like horses, the toil they impose upon them being much harder than what they usually enjoin unto the negroes, their slaves. For these they endeavour in some manner to preserve, as being their perpetual bond-men; but, as for their white servants, they care not whether they live or die, seeing they are to continue no longer than three years in their service.

Esquemeling asserts in his book that the only way to escape eternal bondage on the plantations of the West Indies was to run away, seize a vessel, and engage upon a life of piracy. What sane person could fail to agree with his philosophy?

After escaping from servitude upon the plantations of Jamaica, Darby Mullins, undaunted by the earthquake of 1692 that devastated Port Royal, built an alehouse in nearby Kingston. His efforts in business were short-lived; the enterprise was a flop, and he was forced to live a hand-to-mouth existence, one which led him to New York. For two years he worked around the harbourfront before taking a voyage to Madeira. While away at sea his wife died, and following his return Mullins signed up with Kidd, an act that was to lead him to Execution Dock, there to be hanged alongside Kidd. There seems to have been an ill-fated star that overshadowed poor Darby Mullins his entire life. Who cannot feel sympathy with him?

Amid the tumultuous jeering and raucous cries of the mob, the macabre procession, in which Kidd and his fellow unfortunates were cast in the leading roles, proceeded from Newgate at a walking pace. Led by the Admiralty's deputy marshal riding in an open carriage, bearing over his shoulder the silver oar that symbolized the power of the Admiralty, the cortège commenced the four-mile journey to Execution Dock. Behind the leading carriage came the marshal himself, the powdered and bewigged Mr. Cheeke, upon whom had fallen the heavy responsibility of arranging the finer details of the execution, and the display of the bodies (after the highlight of the event) so that all could see that justice had been done. Following in a black-draped tumbril came the condemned men, whose bodies would soon hang high and dry for all to view as a deterrent to those contemplating a pirate's profession. The pomp and ceremony of the procession was intended to strike awe and fear into the hearts of the populace, and respect for the law of the land. To this end much effort and expense was exerted by authority.

The file of carriages, with their bevy of official attendants, slowly clattered its way down the cobbled streets, along Cheapside, past the site of St. Paul's Cathedral where rebuilding was still in progress after the Great Fire, past the Royal Exchange and the pump at Aldgate, then came to the square battlemented keep of that grim edifice the Tower of London, the sight of which was enough to terrify any condemned man, and finally down to the dark ominous expanse of the brooding Thames itself. As the retinue continued on its way, the numbers accompanying it swelled, as the curious citizens, anxious to make the most of this merry day, swirled along in the wake of the procession. With the jeers of the crowd constantly ringing in their ears, the bound men in the black-shrouded tumbril were jolted back and forth, with scant regard for their comfort in the little space of time remaining to them.

The Reverend Lorrain had gone on ahead to the place of execution. There the gallows stood up high and dry out of the Thameside mud, which at high tide would be awash around the base. For two hours the solemn procession wound its way through the hovels from Newgate until finally, in the mid-afternoon, it arrived at its destination. Lorrain was constrained to anger as soon as he cast his eyes upon Kidd. The condemned man was drunk! Lorrain later wrote that the alcohol "had so discompos'd his mind that he was now in a very ill frame and very unfit for the great work now or never to be perform'd by him."

Still, the condemned Kidd, despite his wretchedness and the fact that he was within minutes of confronting his maker, refused to acknowledge his guilt. Throughout his trial he had maintained his innocence, and even at this eleventh hour he was not about to change his attitude. He had made impassioned pleas and arguments to his judges, and written in profuse detail to those he had thought his friends, but in the end nothing had availed him. Surrounded by the baying mob Kidd made a last speech, as was the right of every felon about to be hanged. He proclaimed once again his confidence in God's mercy, despite his innocence, and forgave the iniquity of those who had committed perjury against him. He denounced those lords that had led him to ruination, and reiterated that the vile murder of which he had been found guilty was a mere crime of passion committed under provocation. He avowed the great sadness of leaving his wife a widow and his children fatherless, and ended by warning seamen to beware of those in high places. It was a speech that lacked any suggestion that might be expected from a contrite and humble heart acknowledging a wrongdoing. Those that were to be hanged that day with Kidd gave more satisfactory farewell speeches. After the speeches, a psalm was sung and prayers said for the souls of the condemned.

It was the tradition to hang pirates four at a time. There was the drunken and unrepentant Kidd, the more contrite Mullins, and two Frenchmen unconnected with either Kidd or any of his crew. Each man's bonds were fastened tight and the nooses slipped snugly around their necks. All, with the exception of Kidd, cried out for the Lord to have mercy on their souls as the wedges were struck out from the trap doors. The trap was sprung, enthralling the crowd with the exhilarating sight of three bodies in their death throes squirming at the end of tautened ropes. The fourth body had tumbled through the trap to fall heavily upon the ground beneath. It was that of Kidd! The rope had snapped, unable to carry his weight. As Kidd lay bound, stunned, and confused in his alcoholic stupor, the hangman reached for a fresh rope, one which he hoped would prove stronger. With little ceremony Kidd was bundled up the steps of the scaffold and hanged a second time. This time the rope held, much to the relief of the official witnesses, and Kidd's life was choked out of him to the jeers and hoots of the gathered assembly. It was six o'clock of the evening of May 23, 1701.

After the four bodies had stopped twitching they were cut down from the gallows. Kidd's corpse, as required by Admiralty law, was chained upright to a post set upon the mud flats. There, the tide was allowed to swirl about its nether regions three times before it was recovered. The body was then coated with tar, bound with iron chains, and the head set in a metal harness to ensure that the skull remained intact upon the torso. It was hung from a gibbet erected on Tilbury Point, on a spot that all mariners entering or exiting the Thames could not fail to see. There it was allowed to rot, the rain lashing it in summer and the frost working on it in winter. Gulls and ravens feasted upon his flesh. Whether anyone recovered Kidd's remains, or whether his remains ever had a civilized burial, is unknown. It is likely that once justice had been done, Kidd's tarred, chained, and harnessed corpse was allowed to decay with no further attentions or kindnesses from His Majesty's officers.

Six of Kidd's crew had been tried along with their captain. All, with the exception of Darby Mullins, had been reprieved and were eventually freed. It is rumoured that two of them, Nicholas Churchill and James Howe, somehow found £315 to gain their release. Interestingly enough, Churchill and Howe were pardoned at the same time as a Robert Hickman, who had been a member of Culliford's crew, and the three names appear together on a release document dated June 20, 1701, less than a month after Kidd was hanged. We shall examine the connection between Kidd and Culliford in a later chapter, but the figure of £315 is the equivalent of 300 guineas, and a suspicion immediately arises that a "hundred guineas per man" was paid by someone for the release of all three — the amount is, frankly, too high to believe that (pirates though they might have been) they would have this much ready cash about their persons. Something doesn't smell right about this transaction, and one is left wondering how many similar transactions were effected to expedite the release of other members of either crew.

Robert Culliford and various members of his crew had been committed to the Marshalsea on August 6, 1700. They were tried at the same time as Kidd, as *The London Post* and *The Flying Post* both report, but were exonerated because they had given themselves up on hearing of the king's proclamation to grant pardons to pirates. Culliford himself was granted bail on August 19, only 13 days after being first thrust into jail, and yet he was re-arrested two months later. The records include the following order, dated October 17, 1700:

> To the Keeper of Newgate or his deputy
> The bodies of Robert Culliford and Ralph Pattison
> sent to yew for safe lodging.

Culliford was eventually granted a pardon signed by Queen Anne and dated April 9, 1702. For almost a year following his trial along with Kidd, he languished in jail on one pretext or another. One is left wondering whether this was the normal bureaucratic nightmare that beset unconvicted prisoners due for release, or whether there was some other, hitherto unacknowledged, reason for his further detention.

Another interesting aspect of the affair is that Nicholas Churchill and James Howe were later reported as managing to find their way back to America, where it is rumoured they dug up gold to the value of £2,300 in the backwoods of Pennsylvania. This sounds rather far-fetched, especially if it was gold brought back prior to their arrest, which would have taken place in Boston or New York. If there is any truth in it, it sounds suspiciously like some payoff for "services rendered." Could it be that Churchill and Howe helped to recover the treasure that Kidd had "lodged in the Indies"?

The hanging of Kidd and the other convicted felons was reported in the press with about as much emotion as his trial:

> *The London Post* (May 19) — The dead warrant is come down to Newgate for the execution of Captain Kidd and the rest of the pyrates next Wednesday at Old Execution Dock at Wapping.

> *The Post Boy* (May 24) — Yesterday Captain Kidd, and three other pirates, were executed at Execution Dock, at low-water mark.

> *The Flying Post* (May 24) — Yesterday about three in the afternoon Capt Kidd; with four other pirates, were carried in carts from Newgate to Execution Dock, where between 6 and 7 they were executed.

> *The London Post* (May 24) — I am told that the corps of Capt Kidd is to be hung in chains at Tilbury Point.

> *The Post Boy* (May 27) — Captain Kidd is to be hanged in chains at Tilbury Point.

The Post Boy carried two other announcements in its edition of May 24, other than that quoted above. These are reproduced below:

> The King went yesterday to Greenwich, and dined with the Right Honourable the Earl of Romney, after which his Majesty went to Hampton Court.

Source unknown

Fate of many a Pirate after his Hanging at Execution Dock.
The corpse was encased in iron hoops and displayed on gallows at Tilbury Point as a warning to sailors. This illustration is taken from a woodcut circa 1900.

The Ordinary of Newgate his account of the behaviour, confession and dying words of Captain William Kidd, and the other pirates that were executed yesterday at Execution Dock in Wapping, will not be published till this afternoon. Printed for E. Mullet at the "Hat and Hawk" in Bride Lane. Beware of sham papers, there being no true account printed but this.

The fact that King William had dined with the Earl of Romney the same day that Kidd was hanged is rather ironic as Romney had helped finance Kidd's voyage to the Indian Ocean. Equally ironic is the fact that after his lunch with Romney, the king would have proceeded upriver by barge to Hampton Court, and in so doing would have witnessed the preparations, if not the spectacle itself, for Kidd to meet his maker. We will never know whether the king felt any remorse towards the fate of his "trusty and well-beloved." Whatever those feelings, William was to die within the year as a result of a fall from his horse.

Paul Lorrain, the Ordinary of Newgate, as the second account shows, was quick to get his latest scribblings into print to satisfy a public demand that would soon evaporate.

Kidd's family in New York suffered stoically the ignominy and shame of his hanging. For some time they lived in quiet seclusion, and after 18 months Sarah Kidd married a prominent politician named Christopher Rousby and lived for a further 43 years in comparative comfort. Kidd's daughters, Sarah and Elizabeth, both made good marriages.

Chapter 2

The Riches of the East

Dipping through the Tropics by the palmgreen shores,
With a cargo of diamonds, emeralds, amethysts,
Topazes, and cinnamon, and gold moidores.
— "Cargoes" (Masefield)

Long before the advent of European voyagers into the Indian Ocean, an extensive trade was carried out over enormous distances between the East and Europe. All the trade routes converged on Constantinople, and after its capture by the Turks in 1453, this trade of centuries was thrown into confusion and disarray. A significant part of the trade that passed through Constantinople originated along the Cinnamon Route, one that began in the islands of the East Indies, stretched across the ocean to Madagascar and Zanzibar, and thence to the Red Sea or Persian Gulf, into Asia Minor. Most of this seaborne traffic was carried in double outrigger canoes.

Herodotus was one of the ancients to describe the source of some of the riches of the East, if somewhat erroneously. Of gold in India, he writes: "… it is produced there in vast abundance, some dug from the earth, some washed down by the rivers."

Of its extraction in the desert: "… there live amid the sand great ants, in size somewhat less than dogs, but bigger than foxes … the sand which they throw up is full of gold … when the Indians reach the place where the gold is, they fill their bags with the sand, and ride away at their best speed; the ants, however, scenting them … rush forth in pursuit."

Of spices from Arabia: "… it is the only country which produces frankincense, myrrh, cassia, cinnamon and ledanum."

Herodotus continues to describe in fascinating detail how giant birds used cinnamon to line their nests, and the artifices to which the collectors resorted to hoodwink these poor creatures in order to rob their nests. So much for Herodotus.

The Gospel of St. Matthew is more succinct regarding the riches brought from the East to honour the birth of Christ: "… and when they had opened their treasures, they presented unto him gifts; gold, and frankincense and myrrh."

In the early fifteenth century Chinese junks dominated the Indian Ocean, taking back to the emperor's court at Peking the exotica of Africa, including giraffes. In contrast, the Portuguese were stumbling southward along the west coast of Africa, in emulation of a voyage of circumnavigation of the African continent that had been first accomplished 2,000 years earlier by the Phoenicians during the reign of Pharaoh Necho II in the sixth century BC.

Following the discovery of America by Columbus in 1492, Pope Alexander VI generously divided the unknown portions of the globe between the Spanish and the Portuguese, and it was the latter who were the first to penetrate eastern waters in an attempt to restore the trade links that had been severed following the fall of Constantinople. The stranglehold the Venetians had hitherto held on eastern commerce was thenceforth to be lost forever. Constrained to the Mediterranean, as they had been by their maritime tradition, the Venetians had neither the vessels nor the skills to compete upon the high seas for this all-important trade. It was the Spanish, Portuguese, French, Dutch, and finally the English that were to become the paramount players in maritime commerce with the Indies.

Dom Vasco da Gama is the European navigator credited with making the first recorded voyage to the Indies, in the process of which he doubled the Cape of Good Hope. Other Europeans, such as Magellan's crew, who completed the first circumnavigation of the world in 1522 following his murder in the Philippines, and Drake and his band of stalwart buccaneers who repeated this feat in 1577–80, may have been the first non-natives to sail directly across the Indian Ocean. However, it is to da Gama that we attribute the initiation of maritime commerce between Europe and the East. He sailed from Lisbon in July 1497, calling at Mozambique, Mombasa, Melinda, and Calicut, returning two years later. In 1502 he commanded a fleet sent out by the King of Portugal, with the express intentions of establishing settlements and trading posts. Calicut was the first of such colonies, though Goa was subsequently to become the centre for the burgeoning trade that ensued. It was at Goa that da Gama died in 1524.

Da Gama was forthright about the purpose of his first voyage. He came, he said, to "seek Christians and spices," and thereupon embarked on some curious means whereby he could convert the natives and, at the same time, rob them of their spices. He is reputed to have tortured the "heathen" Muslims with boiling pig fat in order to extract information, and made such a nuisance of himself that one ruler built a stockade to defend the water supply to his city. Da Gama took great delight in blowing this up before dealing with the city in the same fashion. Irritated by the trading measures employed by the Portuguese, the natives understandably became restless. Reprisals followed, and before long a cruel and merciless tit-for-tat was being exchanged. The spiral of violence escalated, resulting in the slaying of 53 Portuguese in one incident, and many merchants being burned alive. An emissary of a local ruler had his lips and ears cut off, the latter being replaced by sewing on the ears of a dog, before the unfortunate man was returned to his master. Amidst this barbarity, with its numerous burnings, demolitions, and tortures, began the seaborne trade with Europe. Before long the Portuguese had established themselves in Ceylon, Malacca, the Spice Islands, Macao, and the Persian Gulf. For a brief time Lisbon became the centre of the spice trade in Europe.

Throughout the following two centuries there was to be great competition between all the European nations eager to grab their share of the rich trade with the Indies. Despite the division of the globe into two parts, the west for the Spanish, and the east for the Portuguese, it was difficult to know when west became east. The Spaniards sailing ever westward soon claimed the Philippines. Hard on the heels of the Iberians came the French, Dutch, and English, and before long each held some degree of control, small and localized though it might have been, in outposts scattered throughout the region. How the English, through the East India Company, managed to become dominant within the confines of the Indian Ocean is a matter of history, and is of little concern to us here. What does concern us, however, is the concept held in popular imagination that the region contained wealth and riches, riches which might be considered ripe for the plucking.

Reference was made in the previous chapter to a report in the London newspaper, *The English Post*, regarding an attack upon a caravan crossing the desert from Mecca to Damascus. A Mr. William Daniel was travelling in the Red Sea region at the time of this incident, having left London on May 4, 1700, some four to five months earlier. From modern-day Yanbu al Bahr, often referred to as Yenbo, he wrote:

> JEMBO is the seaport town of that famous city Medena, where lies the body of their prophet Mahomet; ... this is the chief city of the Banioquebys or Bengebres, formerly called Saracens, living mainly upon robberies, being very numerous, and able in 24 hours to raise 50,000 men ... there arrived an express to the Governour, from his brother, to the great joy of the people of that town, with the news of their having robbed and destroyed the whole caravan of pilgrims and merchants in their return from Mecca to Damascus, and other parts of Asia, consisting of 70,000 men, giving a glad account how they had barbarously murdered those that resisted, stript the rest stark naked in that wild, scorching, and intolerable desert; and most savagely forced their women away with them. The number of these villains was computed at 100,000. This news not only affrighted him, but his janizaries. However they embarked and August 29th arrived at Judda [Jeddah].

The early accounts of travellers in the East are very illuminating as to the perceived notion of the region's wealth and the behaviour of the inhabitants. These accounts undoubtedly coloured the perceptions and attitudes of Europeans in general. They help us to understand the motivations of Kidd, his backers, and his crew regarding the outcome of a good voyage.

One of the first travellers to make careful notes of his perambulations around the region was a Mr. John Albert de Mandeslo. He travelled very extensively in the years 1638 to 1640. We are indebted to him for his journals, from which the following extracts are taken:

On the city of Gamron or Bandar Gamron:

> Latitude according to the Dutch is 27°. Its situation is upon the Persian Gulph, the entrance at the haven in which ships may ride at anchor without the least danger, at 5, or 6 fathom water, being defended by 2 strong castles, and a square redoubt. The castle is fortified with some antick round bastions, but well provided with artillery. The houses of Gamron are of brick, made of a mixture of stiff clay, sand, shredded straw, and horse dung; whereof having sett one layer, they cover it with a layer of straw or faggots, and so alternatively till they have raised it to 6 or 7 foot high; then they set it on fire, and burn it to brick. The streets of this city are very narrow, irregular, and not kept clean, which together with the excessive heat of the climate, and the changeableness of the winds, renders the air very pernicious here. The English and the Dutch come thither by sea, and besides their ready money, bring divers commodities both out of Europe and the Indies, which they exchange for Persian tapistry, raw silk, cotton, rhubarb, saffron and rose water, which is made in vast quantities.
>
> The pearl-trade is also one of the chiefest at Gamron, which are taken near the isle of Bahram, 6

Lgs from this city. The fisherman's head is enclosed in a bag of boiled leather, which has a pipe reaching up above water to fetch breath through; he rakes together all the shells he meets with at the bottom, and having filled his bag, which hangs about his neck, at a certain signal given by him, he is drawn up into the boat which waits for that purpose.

On Gujurat:

The winter begins in Guzuratta in June, and holds until September, but the rains are not as at Goa. There are but two winds which reign on this coast, viz the N and S winds, which blow each for 6 months without intermission. The greatest heat is in April, May and the beginning of June; but the sultriness of the season is somewhat temperated by frequent breezes of wind, which however bring this inconveniency along with them, that they raise the dust to such a degree, as robs you of the very sight of the sun at noon-day. The chiefest commodities of Guzuratta, are calicoes and silk stuffs, as satins, taffatas, petolas, commerbands, ornis of gold and silver, used for veils for women, brocados, tapestry, streaked carpets, quilts, tents, bedsteads, and cabinets, lacque, seals, beads, chains, buttons, and rings of ivory, rock chrystal and agat. There is also a great deal of saltpetre, vented at Suratte ... borax, well known for its usefulness in refining of gold and silver ... there is abundance of amfion, or opium. The province of Gusuratta produces abundance of cummin, ginger and mirobalans, which they preserve with brown sugar; besides which they have several physical drugs. Diamonds are likewise one of the chief products of this Province, but not many; yet have they good store of pearls, emeraulds, garnata, agats, alabaster, red marble, and jasper stone, which are better pollished here than any where else.

On Indian trade:

Their vessels are generally slightly built, and their great guns kept above deck; and they seldom venture any farther than to Java and Sumatra, or to Aden and Meca, upon the Red Sea; whither they go with a vast number of pilgrims in the beginning of March, and return not till September for fear of the tempests, which from June till then are very violent on that coast, whereas otherwise this voyage might be performed in 2 months.

They carry to the coast of Aden calicoes, indigo, champhire, tobacco, alum, sulphurs, benzoin, pepper and other spices, mirobalans, and many other preserves; in lieu of which they bring back coral, amber, a certain dye called misseit, coffee, berries and opium, but their best returns are in ready cash. Their coasting vessels which go to Cambaya, and Broitscha, and sometimes to Persia, go away in January and February, and return in April or May, and bring with them brocadoes, silk stuffs, velvets, camlets, pearls, almonds, raisons, nuts and dates, but especially rose water. The ships that go to Achin in the isle of Sumatra, are of 200 and 300 tuns burthen, carry thither the products of their country; in lieu of which they bring back brimstone, bezoin, champhire, porcelain, tin and pepper; they set sail in May and return in October.

The Malabars also drive a great trade at Suratte, Cambaya and Broitscha, they bring thither the bark of the cocoe-trees, which is used for making cordages of ships; The pith of the same tree ... which they use for caulking their ships, besides rice and other provisions; these they exchange for opium, saffron, coral, calicoes, and other stuffs. They come to the coast of Suratte, in December, and return in April. Formerly the Portuguese used to be the sole masters of the trade of Guzuratta, by means of their forts at Daman, Diu and Goa; but since the English and Dutch have made their settlements in those parts, they have been forced to confine their trade to Goa ....

On winds off the Malabar Coast:

The S.W. winds which begin to blow here towards the end of June, bring the winter season along with them which continues for 4 months all along that coast, from Diu as far as the Cape Comory; at which time the frequent tempests make the sea so turbulent, that there are few havens where ships can ride with safety. This is the more to be admir'd, inasmuch as in the same months the Coast of Coromandel, which extends along the same peninsula on the other side, and lies under the same deg of elev nay, in some places it is not above 20 Lgs distant from the Coast of Malabar, is bless'd with the most pleasing season of the year.

On a seafight off the Malabar Coast:

Jan 22, 1638-39 ... In the evening we saw the whole Dutch fleet under sail, whence we judged that the admiral, whose name was van Ceulen, would have come aboard of us, as he promised he would; but we lost sight of them by night. Jan 23 ... In the morning we had sight of them again, and supposed that they steered their course towards Ceylon, to assist that king against the Portuguese. About noon we found ourselves out of sight of the land at 13° Lat.

We intended to go for the Coast of Malabar, upon information that an English ship richly laden, coming from Bantam was taken by these after a brave defence, in which it had blown up above 1200 of the Moors after they were entered the ship; our intent was to redeem the master and the mate with 14 prisoners that were taken aboard her, but coming the same night to an anchor in the harbour of Cananor, we found three English ships, the Dragon, the Catherine, and the Seymour, commanded by Captain Weddel, a very experienced sea officer, who had served at the taking of Ormus (Hormuz), by whom being informed that most of the prisoners were set at liberty, we resolved to leave the Coast of Malabar.

On the Maldives:

Near the Cape of Comorin, along the Coast of Malabar, for a tract of near 140 Lgs by sea, extend the Isles (by some accounted 1000 in number) call'd Maldivas, or Maldivar by the Portugyese; having the Cape to the N some of which, being so very low, that they are often subject to inundations, are not inhabited, others are. The Malabars are opinion, that they were torn from the continent by the violence of the tempestuous waves of the sea, which in some places is so slender a distance from the continent, that a brisk active fellow might leap over it. The capital city which has given its name Maldives to all the islands, is built upon 4 small isles, being residence of the king, who commands over all the rest, and a place of good trade, tho' they produce naturally scarce anything but cocoes, but the industry of the inhabitants supplies, in some measure, the defect of nature here, there being not any nation in the Indies more ingenious in making garments of silk and thread (brought thither from the continent) than they.

On Ceylon:

Ceylon affords very good pepper, but their staple commodity is cinnamon. The Kingdom of Candy has certainly both gold and silver mines, but are not cultivated, by an express inhibition from the king; neither must their precious stones be sold to any but the king, but as they have such plenty of them, that they are found among the gravel that is washed down from the adjacent mountains, and carried along with the currents of the water, so it is impossible to prevent their being sold to strangers.

On Pegu (Burma):

Pegu affords no other spice but ginger, and scarce any other commodity is exported, except rice and silver, in exchange for which they bring thither stuffs and calicoes, pepper, cinnamon, opium, sandalewood, etc. They will pawn their children to borrow money, but if the creditor enjoys them carnally, they are free, and the debt is paid.

On Siam:

Their punishments are so severe, or rather cruel, that such as are used among us, are not as much known here: for the slightest crime deserves banishment or transportation; theft is punished with the amputation of hands or feet. The common way of executing criminals is to cast them alive into boyling oil. They have three sorts of trials for want of sufficient evidence; by fire, water and oil; in the water trial, both parties are let down to the bottom of the river, along a great pole, and he who can stay longest under water, obtains thereby his justification, as does he who can hold his hand longest in boyling oil, in the trial of oil; in the fiery trial they are to make 5 or 6 steps through a great fire very slowly, 2 men leaning hard upon their shoulders ...

On Sumatra:

The pepper of Sumatra is next to that of Cochin, the best of all the Indies. It is commonly planted at the root of trees, or propped up with canes as we do our hops. The leaves are not unlike those of the orange tree, but somewhat less, and picquant; the fruit grows in little branches like juniper berries. It is green whilst upon the tree, but grows black after it is dry'd, which is done in December and January ... It is certain that there is more pepper consumed in the Indies than in Europe, because the Indians put handfuls of it in all their sauces, but not beaten or grinded.

On Java:

In Tuban, next after Bantam in Java — Their chief traffick lies in pepper, which they exchange ... for calicoes, cotton and silk, and carry these commodities to Banda, Ternate, and the Philippine Isles, to truck for cloves, mace and nutmegs.

On the Moluccas:

The island of Amboyna, is so near the Molucques that some have accounted it among their number. Its circuit is 24 Lgs at 4° beyond the Line, and 2 Lgs from the isle of Ceram. The chief city has to the W of it, a very fair bay of 6 Lgs where there is safe anchorage, and a good shelter for ships against the winds. … The inhabitants were heretofore savages, and barbarous, nay cannibals, who apply'd themselves to no agriculture, which made the country appear like a wilderness; but of late years they have appl'd themselves to the cultivating of the ground, which being very fertile, produces great quantities of oranges, limons, cocoes, bananas, sugar-canes, besides cloves. They continue still to be a sort of ignorant people, the only skill they show, being in the management of the dart, which they do with much dexterity, that at 60 paces distant, they will hit a crown piece. They are famed for … their small galleys, which in swiftness exceed any in Europe. It was first discovered by the Portuguese, in the year 1515. But the Dutch afterwards also got footing there, the Portuguese being resolved to spoil their commerce, set upon 5 Dutch vessels in the port of Banda … Stephen Verhagon landed 2 years after, viz Feb 21, 1603 landed a certain number of soldiers near Amboyna, in order to attack the castle, but whilst he was landing his artillery, the Portuguese governor … surrendered the place without a cannon shot; though the garrison consisted of 600 Portuguese.

But the chief product of these islands [Moluccas] is the clove, call'd clavos by the modern Spaniard, by reason of its resemblance to an ordinary nail. The tree that bears it … resembles the laurel, its leaves being however somewhat narrower, like those of the almond tree; shooting forth its branches at the top, not unlike the myrtle. The fruit is white at first, grows green by degrees, and brown when it comes to maturity, but does not turn black till it be dry'd in the sun, which is done in 2 or 3 days.

This tree grows naturally without planting, or cultivating; bears fruit in the 8th year, and lasts 100 years. The fruit is gathered but once every other year, because the inhabitants break off the buds the first, that they may have a more plentiful crop the second year. The fruit is ripe from August to January. … As the Molucques yield more cloves than any other of the islands hereabouts, this has misled some to affirm, that they grow only here, it being certain they yield yearly 6000 barrels of cloves (550 weight to a barrel) tho' at the same time the isles of Ires, Meytarana, Cavaly, Sabugo, Marigoran, Gamoconora, Amboyna, but especially the isle of Veranula produce considerable quantities, but not so good as those of the Molucques.

On tortoises (turtles) in the Indian Ocean:

Tortoises (the meat of which is as fine as veal) are in such plenty here, that the seamen draw them at pleasure into the ship with hooks, The Dutch speak of tortoises of such bigness, that ten men might sit upon one shell.

Some time after William Daniel had made his journey in 1700, a Mr. Tavernier travelled into India, Burma (Pegu), Ceylon and various islands in the region. He writes as follows:

… taking ship at Bander-Abassi, or Ormus … That sailing is not safe at all times upon the Indian, as it is upon the European coasts. You must observe the proper seasons, which being past there is no venturing. The months of November to March are the only time of the year to embark for Surat, to Ormus; but from Surat you must not stir after the end of February, for then the western winds, that bring rain along with them into India, begin to blow; but during those 4 months there blows a NE wind, which carries the ships from Surat to Ormus in 15 or 20 days; and this wind veering a little to the north serves also for those that are bound for Surat; but it takes them up to 30 to 35 days, for which they are made amends in March, and the beginning of April, for then the western winds blowing full in their stern carries them thither in 14 or 15 days.

The king of Golconda (7 miles west of Hyderabad) has vast revenues ... The diamond mines raise him a great revenue, and all they that he allows to dig in them. This prince wears upon the crown of his head a jewel almost a foot long, which is said to be of inestimable value. It is a rose of great diamonds, 3 or 4 inches in diameter ... Besides this jewel, he hath other considerable pieces, and such numbers of precious stones, that if there were merchants who could give him the worth of them, he would have prodigious sums of money, and be the richest king of the Indies.

Palicate ... It is a fort that belongs to the Dutch that live upon the Coast of Coromandel, and within it are usually 200 soldiers. It is the chief factory they have in the Indies, where lives the superintendent of all the rest which are in the territories of the king of Golconda. The trade managed there by the Dutch is in cotton cloth, of which they have large warehouses full. Here also they refine their saltpetre, which they bring from Bengal, and make gunpowder with which they furnish their other factories.

Great store of salt-peter comes from Agra to Patna, but that which is refined is 3 times the value of that which is not. Cardomum, which is the most excellent of all spices, grows in the territory of Visapour, and because there is no great store of it where it grows, it is only made use of in Asia, at the tables of the greatest princes. Ginger grows in the dominions of the Great Mogul, and is brought in great quantities from Amadabat, where it grows more than in any other part of Asia; pepper is of 2 sorts, the small and the great; the small comes from Bantam Asken, and some other parts of the East ... the great pepper comes from the coasts of Malabar, and some from Visapour. Nutmegs come from the Molucca islands, and also from the islands of Banda ... Cloves grow at Amboyna, Ellias, Seram and Bouro. Cinnamon comes at present from the island of Ceilon.

... The Hollanders are at a great charge in Ceilon to gather their cinnamon, because the king sends his forces upon them, when they are gathering to surprise them, and take it from them, so that they are forced to have a guard upon their workmen of 7 or 800 men; and this makes cinnamon dearer, and so much the more because the Dutch have spoiled the trade for it from the countries of the raja's about Cochin.

At Raolconda, a town of 5 Lgs distant from Golconda, and 8 or 9 from Visapour, ... is a diamond mine discovered not above 200 years ago. In it are found the cleanest stones, with the whitest water; but being forced to fetch them out of the rocks with a great iron leaver, and many blows, they often flaw the diamonds, and make them look like chrystal, and this is the reason there are so many soft stones found in this mine, though they make a great shew.

At Gani, or Coulour, 7 days journey from Golconda, eastward is a diamond mine. It lies between the town and a mountain, and the nearer they dig to the mountain the larger stones they find, but there is none at the top. This mine was found not above 100 years ago by a country-man, who digging his ground to sow millet, found a large diamond of 25 carats weight. Upon this the rich men in the town fell to digging in the place, and found as they still do, bigger stones than in any other mine, viz some above 40 carats, and one of 900, which Margimola presented to Aureng-zeb; but the mischief of these stones is, they partake of the quality of the soil, and are few of them clean, but some are black, others red, and others green and yellow.

The 2 biggest diamonds in the world, for cut stones, belong, the one to the Mogul, which weighs 279 and 9/16th carats, and the other the Duke of Tuscany, which weigh 139 carats, both clean and well shaped.

There are but 2 places in all the East, where coloured stones are found, and they are in the kingdom of Pegu, and island of Ceilon. The 1st is a mountain 12 days journey, or thereabouts from Sireri towards the NE. It is called Capelan: in this mine are found great quantities of rubies ... yellow topazes, blue and white saphires, jacinths, amethysts, and other different colours. ... The other place, where rubies are found, is a river in the island of Ceilon, which descends from certain high mountains in the middle of the island: it swells very high when the rains fall, and when it becomes low again, the people make it their business to search among the sands for rubies, saphires and topazes. All the stones that are found in this river are fairer and clearer than those in Pegu.

There is a fishery for pearls in the island of Ceilon: for their roundness and water, they are the fairest that are found, but rarely weigh above 3 or 4 carats.

As for ambergrease, there is no man in the world knows what it is, or how it is produced. It is most probable that it must be in the eastern sea, though some has been found on the coasts of England, and other nations of Europe. ... A Portugal sailing from Goa to the Manilles, after he had passed the Streights of Malacca, found a piece of 33 pound weight, and a Middleburgher a piece of 42 pound weight upon the coast of the island of S. Maurice (Mauritius)

Daniel, Mandelslo, and Tavernier each give vivid portrayals of life in the Indian Ocean region in the period prior to or following William Kidd's fateful voyage. They describe in meticulous detail the wealth in gold, jewels, and spices that was available to the intrepid trader in exchange for cash or for merchandise, which often took the form of slaves. The same wealth could also be viewed as a source of plunder to be taken by force of arms. We are deeply indebted to the writers of these travelogues in recording their various odysseys, and the perils that beset them.

At the time Kidd's ship, the *Adventure Galley*, entered the Indian Ocean, the Dutch Verenigde Oostindische Compagnie had managed to engineer a virtual monopoly of the clove trade. The price of cloves on the European market had risen astronomically, and there was little difference in the value of cloves and an equal weight of gold. The Dutch had extended their control over nearly all the clove-producing islands in the Indies, destroyed the clove trees on the outlying islands that could not be effectively policed, and concentrated production at Amboyna. It was at Amboyna in 1623 that the Dutch forcibly removed a small English trading post in what later became known as the Massacre of Amboyna. The Dutch were little better than the Portuguese in the methods they used in establishing control of mercantile trade, which they believed was their prerogative.

The lure of the riches of the East spawned lust and greed among the European adventurers and their commercial backers, which reached its height towards the end of the seventeenth century and beginning of the eighteenth. This avarice led to intense rivalry and hatred, which was to develop into international hostility, often culminating in war. Privateers appeared on what hitherto had been relatively placid waters, and privateering inevitably degenerated into piracy. The abundance of wealth being transported by sea included, as we have seen, silks, brocades, muslins, dyes, and foodstuffs, drugs, tobacco, opium, spices in great variety — including cloves, the costliest of all — with massive quantities of pearls, precious stones, ivory, and gold. The very stuff of pirate dreams! And, of course, there was the prospect of gold coin! It didn't matter if they were Islamic dinars or ancient Persian tetradrachms that filled the pockets of a pirate; back home in North America it was all warmly welcomed. William Kidd, his backers, and his crew might be forgiven while salivating in their sleep at the prospect of such riches so ripe for the taking.

Chapter 3

Piracy in the Indian Ocean

> 'Ha! Ha!' quoth he, 'full plain I see,
> The Devil knows how to row.'
> — "The Rime of the Ancient Mariner" (Coleridge)

For centuries, long before Europeans penetrated the vastness of the Indian Ocean, the region had been beset with pirates. They infested its waters wherever a maritime trade could be preyed upon with minimum effort and maximum effect. One of the great routes of seaborne commerce, as we have seen, lay through the Persian Gulf, perhaps the oldest of any. Archaeological evidence has traced this trade link back to 5000 BC, when the arteries of commerce linked the ancient civilizations of Mesopotamia with India and the East. Complementing the trade in goods was the traffic in slaves, an essential counterpart.

The institution of slavery, more odious than that of piracy itself, is described in many ancient records and accorded a degree of legitimacy that clashes with modern attitudes. The Mosaic Law contains rules for the treatment of slaves, and the numerous civilizations of Asia institutionalized slavery, as did the Greeks and Romans, whose empires depended upon it. The Arabs were no different, and the hinterland of East Africa was virtually a private reserve for Arab traders until the coming of enlightened Europeans. In fact there is evidence that even today, the trade in humans for profit has not been eradicated within the confines of the Indian Ocean. Along with the practice of slavery went piracy, and it was along the trade routes that piracy flourished regardless of the nature of the goods being transported, even if they were in the form of human misery.

The native pirate did not possess the means to undertake long sea voyages, and thus he tended to command a relatively small region in which he could dominate his more peaceful neighbours by terror and thuggery. He positioned himself along those strategic stretches of navigable water that saw a sizeable trade, and where the chances of retribution were slight.

Though piracy first became evident in the Arabian Sea and Persian Gulf regions, it spread rapidly. Robbery at sea is little different from robbery on land, and once man learned how to build a boat, he soon learned how to rob the weak and unwary who took to the water with desirable goods. Before long the shorelines of the Indian Ocean abounded with native pirates. These pirates were to meet their future match in the European pirates, who sailed in better designed and formidably armed vessels and possessed superior sailing and navigational skills. Let us spend this chapter looking at the history of piracy in the Indian Ocean, before devoting ourselves to the particular career of William Kidd, with whose name Indian Ocean piracy is often commonly associated. The following is not a full account of this piracy, but it is hoped that the selected tidbits recounted will help the reader to appreciate the overall history as it relates to piracy, in which Kidd played a small but unique role.

Though the ancient civilization of Mesopotamia was well endowed with bitumen, clay, and agricultural products, it lacked hard building stone, metal ores, and good timber. The Tigris and Euphrates rivers were natural thoroughfares that led to India, the Yemen, and beyond. A vast network of trade links slowly developed, which unfortunately attracted the attentions of pirates, who viewed this trade with covetous eyes. A particularly hazardous stretch lay through the Strait of Hormuz at the entrance to the Persian Gulf. This constriction was an admirable location at which to ambush vulnerable trading vessels, and as a consequence, pirates throughout the centuries congregated in clusters around its rock-bound shores from Cape Musandam to Bahrain.

A local tribe of Arabs, known as the Joassamees, took full advantage of the situation. The town of Ras-el-Khayma, on the Persian Gulf side of the promontory, grew as a result of the inhabitants waxing fat upon the profits of plunder. It stood on a narrow tongue of sand, one side of which gave access to the waters of the gulf, the other to a small creek which afforded a safe harbour. The location was well protected by a fortress and various stone towers. During hostilities with the British in 1816, the town could muster 60 large boats manned with crews of between 80 and 300 men each. With support from allies in the immediate vicinity the Joassamees could field at least 8,000 men. This gives some indication as to the strength of the pirates and the extent to which they relied upon piracy for their livelihood.

The Joassamees naturally fell afoul of local authority in the form of sheikhs, who viewed piracy as a contravention of Islamic law. Numerous forays and skirmishes, and a major battle or two, occurred over the ages without outright victory being won by either party; neither peace nor total anarchy prevailed. The Joassamees were like a rash that would not go away but went into frequent remission. The situation came to a head during the early nineteenth century through the intervention of the East India Company.

The East India Company had persevered through the years in setting up trading posts throughout the gulf, and with these posts came various factories at which the merchandise purchased from native sources was readied for the European market. The vessels operated by the Company were generally well manned and, what is more important, well armed. These large ships were coveted by the Joassamees, but their discretion overcame their valour and they were allowed to pass without fear of hindrance for many years. It was not the policy of the Company at the time to be drawn into local policing activities, unless their profits were likely to be affected as a result of the disruption to trade. Clearly, the practice of piracy within the gulf waters was bound to impinge upon the Company's ability to carry on mercantile trade in a peaceable manner if a firm stand was not taken, and the sooner that stand was taken the better.

The relatively peaceful situation within the gulf, whereby the Company shut its eyes to the backdrop of tribal disputes, piracy, and localized anarchy, came to an abrupt end in 1797 when a number of Arab dhows approached the Persian representative of the Company at Bushire for gunpowder and shot. The unsuspecting agent sold them these necessities in the belief that they were to be used in the settlement of some local dispute, but his thinking couldn't have been further from the truth. No sooner had they received these supplies than the Arabs distributed them throughout their flotilla and turned their guns on the sole vessel of the Company, which lay at anchor within the harbour. It was the *Viper*, a small armed frigate. The timing of the Arab attack was opportune as the crew was enjoying breakfast and their commander was ashore. Despite a vicious and sudden cannonading, the crew reacted with well-trained naval discipline and managed to repulse the boarding parties. After some desperate exchanges the English drove off the attackers, but they suffered many casualties, including the senior officers, in the process. The command fell to a young midshipman, the anchors were weighed, sails unfurled, and the chase ensued well out to sea. The Arabs eluded both capture and destruction, but a good number of years elapsed before they regained enough confidence to attack another Company ship. Meanwhile the attack had jolted the Company into finally realizing the systemic danger these pirates posed to peaceful trading in the gulf. From then on they took greater precautions, but the time would come when the gulf pirates became better organized, better equipped, and better led. They became a very hostile element that impacted severely and continually upon European trade for many years to come.

It was not only Arab pirates that were encountered, and against whom defences had to be mounted, though these were in far greater number than any others. On occasion, privateers from nations at war with England would venture into the gulf on the lookout for Company vessels to attack. In 1804 a French privateer caught up with a small Company ship to the west of the Strait of Hormuz, and in its attempt to escape capture, the ship was driven onto shoals and promptly sank. The French privateer rescued the passengers and crew and, with due consideration for their welfare and safety, took them into Bushire. Here they managed to purchase a dhow in which they planned to continue their voyage to Bombay; however, on reaching the mouth of the gulf, in close proximity to the place they had suffered the previous sad encounter, they were attacked by the Joassamees. After a token resistance, being over-whelmed by numbers and without armaments, they were captured and taken to Ras-el-Khyma, the pirate stronghold. Here they were held for ransom, but as none was paid, for many months they lan-guished in the most appalling conditions. The pirate leaders decid-ed that they should all be put to death by having their throats cut, and with this certain fate hanging over them, a plan was conceived. They volunteered to disclose the location where the first ship had sunk, and suggested that the ship's hold contained booty. This, it was hoped, would prolong their lives if not purchase their freedom.

Arriving at the wreck site the divers in the employ of the Joassamees soon managed to locate the ship's remains and com-menced their salvage; accustomed as they were to diving for pearls in the waters off Bahrein, the shallow shoals presented no difficul-ties. The crews of the pirate ships joined in the general looting of the wreck, leaving the vessel with the captured English on board only lightly manned. Seizing their opportunity, the captives endeavoured to overcome the few Arabs on board, cut the anchor cable, and set sail. The attempt to liberate themselves failed and they were taken to the nearby island of Kenn, where the pirates commenced the wholescale massacre of the inhabitants. During this frenzied assault on the natives, the English captives effected flight, seeking refuge in various clefts and hiding places, until the pirates, satiated with blood and replete with plunder, eventually left the unfortunate place. The marooned English managed to find a boat which they could repair and the materials to make a raft, and after a few days they attempted once again to reach the Persian main-land. During this perilous voyage, one of the vessels sank with the loss of all hands, and the party was reduced to half its number. The survivors marched west along the coast back to Bushire, a task which took many months and during which there was further loss of life, the dead being buried along the trail.

One of the most feared pirate chiefs in the Joassamee camp was Rahmah-ben-Jabir, whose followers numbered 2,000 men. During his command he displayed an inconsummate love for butchering all those who crossed him, even for the most trivial of reasons. Not content simply in slaying those defeated in battle, he would put to death in the most barbaric manner those who later submitted. Even members of his own crew, suspected of muttering against him, were murdered in cold blood with the especial cruelty reserved for those believed to be mutinous. He kept a tank of water on board one of his dhows into which he would thrust selected victims, shutting the lid tightly upon them until they had either suffocated or drowned, after which he would fling their corpses overboard. He delighted in watching the sharks feed upon the bodies of his victims. With this odious reputation preceding him wherever he went, and with his ragtail following in attendance, he was feared throughout the length and breadth of the gulf. The inhabitants of the numerous settlements treated him with the utmost courtesy and deference. Even the agents of the East India Company gave him the respect he believed he deserved whenever he made his periodic appearances. It is said that Rahmah-ben-Jabir dressed simply, but he never removed his shirt from the day he put it onto his back until it fell off him in tatters. His personal hygiene was non-existent and, as might be expected, his habits were equally filthy. It is reported that at one meeting with a Company factor, he and his entourage spent their time hunting for the abundant vermin that infested their persons, crushing them with their fingers and flicking the remains upon the ground.

Despite his total lack of attention to his personal appearance and hygiene, Rahmah-ben-Jabir was a very brave man. He entered into battle with great enthusiasm matched with optimism, and suffered many wounds with a degree of stoicism rarely exhibited by Europeans or others. He lost the use of one arm in battle, as well as the sight of both eyes, but this neither served to diminish his appetite for fighting, nor to lessen the power that he held over his adherents. In the end he went down fighting. A small armada had been dispatched by the Sheikh of Bahrain to destroy him, and after the sheikh's men had gained the upper hand, and with disgrace staring him in the face, he blew up his own ship by setting fire to the magazine. This singular act not only resulted in his own death but also that of his son and most of his crew, and the destruction of several of the sheikh's vessels that were unfortunate enough to be in the middle of the fighting. Upwards of 300 men are said to have perished in the conflagration, only one of Rahmah's crew being saved.

Though many of the Arab pirates practised indescribable cruelty, this cruelty was not confined to their race. One of the most bloodthirsty pirates, who carried out numerous acts of barbarity, was an Englishman named Ben Johnson. While in the Red Sea in 1750, he deserted from the East Indiaman on which he was serving and entered the service of a local sheikh who was in need of a commander for his pirate fleet of 14 vessels. He is reputed to have attracted 200 other Englishmen to his cause, and before long he and his ships proved to be a terror to peaceful maritime trade in the Arabian Sea. He converted to Brahminism, but does not seem to have fully digested the peaceful tenets of that religion, as subsequently he plunged ever deeper into barbarity in all its cruellest forms. He raided a place of Hindu pilgrimage on an island close to the entrance of the Persian Gulf, put to death 2,000 priests and cut off the noses and lips of 700 of the womenfolk, sparing only the prettiest, whom he and his crew took away along with the booty. Towards the end of his career, he contrived to escape from his master and make his way to Constantinople, where he lived to a good old age on the immense wealth he had won through his piratical and merciless exploits.

At the opposite extremity of the Indian Ocean to the Persian Gulf lies the Strait of Malacca. This waterway, like the Persian Gulf, is one through which trade has passed during the millennia. It too offered considerable opportunities to make an easy living by waylaying the innocent traveller and merchant upon the high seas. Here, among the numerous creeks, backwaters, and estuaries that fringe the Malayan and Sumatran coastlines, lay rapacious natives awaiting their opportunity to seize unsuspecting prey. In fact the entire East Indies archipelago, with its thousands of miles of coastline and its innumerable tiny islands, and its lack of any centralized power, religion, or moral government, afforded an excellent prospect for the piratical fraternity. It still does today, as newspaper headlines testify from time to time. This should not be interpreted to suggest that the tribes inhabiting the region were totally lawless, for many sustained themselves through agriculture and had strong ethic principles and a community spirit based upon religious belief and practice, and had no inclination towards this despicable trade. Java was one such island which gave little, if any, support to pirate communities.

The most confirmed pirates in the region were the Malays who inhabited the small islands at the eastern extremity of the Strait of Malacca, further east to the coasts of Borneo and the Celebes, and northwards up into the Gulf of Siam. The practice of the Malays, of which the Illanoons made up one of the most fearsome groups, was to lie concealed along stretches of coast until an unsuspecting vessel was either becalmed or ran aground. That short interval at eventide, when the wind changes from onshore to offshore, was the ideal time to commence a forceful attack, one that could be pressed home with advantage. Sailors aboard the target vessel would either be busy in altering the set of their sails, or resting in a becalmed state. The pirates would then sweep out from their hiding places in their proas, often over 50 feet in length, with crews over 30 strong per proa, armed to the teeth and with great co-ordination. When they mounted an attack they would put up strong bulwarks covered with buffalo hides to defend themselves from missiles and gunshot. Occasionally, much larger proas, or praams, with swivel guns would be employed with significantly larger crews all armed to the teeth. They would station themselves around the target vessel, engaging their enemy in such a manner as to keep them fully occupied, but with little risk to themselves. When the enemy had been thoroughly exhausted they would then make their attack, swarming aboard with the object of killing everyone in sight. Few escaped with their lives, except perhaps a few females who would be taken off to the villages for the pirates' pleasure and amusement.

The native princes, if that is how they can be termed, collaborated with the pirates, supplying the adventurers with arms, ammunition, and opium, taking in return a share of the female captives, cannon, and booty. The pirates formed an indispensable part of any self-respecting rajah's forces to aid him in the settlement of the interminable local disputes that were ubiquitous throughout the general region. In fact they constituted his navy.

When European trading vessels first ventured into the East Indies, they were received with curiosity mixed with awe. The European ships were larger and better than any built locally, and they were better manned with better firepower and better discipline. However, greed overcame curiosity and awe, and the sight of such magnificent ships induced covetousness. Inevitably European vessels were perceived as the most desirable of acquisitions. Before long trouble ensued and any ship venturing into these waters had to be on constant alert. This vigilance was often prematurely discarded with dire consequences for the crews concerned. The natives would mask their intentions under a tissue of falsehood and deception, giving an aspect of compliance to those against whom they had piratical intentions. Many hundreds of ships of European and later American registry would meet their fate in this manner, as would their crews, who would be butchered as a result.

One of the most notorious of the East Indian pirates was Angria, whose brother, the sultan of Timor, had been deposed by the British when they assumed temporary control of Timor. Nursing an understandable grievance, Angria commenced a vendetta against British shipping, and his first victim was a merchantman, the *Elphinston*, which he captured off Bombay. He treated his captives with some consideration, putting 47 men into a small boat with no water and casting them adrift in the hottest month of the year. Only 28 managed to reach Bombay alive. Less considerate acts plunged Angria deeper into the beastlier aspects of piracy, which included flaying with whips, or cutting skin off his victim's back before flinging him to the sharks. He is reported to have murdered more than 500 Englishmen in cold blood. Three years into this exciting career his vessel was chased by HMS *Asia* into Timor and, after a siege lasting 12 months, Angria was eventually shot by one of the Timorese.

In 1831 the *Friendship*, of Salem, Massachusetts, was captured at Qualla Battoo on the coast of Sumatra. The *Friendship* was there to purchase pepper, and many of the crew went ashore to assist in the weighing and transporting of this commodity. One of the pepper boats came up alongside carrying an uncommon number of labourers to assist in stowing the pepper bags on board, but fierce hand-to-hand fighting commenced instead. Other proas quickly joined in the action, having lain in wait along the nearby shore. These each carried 50 men, and the crew of the *Friendship* was soon overwhelmed. A nearby chief, friendly to the Americans, and with whom much business had been transacted on previous occasions, joined in with his men, but they were beaten off by the pirates who had now taken over the ship. News of the capture was carried to other American vessels further down the coast, and by the time they arrived on the scene, the *Friendship* had been looted. Everything moveable had been taken, and since the pirates had been unable to raise sail, endeavours had been made to set her on fire. An attempt was made to warp the charred remains of the embattled ship to a safe location where repairs might be effected, but the ship was run aground and sadly had to be abandoned. None of the cargo, which amounted to a value of $30,000, was recovered, and taking into account the value of the vessel, it was a huge financial loss for the pepper merchant concerned. This is one occasion when maintaining vigilance would certainly have avoided disaster.

Revenge for this incident was soon forthcoming. Exactly a year later, the United States government sent out a frigate masked as a merchantman, which anchored off Qualla Battoo. The overconfident pirates attempted the same ruse, but this time the element of surprise worked against them. Over 100 pirates were killed and their settlement razed to the ground. With 32-pound shot coming at them, the pirates and those in league with them suffered a severe lesson. There were many other lessons of a similar nature that had to be learned by the inhabitants of the region before foreign trading vessels could travel with any degree of comfort, or security, through the Strait of Malacca. Some lessons are never learned, and even today the Strait of Malacca is no place for the unwary or the naive seaman to be afloat.

The Persian Gulf and the Strait of Malacca were by no means the only parts of the Indian Ocean where piracy flourished before the advent of European vessels in large numbers, accompanied by their own peculiar brand of pirate. Two other regions of the Indian Ocean that received similar attentions, because of the riches flowing that way, were the Strait of Aden or Babs-al-Mandab, known as the Babs, and the Malabar Coast of India. The Babs attracted a considerable amount of maritime traffic. Ships passed through the narrow entrance to the Red Sea in great numbers, bound for the Red Sea coast of Egypt, the Gulf of Aqaba, and the Arabian ports along the Hejaz. Vast volumes of merchandise were transported from the Orient and these shipments were attractive to pirates for the value of goods carried. But through the strait also came the many pilgrims to Mecca undertaking the annual hajj. These Muslims, from as far away as Southeast Asia, carried with them immense amounts of personal wealth in the form of gold, silver, jewels, precious cloths, and sumptuous delicacies, all most tempting to the pirate who made the Babs his hunting ground. The Babs was like a huge funnel through which poured enormous quantities of mouth-watering goods that were irresistible to any pirate with red blood coursing through his veins.

South of the Strait of Babs-al-Mandab lay the long stretch of East African coastline that was the particular preserve of Arab traders, and over which the Sultan of Muscat claimed jurisdiction. Often known as the Fever Coast, it stretched as far south as the island of Madagascar. Ideally located for piracy in these waters was the cluster of islands around Zanzibar, the local terminus of the slave-trading empire of the Arabs. These islands, lying full in the track of the monsoons, afforded easy and convenient access to the Red Sea, India, and the Persian Gulf, and the trade routes that carried an abundance of shipping and commerce, whether in slaves, pilgrims, gold, ivory, frankincense, or any other commodity. The islands possessed good harbours, but above all else they were free of the dreaded malarial fevers that were endemic on the mainland. The Arab pirates, because of the Koranic code, could not sell fellow Muslims into slavery within regions dominated by Islam, but to overcome this restriction they sold them into China, taking the cautionary measure of castrating the males. This was to humour the Emperor of China, who was keen to ensure that his subjects would not be contaminated by interbreeding as a consequence of this profitable relationship. Castrated slaves were branded with a distinctive mark on their forehead.

The Malabar Coast of India was somewhat less profitable than the Babs, but it too suffered the attentions of numerous pirates of homegrown origin. A considerable amount of trade flowed up and down the coast between such legendary places as Cochin, Calicut, Tellicherry, Mangalore, Goa, Bombay, Surat, and beyond. There was no native power to exercise control over the predators that were attracted to this region. The Laccadive Islands, lying some 100 miles off the coast, also provided a suitable base for pirates preying on this coastal traffic, provided they had the vessels and attendant skills of seamanship and navigation to seek this refuge where they were virtually secure from retaliation. Following the arrival of Europeans in these waters, the locals were quick to take advantage of their opportunities to learn some of the skills necessary to advance their profession, and the coastal pirates grew stronger and more cunning by this transfer of knowledge.

Many of the native communities within the Laccadives were decimated by pirates taking a fancy to their islands. Once an island had been selected as a pirate base, the native inhabitants would be slaughtered, if not fortunate enough to be impressed, and their womenfolk raped and forced into menial and domestic work serving the pirates for as long as the pirates wished. The Malabar Coast might not have had as much tempting trade passing along it as funnelled through the Babs, but there was one redeeming feature. The targetting of Muslim pilgrims by the pirates lurking in the Babs caught the attention of Muslim rulers who treated it as an insult to Islam, and invited retribution. In the case of the Malabar pirates, no such retribution could be invoked as no religious taboos had been violated. Hindoo rulers may have given vent to their wrath at the attacks upon the coastal trade off their domains, but their ability for armed reprisals was limited. All they could do was curse or weep as the occasion warranted. Their cursings were to diminish and their weepings to cease by the time the Royal Navy had become firmly established in the Indian Ocean, but this did not happen until the latter half of the nineteenth century.

There was only one region within the bounds of the Indian Ocean that does not seem to have been bedevilled to any great extent by native pirates. This was the long stretch of East African coastline below Madagascar. Before the arrival of the Europeans there was little trade along this coast, except by Arab slave traders who, since they were the predators, were far better equipped. Their armed ships and seamanship skills enabled them to repel any attempt by indigenous Africans to seize their vessels and the commodities they carried. Furthermore, there was no maritime tradition among African tribes, and many Africans viewed the sea with fear and trepidation, considering those that the sea carried upon its bosom as fiends. When Europeans first landed on the Zululand coast, their ships, the armaments they carried, and the white skins of their crews all combined to strike fear and dread into many of the Zulu tribes. These initial emotions were soon to evaporate as familiarity bred contempt.

The island of Madagascar, or Isle of Saint Laurence as it was first named by the early Europeans, was regarded favourably by the first European traders and settlers. In fact, the English made tentative steps to colonize Madagascar as early as 1644 by establishing a settlement at Saint Augustine Bay, but the colony failed tragically, mainly through disease, and no further attempt was made. However, intrusion by Europeans into the island's affairs soon realized the potential of trading with the numerous native kings and princes. There was a vast fortune to be made in trading guns and powder in return for captives won in battle, and the native rulers were encouraged to take up arms supplied by the European traders in order to settle their disputes. In the process, captives were safeguarded for resale to their European benefactors instead of being massacred. It is certain that the trade in slaves from Madagascar never attained the scale of that from West Africa, but it gave the slave traders another source from which to reap much profit.

Ironically the Madagascar trade was centred on New York rather than in Europe, and New York merchants waxed fat upon the proceeds. They exported commodities such as cloth, knives, tools, cooking utensils, liquor, and all the necessities for an improved lifestyle for the natives along with the means of waging war. Since this trade had not been sanctioned by any legally constituted authority, there was little exercise of any control in its practice. In the final analysis, its success depended upon the trust that could be engendered between the various parties concerning the maintenance of power within the community for the chiefs, or the profits that could be gained by the traders. To the credit of this primitive thinking many satisfactory alliances were forged, and the steady stream of guns into Madagascar was only equalled by the steady stream of misery being loaded onto ships destined for the West Indies and North America. Many trading alliances stood the test of time but many did not, either due to a shift in power politics on the island or to rivalry between the traders. In this relatively lawless state it was inevitable that the European pirate soon saw his opportunity to cash in.

The European buccaneering fraternity does not seem to have made its presence felt in the Indian Ocean until the latter part of the seventeenth century, shortly before Kidd appeared on the scene. The West Indies had, up to this time, attracted European adventurers in large numbers ever since the Spanish conquest of the mainland and the huge bounty of riches that streamed back to Spain as a result of this colonization. Plundering of Spanish vessels, carrying vast amounts of wealth in the form of gold and silver, jewels, plate, and valuable artifacts torn out of Aztec and Inca domains, had become a national pastime for English, French, and Dutch pirates. Countries at war with Spain gave a legitimacy to this plundering by issuing letters of marque, permitting ships sailing under their colours to attack enemy shipping. The buccaneers were quick to take advantage of the political situation, knowing they were the backbone of their nation's ability to harass the enemy on the high seas. However, during the seventeenth century, European powers were becoming sensitive to the fact that the privateers were beginning to unduly affect the ability of their diplomats to conduct sensible relations with other nations, some with whom they were at war and others with whom relationships were strained. The privateers, whose actions bordered on piracy, were to become a wild card in the sphere of European politics in the West Indies, and, as may be expected, moves were made to suppress them. As a consequence, the pirates migrated out of the West Indies in a bid to seek alternative hunting grounds where the niceties of the law would not duly affect the business of filling their pockets. As privateering and piracy followed in the wake of trade and colonization, the allure of the Indian Ocean beckoned and the pirates followed their natural instincts.

The burgeoning trade with India meant that vessels of Portuguese, Dutch, and English nationalities were constantly rounding the Cape of Good Hope, and in their transit from the coasts of India, would pass in close proximity to the island of Madagascar. Many sought out the Comoros, where fresh water and provisions were available, and as a result the waters around the northern tip of Madagascar had the potential to become happy hunting grounds for pirates. It was at Isle St. Marie, towards the northeastern extremity of Madagascar, that an interesting pirate community grew up.

St. Marie is a narrow island about 40 miles long that lies off the mainland of Madagascar, separated from it by a channel some 18 miles wide. The island is low-lying, with a high point midway along its length rising to some 370 feet above sea level. Toward its southern end is a fine harbour that looks westward to the hills of Madagascar, which rise to over 3,000 feet. It is a picturesque spot, with the modern town of Soanierana Ivango across the channel on the mainland, and that of Ambodifotora on the island, in close proximity to the old pirate harbour. These are the two largest settlements in the area. The eastern coast of Madagascar is characterized by steep cliffs and the pirate harbour is one of the few safe anchorages along that stretch of coastline. At the entrance to the harbour is a small island, which gives the advantage of providing an excellent defensive position to ward off, or give notice of, unwelcome intruders. Recent findings have disclosed the presence of old fortifications on this strategically situated knoll of limestone, and the discovery of a vast network of tunnels and chambers has led to much speculation that the island may have been one of the fabled pirate banks, that is, a place when pirates stashed their goods while out "on account."

In the heyday of Indian Ocean piracy there were few native residents on St. Marie, and they could be easily dominated by the European intruders and forced to be accommodating. The same could not be said about Madagascar proper, where the numerous local kings and tribal chiefs squabbled with each other in an atmosphere of constant discord bordering on active war, to which they resorted at frequent intervals. Trade abhors uncertain politics, and so St. Marie became the emporium through which trade was conducted with the mainland. The pirate harbour flourished to such an extent that it is claimed that at one time over 1,500 pirates and traders made it their centre of operations. The first factor to set up a permanent base did so in 1691, and from then on a very sizeable and profitable trade was conducted, with merchandise of all sorts imported mainly from North America. Guns, powder, sails, rigging, clothing, pots and pans, knives and axes, and of course prodigious quantities of liquor to satiate the thirsts of the pirates all found their way to the island from reputable and less reputable New York merchants, and this was exchanged for slaves captured on the mainland. The Madagascar slave trade, though not the most profitable, was successful enough to catch the eye of merchants not too delicately disposed towards the trade. A great deal of booty won by the pirates upon the high seas found its way onto homeward-bound vessels and, in this manner, goods appeared in the American colonies that had previously only been dreamed of. Spices, drugs, and exotic textiles of oriental manufacture all began appearing in North American communities. Many a wife or daughter of a wealthy colonist began to display herself in rich brocades, silks, and other fripperies, with little thought of the price that had been paid in terms of lives expended. Much of the booty brought back to New York was transhipped to Europe, where Asian commodities brought a much higher price than in the colonies.

St. Marie was an ideal place for a trader to capitalize upon stolen goods, where the pirate community gave him a regular clientele. When the pirates were replete with alcohol, the terms were not harsh for relieving these hard fighting men of the booty they had seized so easily from their prey. It was a case of easy come, easy go. Furthermore, this self-same clientele could be contracted to do some slave-trading when in a sober frame of mind. The natives on the island provided a ready source of labour, and the womenfolk recruited provided, albeit with reluctance, the comforts of home that the pirates so sorely lacked. The only fear the pirates had was that an attack might come unexpectedly from some agency, such as the East India Company, bent on seeking out and destroying them. It was put out, therefore, perhaps with a great deal of exaggeration, that Isle St. Marie was a heavily fortified base, and that there was a greater number of pirates resident there than was actually the case. To their credit, neither the East India Company nor any man o' war attempted to penetrate the imagined stronghold that St. Marie had become, and the deceit that was spread throughout the Indian Ocean about the defences of the pirate base paid handsome dividends.

Kidd was to sail into a region that, immediately before his arrival, had witnessed an incident that would be retold countless times in pirate communities, and which proved to be the stuff of which legends are created. It was an incident that was bound to ensure that Kidd's arrival would be viewed with great hostility, both by the East India Company and the Mogul, with whom good relationships were fundamental to their mutual benefit. The man responsible for this singular event was Henry Avery, a Devonshire man. Avery had set out from England in 1693 as second mate on the *Charles* with the intention of participating in a naval expedition against various Spanish colonies in the West Indies. After a long and tiresome wait for the squadron to be assembled, the crew, including Avery, became restless and decided to take the *Charles* for themselves. They promptly went "on account" along the coast of West Africa, encountering some action on the way that proved to be both satisfying and rewarding. Other men joined them and they renamed their vessel the *Fancy*. Finally they reached Madagascar and revictualled at Johanna in the Comoros. An appearance in the harbour of three East Indiamen caused the *Fancy* and her crew to put up sail with some dispatch in order to evade closer attention by the Indiamen.

In February 1695, shortly after the escape from Johanna, Avery was to bedevil the relations between the East India Company and the Mogul. He issued a declaration that he would not attack any Company vessel if the Company flew certain flags in a certain way. This proclamation served only to convince the Mogul that the East

India Company was in league with pirates, and helped to confirm the rumours being circulated by the Dutch that all pirates were indeed English.

The *Fancy* sailed north to the Babs, enticed to this particular honey pot by the anticipated annual sailing of the Muslim fleet from Surat to Mocha. Vast pickings were on offer from the hordes of pilgrims intent upon making the pilgrimage to Mecca, and the traders that would be accompanying them bent on taking cloth and spices to Arabia in return for gold and coffee. However, the *Fancy* was not the only pirate vessel eager to capitalize upon the opportunity. The *Portsmouth Adventurer* (Capt. Joseph Faro) and the *Dolphin* (Capt. Want) quickly appeared. Subsequently the *Pearl* (Capt. William Mace), the *Amity* (Capt. Thomas Tew), and the *Susannah* (Capt. Wake) arrived within three days of each other. Since all these vessels originated in North America, Henry Avery might be forgiven for believing all American ships were pirate vessels. It may be noted that some of these names are recorded on the commission given to Kidd by King William when he was ordered to sail against pirates (see Chapter 4).

The pirate fleet now possessed great strength in numbers; the *Fancy* alone boasted a crew of over 150 men and 46 cannon. It was during the night that the Muslim fleet sailed from Mocha and passed through the Babs, and if it had not been for a straggler, the fleet might have evaded the pirates lying in ambush on the southern side of the strait. The pirates, once alerted, put up sail with alacrity and pursued the Muslims across the Arabian Sea, catching them off the coast of India. Here, Avery managed to close with the *Fath Mahmamadi*, which was carrying a cargo containing between £50,000 and £60,000 in gold and silver alone. A few days later the pirates surrounded the *Ganj-i-Sawai*, later referred to as the *Gunsway* by the English, which was a formidable vessel. Armed with 40 cannon and defended by 400 rifles, the *Gunsway* put up a resolute fight, but was severely crippled by a lucky cannon shot that took away part of the mainmast. Hand-to-hand fighting ensued as the pirates swarmed aboard. It is said that even the slave girls on board joined in the defence of the stricken ship and proved themselves effective in battle. No doubt this shock tactic by the defenders had some immediate effect upon the pirates, but might only have fuelled their desperation to take the ship. After several hours of combat, the *Gunsway* fell to the pirates, and the booty, when shared out among the pirates, amounted to £1,000 per man. Shorn of anything of value, the *Gunsway* was then set free.

After this epic event, which has gone down in the annals of pirate history, Avery seems to have disappeared. Some of his men returned carrying ivory tusks, jewellery, exotic cloth, and souvenirs from their exploits; one was even arrested when over £1,000 in foreign gold was found hidden in the lining of a cloak he wore. Legend tells us that Avery, carrying with him vast wealth, soon dissipated that which could be easily spent, leaving him with a cache of diamonds that were not as readily converted into cash, and that from then on he was in the grip of unscrupulous merchants who "fenced" the jewels for him. He is reported to have lived quietly and modestly at Bideford in Devon for many years and eventually to have died a pauper.

A report from the East India Company's factory at Bombay dated October 15, 1696, indicates the serious concern the Company displayed to the disruption of trade being caused by pirates:

> Besides the Gunsway, the Mogul's own ships were robbed last year near Surat, and barbarously used. Abdul Gophoor has had a ship robbed of a great sum of money in the Gulf of Persia, and today we have news from Mocha, of two of the Company's ships being taken. The loss of one of them in which was 60,000 rupees, has almost broke some of the merchants in Bombay, as the loss amounts to £75,000. The E.I.Company lost 80 tons of good new coffee in her. They were taken by two small pirates, of 13 and 14 guns, each with 150 Englishmen as crew.

Another piratical haunt, somewhat less renowned than St. Marie, was the Nicobar Islands in the Bay of Bengal. This island chain stretches over 180 miles in that vast space of ocean between the northern tip of Sumatra and the Andaman Islands, which are a northerly extension of the Nicobars. They are extremely isolated and have few inhabitants. They have the added advantage of being in close proximity to the trade route between the islands of the East Indies and the Indian subcontinent.

Once an India-bound vessel had managed to elude the attentions of the Malay pirates in the Strait of Malacca, it had to run the gauntlet of the Nicobar chain. However, there was one redeeming feature, if it can be considered as such, that the Nicobars are 250 miles distant from the nearest land mass, and for this reason the pirates were not very numerous. Because of the vast ocean distances involved, the Nicobars were mostly restricted to pirates of European ancestry, with their larger, better built vessels and their higher quality seamanship and indisputably superior discipline.

One of the most skilful of the resident pirates in the Nicobars was named Worthington, who led a very rewarding life in consort with the islanders. Worthington had deserted from the British Navy, and, with a gang of Malays, managed to find refuge upon Nancowry, an island in the group that possesses a magnificent harbour. For many years after Worthington set himself up in the piracy business on the island a great number of ships were lost in the vicinity. These losses were attributed to the gales and cyclones that beset the region during certain times of the year. No one suspected that the ships were lost through acts of piracy.

Worthington's methods were unique in the fact that he possessed no ship. His technique was to allow vessels to enter the harbour at Nancowry and to attack when the crews least expected. After seizing the vessel and butchering the crew, he and his gang would remove any contents considered of value to either themselves or the natives, then take the ship out to sea and scuttle it. As this practice was akin to that adopted by the Malays in the Strait of Malacca, it is evident that he had learned much from his apprenticeship while at sea in the service of the Royal Navy, and from his Malay subordinates. Since no witness escaped, no one lived to recount the tale to any authority. After he had retired from this business, his successors made a fatal mistake in allowing a sole survivor to escape, and the inevitable retribution came in the form of a British warship. The rats' nests of pirates that had made the Nicobars their base was exterminated. In 1869, the British finally took control of the Nicobars and the natives were encouraged to refrain from unsociable acts. The only ferocity displayed by the islanders in recent years has been the ceremonial murder of persons considered dangerous to society — those possessed by evil spirits or doctors who fail to provide a promised cure to an ailing patient.

During the eighteenth and nineteenth centuries, the British navy waged a relentless war on piracy within the Indian Ocean region, to the extent that it became a virtual "British lake" under a civilized and central authority, with a powerful navy at its command. Acts of piracy eventually petered out and merchantmen of all nations could pass freely without let or hindrance. The rise of the British Empire during this period, which reached its zenith by the end of the nineteenth century, not only eradicated piracy, but suppressed slavery and fostered peaceful trade within the Indian Ocean. However, with the decline of the British Empire has come a resurgence of piracy; the following Associated Press report appeared in the *Journal-Pioneer* of P.E.I., Canada in the latter part of 2001:

> KUALA LUMPUR, Malaysia — Pirate attacks mounted worldwide in the first six months of this year buoyed by Indonesia's sinking economy and straggling sea patrols.
>
> Southeast Asia remained a pirates' paradise, contributing 85 of 165 attacks across the globe from January through June ... The worldwide total was up slightly from 161 cases recorded in the first six months of last year, and 115 in the same period of 1999 ...
>
> "It is common knowledge that attacks originate from Indonesia," it [the report] said. "Declining economic conditions and lack of maritime patrolling have

exacerbated the piracy threat in Indonesia and surrounding waters."

Indonesia, the world's fourth most populous country, nevertheless recorded fewer attacks in the first half of this year — 44 off its archipelago's 13,000 islands compared to 56 in the same period of 2000.

Bandits picked up the slack in neighbouring Malaysia, where attacks doubled from seven in the first six months of last year, despite the Malaysian Navy boosting efforts to battle piracy.

The Philippines — struggling to contain cash-rich rebels rolling in ransom from chronic kidnappings — also grew more afflicted, with four cases reported so far this year compared to one in the first half of 2000.

Chapter 4

Captain Kidd and His Commission

> *There lies the port: the vessel puffs her sail.*
> — "Ulysses" (Tennyson)

Kidd is a fairly common surname, particularly in Scotland, and for this reason there is a great deal of uncertainty surrounding the parentage of William Kidd and the circumstances of his upbringing. Even his age at the time he was hanged is not known with any certainty, let alone details of his life before he set out on that fateful voyage to the Indian Ocean, as a result of which he became a perceived thorn in the flesh to the East India Company.

Paul Lorrain, chaplain and Ordinary of Newgate, is the only reliable witness to Kidd's age at the time of his hanging, stating that he was "born in Scotland, about fifty-six years of age." This places Kidd as having been born about 1645. The generally accepted place of his birth is Greenock, but researchers have sought vainly for any confirmation of this in parish records. There is a general belief also that his father may have been a minister of the church, though once again there is no confirmation. Since Kidd was without doubt fairly well educated in the sense that he could read and write, had a good hand, and was proficient in the art of navigation (which required a firm grounding in the science of mathematics), it is not unlikely that his father was a minister of the church who gave his son a solid basic education. Kidd's early life would have been during the Cromwellian period, when religious fervour and dissent ebbed and flowed around the British Isles. The fortunes of Kidd's father, if indeed he was a member of the cloth, could well have ebbed and flowed in tandem with the politico-religious struggles endemic at the time.

Another notion regarding Kidd's parentage is that his father was a boatswain. This arises from a line in a play produced in 1702, a year after his hanging. The play, titled *Dialogue between the Ghost of Captain Kidd and the Napper in the Strand*, has the napper accusing the ghost — "Thou son of a boatswain begot in a skuller." A skuller (or sculler) is a small rowboat, and the line suggests an exceedingly humble birth for Kidd, if this is true. Whether the playwright knew this as a fact or was merely indulging in literary licence, we have no knowledge. On the whole it sounds unduly dramatic, and thus doubtful. However, as the play was written within a year of Kidd's hanging, some credit must be given to the statement. If the playwright asserts correctly that Kidd's father was indeed a boatswain, then Kidd must have been self-taught to a greater extent than if his father had been a minister. This would imply a high degree of self reliance and resource in his character.

Kidd's early life is equally as puzzling as his birth and parentage. Some evidence has been presented to suggest that he first went to sea in 1659 when only 14 years of age, on a ship bound for the West Indies, and thereafter made a number of voyages to distant parts. The same source credits him with having been pressed into the service of the Royal Navy during Anglo-Dutch hostilities in 1673, serving on the *Royal Prince*, a first rater of 1,400 tons and 100 guns, the flagship of Sir Edward Spragge, and in which he saw action. On cessation of hostilities he reverted to the merchant service. From 1680 onwards he appears to have been engaged in trading ventures to the West Indies, and during this period to have used New York (taken by the British from the Dutch in 1664) as a trading base. By 1690 Kidd seems to have amassed a modest amount of wealth, and some of this is likely to have been gained from various privateering ventures against the French in the West Indies, as well as more honest trading activity. On May 16, 1691, he married Sarah Oort, a rich widow who it is said was scarcely literate. Sarah Oort, née Bradley, had been married twice before, firstly to William Cox, a respected merchant in New York, and then to John Oort, merchant and ship's captain. There were no children from these previous marriages.

One of Kidd's neighbours in New York was a ship's captain called Giles Shelley, who frequently went voyaging to the Indian Ocean. Whether Shelley was a pirate has never been determined, but he did carry out a very remunerative trade with the piratical brethren who had centred their activities upon Madagascar. It was claimed later, when details of this trade emerged, that Shelley retailed rum to the pirates for over £3 per gallon (which cost two shillings in New York), and Madeira wine for over £2 per gallon (which cost three shillings). The profit in conducting this trade, which included other tradeable commodities, such as weapons, gunpowder, and naval supplies generally, was immense. As far as is known, Kidd, during his residency in New York, had never voyaged to the Indian Ocean, but it is possible he had taken lengthy voyages in his years of early manhood, perhaps in an East Indiaman. Since New York, at the time, was a hotbed for piratical collusion of one sort or another, it can be concluded that Kidd had heard a great deal about the mouth-watering riches and trading profits that could be won in that far-off region of the globe. As has been said before, Kidd could have turned pirate at any time of his career, and the temptations to do so while resident in New York must have been great indeed. But he did not. He resisted those tempting visions of immense wealth, so readily available to a man of lesser integrity. Without any shadow of doubt, by 1695 he had become a man of substance, with much to lose by indulging in dubious activities bordering upon, or crossing into, illegality.

By the summer of 1695 William Kidd would have been about 50 years of age, and it might be supposed that he was in the sort of mid-life crisis that afflicts most men about that age. He was modestly well off, his trading vessels were engaged profitably, and it must be supposed that he owned one or two ships by this time. There was little reason for him to go to sea himself, as with the financial resources resulting from his marriage he could have well afforded to employ others. The prospect of retirement from the sea for good was likely not very attractive, despite the fact that he had a pretty wife, two young daughters, and owned a good deal of potentially valuable real estate on Manhatten Island. However, he decided to captain his own vessel, the *Antigua*, on a trading voyage to London, and this was to prove a fateful decision. It has been claimed that he travelled to England to seek a privateering commission, though there is no evidence to this claim. If this is true, however, it would suggest that Kidd yearned after the old, more youthful days of yore, when he had participated in privateering actions in the West Indies. There are few men of advancing years that do not dwell on the glorious exploits of their youth with a degree of regret that they are unable to relive them. Kidd may well have been one of the same mind, and if so, it was the last throw of the dice in more ways than one.

William Kidd arrived in London in August 1695. On his arrival he settled himself upon his only relation there, a Mrs. Hawkins who, although a distant relative, gave him a warm welcome in her home in the riverside community of Wapping. It is ironic that this same community was to witness his corpse dangling from the hangman's gibbet a mere six years later.

Kidd could not have arrived in the metropolis at a more opportune time, if it was indeed a privateering commission he sought, though the commission he was to ultimately receive might have been far different than the one he might have imagined. England and France were still at war, though the Battle of La Hogue in May 1692, won decisively by the combined Anglo-Dutch fleet, had removed any threatening French presence from the English Channel, at least for the time being. The same could not be said for more distant waters where French privateers preyed on English and Dutch merchantmen with impunity. This situation was to continue until the signing of an Anglo-French peace agreement two years later in 1697. However, it was not only the French privateers that were disrupting English merchant shipping; it was also pirates. The fact that many of these self-same pirates were of English nationality was proving a severe embarrassment to the government of the day. Because of their predations, considerable difficulties were being encountered by English trading companies having outposts abroad. One of these was the English East India Company.

The English East India Company, more usually referred to as The East India Company, or more colloquially as "John Company," or just "The Company," had been formed in 1599 for the purpose of trading with the East Indies, its first charter having been signed by Queen Elizabeth I a year later. The first few voyages resulted in large profits being realized, and the Company applied for, and was granted by the Crown, substantial additional powers, including the ability to seize and confiscate the ships and goods of traders in contraband, where such illegal trade impacted upon the Company's interests. In the seventeenth century the English, French, Portuguese, and Dutch were all vying for footholds in eastern waters, and merchants of all nations felt the need for vessels not only to be fitted out for defence, but also for attack. In the early days of the East India Company an English fleet off Surat had attacked four Portuguese men o' war escorting 200 merchantmen. The English victory was so complete, and the Mogul so impressed, that a treaty was made with the East India Company in 1613 permitting it to trade within his extensive dominions.

Throughout the seventeenth century the fortunes of the Company increased in a spectacular manner. By virtue of the treaty with the Mogul it held an essential monopoly on most trade with India, and from this foundation its influence spread into the East Indies, to Amboyna in the Spice Islands, and beyond. Though a treaty had been signed with the Dutch East Indies Company in 1619, whereby the two companies were to work harmoniously for their mutual benefit, this did not prevent the Dutch from attacking and massacring the leading members of the English factory at Amboyna. From thenceforth the two companies demonstrated unaffected antagonism to one another's pretensions in the region. Despite such rivalry, even in times of official Anglo-Dutch peace, the period was marked by virtually constant bitterness and unrelenting hostility.

By 1689, the East India Company felt capable and confident enough to confront the Mogul militarily, erroneously believing that there was sufficient moral and political backing for its cause back in England. The Company's arrogance was doubly compounded in banking upon further military muscle being made available to them if need be. In this way they could wage a war that would increase their sphere of influence and enhance their profits. Their gamble proved to be a mighty mistake. The Mogul emperor at the time, Aurangzeb, might have been engaged in putting down an insurrection in the southernmost part of his domains when war was sprung upon him, but he still had vast military resources at his disposal. The result was that the Company experienced a crushing and devastating defeat. From that point on the relationship between the Company and the Mogul was, understandably, not quite as trustful as it had been hitherto. In addition, the Company faced a number of problems which impacted upon their profits, ranging from the consequences of the war with France, to the resentment of English textile workers objecting to the importation of foreign cloth. There was also the matter of paying war reparations to Emperor Aurangzeb for starting, and losing, a foolish and ill-judged war. The value of the Company's stock plummeted by 70 percent from its previous high in 1685 to an all-time low in 1691. To add insult to injury, the monopoly on their trade with India was being viciously contested by enemies back in England. By 1698 this monopoly was to be broken by the grant of a charter to a rival. This rival, known as the New East India Company, proved to be no less aggressive than the Dutch.

It was against this backdrop of war with France and the intense trade rivalry in the Indian Ocean, with its uncertain fortunes for the contestants, that William Kidd might have sought his privateering commission during the latter half of 1695, if he was so inclined. Apart from Mrs. Hawkins and her immediate family, there was no one whom Kidd could approach in the metropolis who might help him to attain such an ambition — with one exception. While in New York the previous year, Kidd had made the acquaintance of Robert Livingston, a fellow Scot, who had preceded him to London by a few weeks. Livingston was indebted to Kidd, possibly for his life, if not for avoiding a very lengthy jail sentence. The favour related to the time when Livingston had been taken to court on a charge of trading with the enemy. New York had been a hotbed of illegal practices to which many an official blind eye had been turned. These included, among others, the connivance of aiding and abetting pirates, smuggling, avoidance of custom duties, non-payment of taxes, and the lesser crimes of illegally distilling liquor and running brothels. Trading with the enemy might have been considered by authority to be more odious than most of these, but nevertheless Livingston was given a fair trial, a trial in which Kidd found himself in the position of foreman of the jury. Livingston was acquitted as a consequence.

Prior to the revolution of 1688 against King James, there had been a gradual polarization in the political strife in England. Two factions had arisen, the Whigs and the Tories. The term "Whig" had originally been used contemptuously to refer to extreme Presbyterianism, but had latterly become associated with those merchants and nobles who, though not necessarily opposed to the monarchy, could not accept the "divine right of kings," a belief that, some 50 years earlier, had lost Charles I both his crown and his head. The Tories, on the other hand, were more supportive of the monarchy, and in view of the fact that many considered the uprooted Stuart dynasty to be the legitimate royal line, were as a consequence viewed with some suspicion by the new monarch William III. Also, the Whig lords had been active in prosecuting the revolution, and, in the process, providing much aid to William by means of money, men, and materials. It was the Whigs, therefore, that more often than not had the ear of the king and were the ascendant political party of the day.

Livingston's fertile imagination had spawned a plan whereby he might enrich himself at someone else's expense, and in the process brighten up his rather tarnished image back in New York. He turned to Richard Coote, Earl of Bellomont, a prominent Whig politician, to hatch out the details of this plan, which, put bluntly, involved robbing pirates of their ill-gotten gains, and in the process putting most of the proceeds into their own pockets and those of their abettors. Bellomont was an impecunious Irish lord who had been nominated for the position of captain-general of the Colony of Massachusetts Bay and that of governor of New York. Two posts with two salaries, a bewitching prospect for any impoverished lord!

Though the former appointment had been approved by King Willam, the latter had not, and Bellomont's desire for this additional sinecure gave Livingston his golden opportunity.

At the time, Benjamin Fletcher was the incumbent governor of New York. Livingston's plan had at its core the object of unseating Fletcher, a corrupt individual, by revealing the extent to which Fletcher aided and abetted the piratical fraternity that had made New York their base of operations. Bellomont's appointment as governor of New York would be certain as a result, or so Livingston hoped. However, as fortune would have it, the king granted the governorship to Bellomont later that same year before Livingston's plan could bear any fruit. Kidd was to play a vital role in Livingston's projections, but to what extent he voluntarily played an active part in its development is unknown. Kidd later claimed that he was coerced into it by Bellomont, who threatened to take his ship, the *Antigua*, from him if he did not comply, and this is likely to be true.

Livingston's plan was simplicity itself. It involved intercepting pirates returning to New York before they entered port. By condemning such prizes by due process of law, much of the booty carried in the pirate vessels would become theirs unless, of course, it could be traced back to the original owners, an unlikely possibility at the best of times! Bellomont must have been truly fascinated at the prospect of feathering his own nest legally and strengthening his political position in the colonies at the same time. A minor problem arose as to how to finance such an operation, which required a fighting vessel capable of confronting heavily armed pirates on the high seas, and to man it ably with a proficient commander and crew. Kidd was an obvious choice, and his presence in London may well have sparked the plan in Livingston's mind long before he mooted the idea with Bellomont.

Bellomont discussed the plan with the king who, though he initially refused to consider it, finally gave it a degree of royal favour, provided that the Crown was not involved in any of the financing. Bellomont then turned to various Whig lords for financial backing and, it must be supposed, the original scheme at this stage began to take on a vastly different form as the lords, eager to make good profit from the projected venture, all had their input into its planning before opening their purses.

The leading individuals who were to become involved in Livingston's scheme were, apart from Bellomont, Henry Sidney (Earl of Romney), Lord John Somers, Edward Russell (Earl of Orford), and Charles Talbot (Duke of Shrewsbury). In addition there was Mr. Edmund Harrison, who was to become a director of the New East India Company (a rival of the East India Company) when it was finally granted its charter in 1698, and who, in turn, was later to be knighted. Harrison had previously helped finance treasure-fishing expeditions to sunken wrecks in the West Indies. In addition there was a certain Dr. Cox.

Kidd was later to write of this period in his life in the following terms:

From Boston following his arrest:

> Livingstone, a merchant of Albany, carried me to wait on my Lord Bellomont at his house in Dover Street, where both my Lord and Livingstone urged me with many arguments to accept the command of this ship under the King's Commission ... I pressed to be excused my voyage to New York, whereupon Lord Bellomont added threats to his wheedles, and told me I should not be allowed to carry my own ship out of the river of the Thames unless I accepted command of this ship ... Livingston carried me to the house of the Duke of Shrewsbury, the Lord Chancellor (John Somers), Earl of Romney and Admiral Russell ... Where he discoursed with them, but would not suffer me to see or speake with them ...
>
> Before I went to sea, I waited twice on my Lord Romney and Admiral Russell (now Lord Orford) who both hastened me to sea, and promised to stand by me in all my undertakings.

From Newgate Prison awaiting trial:

> I did not seek the commission I undertook, but was partly cajold, and partly ensnared into it by the Lord Bellomont, and one Robert Livingston of New York, who was the projector, promoter, and chief manager of that designe, and who only can give your House a satisfactory account of all the transactions of my own. He was the man admitted into their closets, and received their private instructions, which he kept in his own hands, and who encouraged me in their names to doo more than I ever did, and to act without regard to my commission.

With the exception of Lord John Somers, who was to become Lord High Chancellor, the leading participants in the scheme — Bellomont, Sidney, Russell, and Talbot — had actively participated in the revolution of 1688 that placed William, Prince of Orange, on the English throne. All four had gathered around William in Holland, and joined his invasion force against England. It can be expected that they had the ear of the king as a token of this loyalty, and this loyalty was reflected by royal assent.

Once Kidd had been irrevocably drawn into the enterprise, he was prevailed upon to do a number of things which ensured that he remained enmeshed and financially committed to the project. He was induced to sign a performance bond of £20,000 in favour of Bellomont, as insurance in the event that he should fail to make a "good voyage." Livingston was also sucked in for a sum of £10,000 in a similar manner. Drawn up in October 1695, the bonds were duly signed, sealed, and witnessed, and affixed with a sixpenny stamp. Kidd was forced to sell his ship the *Antigua* in order to raise the necessary funds. On the other hand, if Kidd was to recover treasure and prizes which after condemnation realized more than £100,000, then he would receive the proposed vessel, the *Adventure Galley,* as a bonus. Bellomont was very effective with his wheedles.

In due course an application was made to the Admiralty for a privateering commission and this was duly granted in December 1695. However, the terms of the commission first granted only related to the seeking out of enemy commerce. Much discussion ensued between the backers of the venture and the lords of the Admiralty to enlarge the scope of the commission to include the taking of pirates, a matter which caused some consternation as to whether a commission to apprehend these villains would be legal. In the end, a commission was granted which met the requirements of all concerned. It was subsequently signed into law by the king on August 24, 1696. It read:

William Rex

WILLIAM THE THIRD, by the grace of God, King of England, Scotland, France and Ireland, defender of the faith, etc. To our trusty and well beloved Capt. ROBERT KIDD, commander of the ship the Adventure Galley, or to any other, the commander of the same for the time being, Greeting : Whereas we are informed, that Capt. Thomas Too, John Ireland, Capt Thomas Wake, and Capt. William Maze or Mace, and other subjects, natives or inhabitants of New York, and elsewhere, in our plantations in America, have associated themselves with divers others, wicked and ill-disposed persons, and do, against the law of nations, commit many and great piracies, robberies and depredations on the seas upon the parts of America, and in other parts, to the great hindrance and discouragement of trade and navigation, and to the great danger and hurt of our loving subjects, our allies, and all others, navigating the seas upon their lawful occasions. NOW KNOW YE, that we being desirous to prevent the aforesaid mischiefs, and as much as in us lies, to bring the said pirates, free-booters and sea-rovers to justice, have thought fit and do hereby give and grant to the said Robert Kidd (to whom our com- misssioners for exercising the office of Lord High Admiral of England, have granted a commission as a private man-of-war, bearing date the 11th day of December 1695) and unto the commander of the said ship for the time being, and unto the officers, mariners, and others which shall be under your com- mand, full power and authority to apprehend, seize, and take into your custody as well the said Capt. Thomas Too, John Ireland, Capt. Thomas Wake, and Capt. Wm. Maze or Mace, as all such pirates, free-booters, and sea-rovers, being either our sub- jects, or of other nations associated with them, which you shall meet with upon the seas or coasts of America, or upon any other seas or coasts, with all their ships and vessels, and all such merchandizes, money, goods, and wares as shall be found on board, or with them, in case they shall willingly yield them- selves; But if they will not yield without fighting, then you are by force to compel them to yield. And we also require you to bring, or cause to be brought, such pirates, free-booters, or sea-rovers, as you shall seize, to a legal trial, to the end they may be pro- ceeded against according to the law in such cases. And we do hereby command all our officers, minis- ters, and other loving subjects whatsoever, to be aid- ing and assisting to you in the premises. And we do hereby enjoin you to keep an exact journal of your proceedings in execution of the premises, and set down the names of such pirates, and of their officers and company, and the names of such ships and ves- sels as you shall by virtue of these presents take and seize, and the quantities of arms, ammunition, pro- vision, and lading of such ships, and the true value of the same, as near as you judge. And we do hereby strictly charge and command you, as you will answer the contrary at your peril, that you do not, in any manner, offend or molest our friends or allies, their ships or subjects, by color or pretense of these presents, or the authority therby granted. In witness whereof, we have caused our great seal of England to be affixed to these presents. Given at our court in Kensington, the 26th day of January 1695*, in the 7th year of our reign.

*Note: This should read 1696 in conformity with our present dating system. Prior to 1752 the British used the Julian calendar and New Year's Day was March 25. Thus March 24, 1695, and March 25, 1696, were consecutive days.

Whether or not Kidd had voyaged to London to seek a privateering commission, he now had one — for better or worse!

Chapter 5

The Sailing of the Adventure Galley

> *The fair breeze blew,*
> *The white foam flew,*
> *The furrow followed free.*
> — "The Rime of the Ancient Mariner" (Coleridge)

The vessel selected for Kidd's projected voyage was the *Adventure Galley*, a three-masted ship akin to a barque equipped with oars, which was finally launched from Castleyard, Deptford, on December 4, 1695. She was of 287 tons' burden, 125 feet long, and fitted with 34 guns, saker or light cannon. Since the Anglo-Moor wars the British had adopted the galley design for many of their vessels, both naval and merchantmen. The double-banking of oars gave certain obvious advantages when the ship became becalmed during a conflict with an adversary, a lesson that the British had learned the hard way during hostilities with the Moors off the coast of North Africa. The navy's *Charles Galley* and *James Galley* were fine examples of the galley design adopted for warfare. These two vessels, 526 and 433 tons respectively, were each capable of carrying in excess of 200 men and 30 guns, and with 26 oars and 3 men at each oar, these ships could attain a speed of three knots. A useful advantage with a becalmed enemy. The *James Galley* had shown her mettle, and the benefit of the galley design, during the recent Battle of La Hogue (1692).

However, it was not only the Royal Navy that had adopted the galley design for its ships; the East India Company and other trading companies had also done so, so there is a great deal of uncertainty as to the actual origins of the *Adventure Galley*. The claim that she was a new vessel at the time of her launch is, frankly, doubtful, as is the idea that she was originally intended for the navy. With fresh hostilities imminent, and rumours abounding about an intended invasion of England by the French, the only sensible conclusion is that she was being refitted for commercial trading at the time Kidd's attention was drawn to her availability. The fact that the *Adventure Galley* was to become so unseaworthy that she sank within three years following her launch from Deptford suggests that she was certainly not a new vessel. If she was new then she was certainly not well built. Since shipyards were notorious for utilizing substandard materials and indulging in dubious workmanship practices, often with the connivance of those in positions of responsibility for the work being carried out, this too is a possibility.

Despite the uncertainties surrounding the history of the *Adventure Galley* prior to her launch at Deptford, the following two months saw a great deal of hasty preparation to make her ready for sea. It is likely that Admiral Russell, a partner in the consortium funding the voyage, would have played more than a disinterested role in these activities. In fact, the securing of the *Adventure Galley* may well have been largely due to the influence Russell had in maritime circles, as Russell had an extraordinary interest in anything that affected his own financial well-being.

Though Kidd protested volubly, at a later date, the manner by which he had become inveigled into the project through the "threats and wheedles" of Lord Bellomont, he was of a vainglorious disposition. It would be expected from his character that he actually revelled in his connection with the lords with whom he had now become involved, and it is more than likely that he threw himself into all aspects of preparation for the voyage with considerable enthusiasm. One can visualize him strutting the decks of the *Adventure Galley*, which would have been littered with the confused mess of a vessel in preparation for a long voyage and teeming with carpenters, sail-makers, riggers, caulkers, painters, armourers, and other innumerable tradesmen. Provisions, fresh and salted, would be hoisted aboard, together with vast quantities of fresh water in barrels. All this required minute inspection, as many an unscrupulous chandler made fit to lessen his losses by foisting questionable goods and tainted supplies onto naive and less vigilant ships' captains. Kidd is unlikely to have been one of these, and it must be supposed that he and his quartermaster were diligent in ensuring that the seeds of potential discontent that often bedevilled ships' crews because of bad fare were not sown aboard the *Adventure Galley*. Kidd could well have been a very proud man, for he was now the commander of a privateer of not inconsiderable size.

There is uncertainty regarding whether Kidd experienced problems in recruiting crew for the *Adventure Galley*. One source suggests that he was limited to hiring 70 men, of which no more than half were mariners, the rest being drawn from the many volunteers that thronged the nearby wharves. A vessel the size of the *Adventure Galley*, with its reliance on oars as an auxiliary mode of transport, implies that a much higher complement of men, even if they were not experienced seamen, would be needed for a full crew. Another source makes reference to his recruiting inmates from some of the London jails, presumably those serving sentences for crimes considered less heinous by the authorities. Regardless of the actual sources from which he drew his crew, Kidd had certain advantages to offer in order to attract able-bodied fighting men. In time of war, the Royal Navy was hard pressed to find sufficient manpower prepared to fight and die for king and country. A berth in a privateer, on the other hand, offered the prospects of escaping drudgery on land, if the navy's predatory eye could be avoided, and the opportunity, if luck was favourable, of returning from a good voyage with a pocketful of gold. Some of the men who joined Kidd in London were to return in manacles.

It was the custom to draw up articles of agreement before the commencement of a voyage, and it can be certain that the men who joined Kidd on the *Adventure Galley* at London signed such an agreement. These articles regulated the various charges and payments to all members of the crew. Esquemeling, in his *Buccaneers of America*, writes of such agreements in the following terms:

> They agree upon certain articles, which are put in writing, by way of bond or obligation, which every

one is bound to observe, and all of them, of the chiefest, do set their hands unto. Herein they specify, and set down very distinctly, what sums of money each particular person ought to have for that voyage, the fund of all payments being the common stock, stock of what is gotten by the whole expedition; for otherwise it is the same law, among these people as with other pirates; no prey, no pay. In the first place, therfore, they mention how much the captain ought to have for his ship. Next the salary of the carpenter, or shipwright, who careened, mended, and rigged the vessel. This commonly amounts unto 100 or 150 pieces-of-eight, being, according to the agreement, more or less. Afterwards for provisions and vict-ualling they draw out of the same common stock about 200 pieces-of-eight. Also a competent salary for the surgeon and his chest of medications, which usually is rated at 200 or 250 pieces-of-eight. Lastly, they stipulate in writing what recompense or reward each one ought to have that is either wounded or maimed in his body, suffering the loss of any limb, by that voyage. Thus they order for the loss of a right arm 600 pieces-of-eight, or 6 slaves; for the loss of a left arm 500 pieces-of-eight, or 5 slaves; for a right leg 500 pieces-of-eight, or 5 slaves; for a left leg 400 pieces-of-eight, or 4 slaves; for an eye 100 pieces-of-eight, or one slave; for a finger of the hand the same reward as for the eye. All which sums of money, as I have said before, are taken out of the capital sum or common stock of what is gotten by their piracy.

The departure of the *Adventure Galley* was to be fraught with problems that depleted the manpower of his ship so severely that Kidd was forced to sail for New York to bring his crew up to full strength. Another set of articles of agreement were signed there and these are reproduced in full in Appendix I. They follow, more

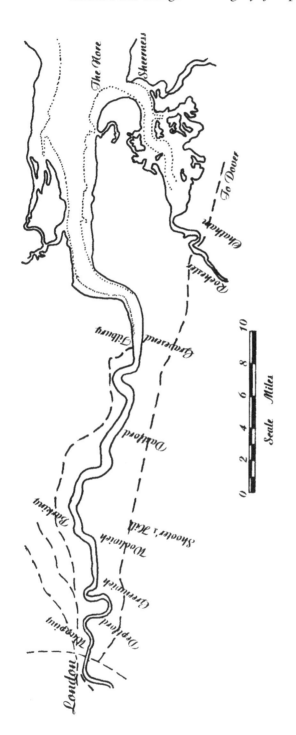

Map of the Lower Thames Valley below Wapping.

or less, along the lines of those given by Esquemeling. There was a considerable degree of democracy practised on such vessels, in considerable contrast to the autocracy on naval ships. This even extended to the honouring of wills of men who had died in pursuit of a good voyage, their widows being assigned the share of booty that their late husbands would have brought home.

In late February 1696, Kidd sailed down the Thames headed for the open sea. During the weeks that the *Adventure Galley* had been preparing to sail, Kidd had earned a reputation for arrogance and boastfulness. This is not surprising, as in view of his humble origins, was he not now in possession of a king's commission that entitled him to fly the royal pennant? One can easily imagine him strutting his quarterdeck full of vainglory. However, before he got very far downriver he found himself decidedly up to his neck in hot water. Naval protocol at the time required all passing ships to recognize the navy's superiority by the dipping of colours, or the firing of a salute. It was a tradition jealously maintained by naval captains. Whether Kidd, advertently or inadvertently, forgot to dip his colours is unknown, but he could not have chosen a worse vessel to insult by ignoring this nicety of tradition — it was one of the royal yachts! It is easy to forgive Kidd for this action. Did he not have an immature crew aboard? Wasn't he unfamiliar himself with his new command? Wasn't the river crowded with other shipping? Those few miles downriver to the open sea must have presented a nightmare to him, without the hazards of pretentious captains making a fuss about such trivialities as dipping one's colours. However, the damage was done and a shot rang out across their bows.

Kidd, now defiant, still did not dip his colours, his men accompanying this defiance with the mariners' gesture of turning their backsides to the adversary and slapping them in unison. This singular attitude was repeated when they were confronted by another naval vessel, HMS *Duchess*, at the mouth of the Medway River, but this time Kidd's ship suffered the ignominy of receiving an official boarding party. At Sheerness the crew was removed and pressed into the service of a navy readying itself to repulse a rumoured invasion from France. The rumours proved groundless, and after a lengthy delay many of those who had been pressed into service were released back to Kidd. Amongst all this irritating fuss and bother, Kidd had to do some fancy footwork. He started without delay for Sittingbourne, Kent, where he sought out Admiral Russell who, mindful of his own personal interest in the fortunes of Kidd's voyage, exerted his authority on Captain Stewart, commander of the *Duchess*. Stewart complied with Russell's orders, but took the opportunity to retain the more skilled mariners amongst Kidd's crew, replacing them with those of his own that he deemed of little use, and some which might have been "bad apples." One of those was later to testify against Kidd at his trial.

The result of all this folly and stupidity on the part of Kidd was the loss of many of his best men. Undermanned though he probably was when his ship slipped its moorings in the Thames, his crew was considerably less experienced when the *Adventure Galley* finally escaped from the clutches of the Royal Navy. Whether Kidd had intended to cross to New York at the time the voyage of the *Adventure Galley* was planned is unknown, but to New York he set sail in order to bring his crew up to fighting strength. There on the New York waterfront he had numerous contacts and would experience little difficulty in attracting able fighting men, ones who preferred the hazards of a voyage with good prospects to fighting the French on the borders of Canada in the service of an ungrateful England. Rather die of disease in the heat of the tropics with a full belly than die in the frozen wastes of starvation!

The *Adventure Galley*, prior to its Atlantic crossing, dropped anchor in Plymouth for a while, and is reported to have sailed from there in May 1696 with a total compliment of 80 men, little more than half the number required for a full crew. On the voyage to New York, Kidd was fortunate enough to fall in with a French fishing vessel bound for the Grand Banks of Newfoundland. This harmless vessel soon submitted to Kidd with its load of salt and fishing gear. It was the first legitimate prize and was taken into New York. The ship was condemned, the proceeds for Kidd yielding between £800 and £900, which he spent on provisioning the *Adventure Galley*.

The crew that Kidd recruited at New York was somewhat mixed. Of the 152 names recorded, the greatest number were overwhelmingly English by ethnicity, but included also were 25 Dutchmen, which is not surprising as New York had been the Dutch colony of New Amsterdam before it was taken by the British. There were also a few sundry Scots, a couple of Frenchmen, some Welshmen, and an African. Brief biographical sketches of some of the crew that sailed with Kidd are given in Appendix II, as far as such details can be determined. Some of these sailed with him from London, some joined in New York, and others were picked up along the way. Attention is drawn to the name of Benjamin Franks, a jeweller by trade, who at 46 years of age was the oldest member of the crew, and that of Darby Mullins, who was hanged alongside Kidd at Execution Dock.

The *Adventure Galley* finally departed New York in the first week of September 1696, and the last sight of North America many of the men were to see was Sandy Hook, the promontory of land that juts out from the New Jersey coast on Lower New York Bay.

The first leg of the voyage was relatively unexciting. The *Adventure Galley* sailed in the company of a brigantine bound for Madeira, and though they caught sight of a sail, it proved to be that of a Portuguese merchantman, and thus an ally which could not be taken. The weeks were spent profitably by Kidd in training his newer hands in handling sails and rigging, weaponry practice and the like, all activities in which proficiency was required if they were to make a good voyage. They arrived at Madeira in early October, and after a day spent victualling, set course for the Cape Verde Islands. These were to be the last islands they would see before being confronted by the immense open spaces of the South Atlantic. At the island of Boa Vista they took on some salt and at the nearby island of Santiago they took on provisions, water, and wood. The *Adventure Galley* was not to catch sight of land again for over three months.

Whatever criticisms may be levelled at Kidd, there is little doubt regarding the quality of his seamanship. He knew his winds and currents and, if he had not navigated the South Atlantic before, he certainly knew how to face these uncertainties. With the northeast winds astern, and the current in his favour, he steered the *Adventure Galley* southwest towards the Brazilian coast, avoiding the prevailing adverse southerlies and north-flowing current along the African shore, and thereby minimizing his time in the doldrums with its flirtatious and capricious winds. They made good passage, eventually steering eastwards to the Cape of Good Hope when they could take advantage of the prevailing westerlies and the eastward flowing currents. It was in latitude 33°50' that misfortune overtook Kidd in the form of a squadron under the command of Commodore Thomas Warren of the Royal Navy. The date was December 12. Warren had left England seven months earlier with five vessels, the *Windsor, Tiger, Kingfisher, Vulture,* and *Advice,* the last of which Kidd and some of his men were to become better acquainted with at a later date, when they were transported to London in chains. The purpose of Warren's squadron of naval ships was to escort a vast flotilla of merchantmen outward bound from England to a variety of destinations. Once out of the potentially hostile waters of the English Channel and the eastern North Atlantic, the merchantmen had split up, going their separate ways. The flotilla had been whittled down to a few East Indiamen that Warren had been instructed to accompany as far as St. Helena. There he was to await a return convoy. Warren's problem, however, was that he could not find St. Helena since his sailing master aboard the *Windsor* had died, and for many weeks before encountering Kidd he had drifted aimlessly among the wastes of the South Atlantic, much to the ire of the captains of the East Indiamen. During this period, the ships under his command had been depleted in manpower through disease and death, largely due to scurvy.

Kidd cursed his bad luck at encountering a flotilla of considerably larger and better-armed ships, even if they were English. Doubtless he knew the demands that inevitably would be made upon him, and the inroads that would be made into his own manpower. His only recourse was to be as pleasant as possible to his unwelcome visitors and to play along with the commodore and his captains. There were constant visits between the various vessels, and it may be expected Kidd kept quiet regarding any intentions he may have had that were not defined by the commission he held. It was a very tense week during which Warren and his party weighed up Kidd, and during which Kidd warily maintained his guard as they wallowed steadily eastwards in tandem. During a night of relative calm, Kidd found the opportu-

nity to escape the attentions of the navy. With his crew manfully plying their oars, the *Adventure Galley* slipped away under cover of
darkness, and when morning broke she was over the horizon.

When Warren eventually reached the Cape (a long way from St.
Helena), he spread the belief around that Kidd was a pirate, though
there is no evidence to support such a contention at the time, but
there is the suggestion that Warren's convictions were more strongly held after Kidd's much publicized arrest some three years later.
Kidd wisely avoided the Cape, where the navy and East Indiamen

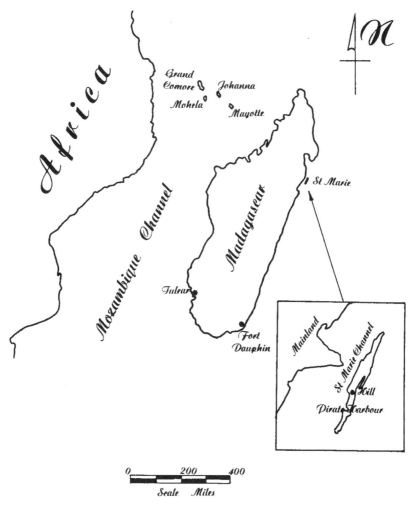

Map of Madagascar and the Pirate Harbour of St. Marie.

frequently called, even though he and his men were by that time in dire straits. Despite the fact that his men were suffering from scurvy, an accompaniment of most long sea voyages, and the fact that his sails and rigging desperately needed overhauling, he set a course straight for Madagascar. There, at Tulear on the southwest coast of the island, he landed in mid-January 1697, some 20 weeks after departing from New York. A period of rest and recuperation, followed by an overhauling of the vessel and its gear, was a welcome prospect. Kidd had proved an excellent seaman and navigator to bring the *Adventure Galley* so far, so quickly, and with no serious loss even though there was as yet no prize.

It was while the *Adventure Galley* was at Tulear that a sloop dropped anchor in nearby Saint Augustine Bay. It turned out to be a slaving vessel from Barbados named the *Loyal Russell*, which had arrived to buy slaves from Madagascar in exchange for European merchandise, rum, sugar, powder, and shot. These commodities were much prized by the numerous kings and chieftains on the island, and the trade was a good way to rid themselves of some of their less fortunate subjects or those captured in war. The *Loyal Russell* had been at the Cape when Warren and his navy ships finally found port. It was from the captain of the *Loyal Russell* that Kidd learned that it was being bandied around by Warren and his fellow officers that he was a pirate. Warren's beliefs were no doubt coloured by the way the *Adventure Galley* had slipped away under cover of darkness, when all Warren really wanted was to poach some of Kidd's crew.

Though many of Kidd's immediate needs, namely fresh water and provisions, were satisfied by his stay at Tulear, he desperately needed fresh sail and rigging, which suggests that some of these essentials carried from London might have been substandard. These commodities could not be obtained from the captain of the *Loyal Russell*. Kidd opted to make a short passage to the Comoros, the islands being a frequent stopover for East Indiamen. There he banked on obtaining the rigging and new sail that he needed to make the *Adventure Galley* fit for the tasks that lay ahead. The captain of the *Loyal Russell* agreed to sail with him. After a month at Tulear, Kidd pulled up anchor and sailed up the Mozambique Channel to the island of Johanna (now Anjouan), which was dominated by its volcanic peaks reaching to over 5,000 feet. He arrived there on March 18.

On the way they fell in with several ships of the East India Company, but none were prepared to render any assistance to Kidd, neither on his arrival at Johanna were any merchants prepared to give him credit for the tackle he so desperately required. Furthermore the *Adventure Galley* was in sore need of careening. He departed from Johanna four days later in search of a careening spot, where the ship could be hauled up on a suitable beach to remove the accumulated tangle of barnacles and weed that had infested the ship's bottom during the outward voyage. Kidd's own report, and those of his men, state that they went to the island of Mohila, some 40 miles away to the southwest. However, Mohila is virtually encircled by coral reef, and though there are gaps in the reef, caused by the discharge of freshwater from the streams flowing into the sea, it is possible that Kidd might instead have gone to Mayotte where there is an abundance of sheltered beach and less coral reef.

Regardless of the island at which careening was carried out, the process of readying a vessel and the carrying out of this task efficiently is one requiring great attention to detail. It is important to select a beach with the right slope and a decent tidal fluctuation, the latter depending upon the ship's draft. A sloping sandy bottom is best. The ship is then warped as far up the beach as possible during high tide and secured with heavy cables. When the tide ebbs, it leaves the vessel high and dry, and the ship is then canted to one side as the tide ebbs by heaving on other cables using block and tackle to control this delicate operation. Frenzied activity ensues to inspect for shipworm, and to remove them by pouring boiling pitch into the wormholes, plugging the holes with oakum, cutting out planks that cannot be saved and replacing them, scraping off weed and barnacles, then after all structural damage has been attended to, and all hindrances removed that might diminish the vessel's speed, the clean, scoured bottom is payed with one or more coatings of pitch. The number of tides that pass depends on the work which needs to be done, as first one side of the ship is careened and then the other.

During all this time the *Loyal Russell* rendered assistance, stripping the ship of its moveables, particularly the guns, and providing men and materials to help with the laborious scraping, caulking, and paying with pitch. The whole operation reportedly took several weeks, during which about 30 of Kidd's crew died from disease, presumably malaria or yellow fever. Other reports, including one by Abel Owen, the cook, suggest up to 50 men died in total and were buried on the island.

After the *Adventure Galley* had been fully careened, righted, and all moveables, including the guns, replaced aboard, Kidd was faced with another headache apart from his lack of sailing tackle. He had lost one-fifth of his crew, and though he might be able to sail without making these losses good — he had sailed from England to New York with less — he could not possibly hope to win a seafight without bringing his numbers up to full strength. Some men from the *Loyal Russell* joined him and without further delays Kidd returned to Johanna to seek more men. The *Loyal Russell* departed Mohila after having spent two months in Kidd's company, presumably to resume the business she was previously engaged upon. It seems rather suspicious that a trading vessel like the *Loyal Russell* should spend so long in Kidd's company, rendering him all manner of assistance, without any apparent return. It makes one wonder whether the ship, named as she was, did not somehow have a connection to Admiral Russell, one of Kidd's secret financial backers. Kidd's later testimony states categorically that the *Loyal Russell* was a sloop from Barbados with a master by the name of French. Also on board were Mr. Hatton and Mr. John Balt, both merchants, the former dying in Kidd's cabin while they were at Tulear. However, this was Kidd's testimony, and as will be seen, Kidd was often not entirely truthful, and when he was, he tended to give erroneous impressions.

Kidd was luckier in his second visit to Johanna, and was able to find new men, including a group that had either absconded or been marooned from an East Indiaman. Some of these had money that they lent to Kidd, which enabled him to buy the sail and other rigging he so badly needed. Towards the end of April 1697, the *Adventure Galley* weighed anchor and headed north into the vastness of the Indian Ocean and the Arabian Sea. The kaskazi wind, the one that comes from the northeast, had petered out, and the kusi was gathering force from the south and would blow steadily from April to November. Kidd must have felt that his luck was beginning to turn.

Chapter 6

The Taking of the Queddah Merchant

Better far to live and die,
Under the brave black flag I fly.
— The Pirate King in *Pirates of Penzance*
(Gilbert and Sullivan)

William Kidd, in his later testimony, reports "that on the twenty-fifth day of April [he] set sail for the coast of India and came upon the coast of Mallabar in the beginning of the month of September." Four months is a long time to sail from the Comoros to India. Few depositions reveal where the *Adventure Galley* actually went during this period, the exception being that of Benjamin Franks, who was to leave Kidd's crew in India by jumping ship. Later, Franks was to be sent back to England to testify at Kidd's trial. Franks reveals that the *Adventure Galley* sailed to the Babs, and it must be presumed that Kidd's intention was to voyage there to seek out pirates, as there was no indication at this time that he was set upon acts of piracy himself, or that he had ever committed a single piratical act. However, temptation was to stare him in the face, and his motley crew, eager for plunder, were to tip the scales and seal their fates.

With the southwest monsoon astern, Kidd would have made a fairly rapid transit up the East African coast, probably arriving in late July or early August. He would have missed the opportunity of intercepting the vast hordes of Muslims en route from India for their intended pilgrimage to Mecca some months earlier, but these same pilgrims would be returning in August and September and that would be the ideal time to make an attack on the fleet. As Mandeslo comments, the Indian traders took with them to the Red Sea various trade goods, but their best returns, carried with them back to India, were in the form of ready cash, most of which would have been gold.

The Red Sea narrows at its juncture with the Gulf of Aden, and the Strait of Babs-al-Mandab is dominated by the island of Perim, which considerably influences the shipping routes in and out of the Red Sea. The stretch of water between Perim and the African shoreline is riddled with shoals, and as a consequence shipping maintains a healthy respect for these waters by keeping to the north side of the island. Those same shoal-ridden waters serve as an excellent refuge for those laying in wait to attack innocent shipping. Like many others before him, Kidd would have anchored on the south side of the island, and, safely masked from the north by the bulk of the island, he and his crew could leisurely occupy themselves as they watched and waited.

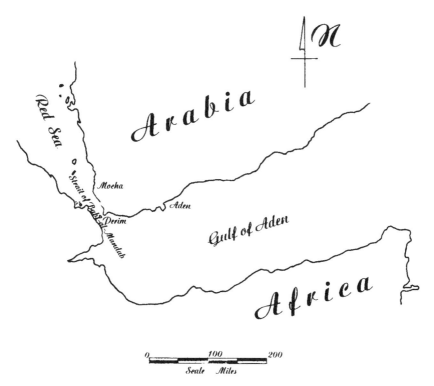

Map of the Gulf of Aden and the Strait of Babs-al-Mandab.

The Gulf of Aden is a torrid place and the land is barren, devoid of any vegetation with the exception of a small amount of nondescript scrub. The African mainland, 12 miles away from Perim to the south, is a wasteland of sand and silt, and the rocky headland on the Arabian side of the strait has similar characteristics, though in distance it is a little closer. Perim itself is a nub of volcanic rock rising out of the surrounding ocean, and the only safe anchorage is on the south side of the island. Here in this cauldron, Kidd and his crew prepared to pounce on a suitable prey, but it is unlikely that any of them appreciated the barren beauty of this hostile place. The high point of Perim lies to the west of the anchorage, and it was to the appropriately designated Signal Hill that Kidd posted his men as lookouts. At the same time, the quartermaster set off in the ship's pinnace to scout the Arabian port of Mocha, which lies some 50 miles to the west. He returned with the glad tidings that a fleet of some 17 vessels was being assembled in the port and appeared to be preparing to depart.

Kidd's presence in the general vicinity had not remained undetected by the Moors. In their search for water and supplies, Kidd's men had made various raids upon the African shore before arriving at the Babs, and news had spread and reached Mocha. It was not difficult to link the presence of European predators to a possible raid on the fleet, and unfortunately for the crew of the *Adventure Galley*, there was a 36-gun armed escort to the Moorish fleet. It was the East Indiaman, the *Sceptre*, a vessel that had accompanied Commodore Warren in his wanderings around the South Atlantic before he encountered Kidd. The *Sceptre* had left Warren's convoy, probably in frustration with Warren's navigational ineptitude, and made her own way to the Cape and thence to India, before being assigned to escort the Mocha fleet back to Surat.

Following the looting of the *Ganj-i-sawai*, or *Gunsway*, by Avery two years earlier, an incensed Mogul had instructed European companies trading with his domains to provide armed protection for his shipping. The English, French, and Dutch were ordered to comply, and protection had to be provided especially for the pilgrim fleets to and from Mocha. With the *Sceptre* were two smaller Dutch vessels whose fighting ability is somewhat questionable.

The captain of the *Sceptre* was a stalwart and proficient mariner by the name of Edward Barlow, and it is largely due to his detailed journal that we have any knowledge of the actual events that later transpired between the Mocha fleet and the *Adventure Galley*. His ship had brought a miscellaneous cargo into Mocha and was returning to India carrying coffee, dyes, and some ivory. Barlow could have anticipated a profitable voyage for his ship, though it is understood that this was his first visit to a Red Sea port.

Robert C. Ritchie, in his excellent biography of Kidd, titled *Captain Kidd and the War against the Pirates*, has given a fine rendering of Barlow's journal, and the following précis is based on Ritchie's work.

The pilgrim fleet finally sailed from Mocha on August 11, 1697, but some three days earlier the *Gunsway* had sailed alone, presumably under cover of darkness, because it totally eluded Kidd and his lookouts. Arguably, perhaps, Kidd had lost the dubious distinction of retaking and plundering once again one of the most famous ships belonging to the Mogul. During the night of August 13, the fleet silently slipped through the Babs by the north channel. However, this time Kidd and his men were more alert and when the sun rose in the morning the *Adventure Galley* was amidst the convoy. To declare its intentions, the crew had hoisted a blood-red banner, so the proverbial cat was now really among the pigeons! If there is a single act that suggests the point at which Kidd elected to become a pirate, then surely the raising of a blood-red flag in such a situation must be that act. At the same time one must be wary of the evidence. Did Kidd in fact raise such a flag?

Barlow, in the *Sceptre*, was the closest of any of the armed escorts to the *Adventure Galley*, and after manoeuvring his vessel into a suitable position, opened fire immediately after raising his own colours, which were those of the East India Company. Kidd's response was to turn away from this surprise attack. Beset by light and fickle winds, Kidd used his oars to good effect, turning his attentions to a large merchantman which, he hoped, possessed less fire power. This may have been prompted by a reluctance to directly attack an East Indiaman, against which he might have come off the worse.

Drawing up alongside his prey, and now within cannon range, he let off volley after volley, to which the merchantman responded ineffectively. Barlow refused to be thwarted by Kidd's change in tactics and lowered his boats in an attempt to catch up with Kidd. With his boat crews straining at the oars, the *Sceptre* decreased the distance between itself and the *Adventure Galley*, and though not within range, commenced some ineffectual fire. Barlow's men took to the shrouds and rigging and, in imitation of pirate practice, began screaming blood-curdling oaths and brandishing their weapons at the fleeing vessel. Kidd pressed on more sail, and with his men also straining at the oars, kept the *Adventure Galley* out of range of Barlow's cannon. Kidd had discovered an indomitable adversary in the *Sceptre* and her captain, and when dawn broke the next morning, Kidd had vanished over the horizon.

Though he was out of sight of the Moors, Kidd still hovered around in the hopes of picking up a straggler. However, forewarned is forearmed and there was no chance of that. The confrontation by the *Sceptre* with an unknown vessel of obvious piratical intentions had induced the merchantmen to close up and cling to the skirts of their armed escorts. With his fresh water almost depleted, Kidd decided that discretion was the better part of valour and he pressed on, with as much sail as he could muster, towards the Indian coast. North of Surat he replenished his water and other victuals, and lay in wait for the slow-moving convoy of Moorish vessels to appear. He may have hoped, also, that other prey might materialize in the form of coastal traffic. Dissent began to grow among the crew; the torrid heat, the lack of water and supplies, and the loss of a prize all contributed to a general sapping of morale. The crew even talked openly of desertion at the first available opportunity, and with such talk it can be expected that the prospect of a successful mutiny might also have been debated. Kidd had a lot of problems on his hands! In addition, the seaworthiness of the *Adventure Galley* was becoming of increasing concern, for the water was rising higher in the bilges every day, requiring more and more pumping to keep the ship afloat.

The *Adventure Galley*, flying English colours, was fortunate enough to encounter a small local trader, and at this point it would appear that Kidd definitely turned pirate. He rapidly overran the smaller vessel, put a shot across its bows, and brought it to. Captain Thomas Parker was brought aboard and while various niceties were discussed by Kidd and Parker, Kidd's crew foraged around their unfortunate victim. They took the hapless crew hostage, tied them up, beat them with the flats of their cutlasses, and hoisted them into the rigging. One hundred pieces-of-eight were found, food requisitioned, and Parker and one of his men were forced to remain on the *Adventure Galley*. Parker had intimate knowledge of the Malabar coast, its currents and its winds, and as such was an important asset for Kidd to retain. Following this encounter, it emerged that Kidd had already been declared a pirate, presumably as a result of his previous encounter with Commodore Warren, and this unwelcome news was being widely broadcast.

On September 3, the *Adventure Galley* sailed into the port of Carrawar, and made itself known to the tiny outpost of the East India Company. The factors of the Company could do little to prevent Kidd's men from taking on the fresh water and other supplies they so desperately needed. One of the strangest encounters for Kidd, however, was coming face to face with an old shipmate by the name of William Mason, with whom he had a proverbial bone to pick. Mason had once participated in an act of mutiny, one that had deprived Kidd of his vessel the *Blessed William* in the Caribbean some nine years earlier (see Chapter 7). However, in the meantime, Mason had turned his hand to a more honest way of earning a living, and though prevailed upon by Kidd to join up again, he resolutely declined.

Though Kidd did not manage to augment his crew while at Carrawar he certainly managed to lose a few, one of whom was Benjamin Franks, who had signed up to go as far as India. The ex-jeweller was now free to find his own way to his family's outpost in India and recommence his profession. About 10 men in all managed to effect their escape, while others less fortunate were returned to the *Adventure Galley* and soundly whipped. The captive Parker was kept secure below decks to prevent his flight, the knowledge he had of coastal waters being of paramount importance to Kidd. The picture of conditions on board recounted by the escapees was frightful. The ship was leaking badly, supplies were depleted, dissatisfaction and fighting was rife, and many of the men were in a mutinous frame of mind. General morale was at a low point and Kidd had to use brute force on more than one occasion to quiet his fractious crew.

Kidd has often been described as a bully, and there is little doubt that he had occasion to bully and cajole the sullen and quarrelsome crew under his command. A large brawny man endowed with a short temper, he cannot be expected to have treated his men with less than the forceful language he considered was merited by the circumstances. Kidd could not administer discipline as the navy did using the cat-o'-nine-tails — he would not have lasted long if he had tried this punishment! Instead he had to wheedle and cajole his men in as coercive a manner as possible. Far from home in a leaky ship, with an insubordinate bunch of malcontents under his command, the prospects for a good voyage did not look promising. The fact that he had now learned that he had been declared a pirate made his situation even more daunting. From thenceforth, vessels flying the English flag would be keeping a watchful eye out for his presence.

Kidd had picked up one tidbit of useful information while at Carrawar: a large Moorish vessel was en route. He lay off the coast in readiness to waylay the merchantman, but instead he was unfortunate enough to encounter two Portuguese men-o'-war who had been dispatched from Goa to seek him out. Throwing discretion to the wind, Kidd ran before them with all the sail he could muster, and during the ensuing chase the two Portuguese vessels became separated, the smaller, faster ship outsailing the larger. Kidd now turned and attacked. Faced with the urgency of some real action, Kidd's men threw themselves into the unequal contest with gusto, and the Portuguese ship was soon ripped apart by cannon fire from the *Adventure Galley*. Before Kidd could board and ransack the crippled ship, her sister vessel approached and Kidd was forced to retreat. He slipped away to lick his wounds, with the loss of about 10 of his men and no reward for the effort. However, the action had put new heart into his crew and Kidd had displayed his vigour and mettle in his cunning tactics. The battle had lasted five to six hours.

Map of the Malabar Coast and Southern India.

Kidd next put into Calicut, further down the coast, arriving there on October 4. He sailed in with style, firing his cannons to announce his arrival. The agents of the East India Company received him with much suspicion and distrust, as they had already heard that he had been declared a pirate. Kidd is reputed to have rebuffed this igno-minious description of himself with as much dignity as he could when confronted by the Company's agents, and much to their relief, he sailed off without incident. Cruising slowly and steadily southwards, further down the coast Kidd intercepted a number of small vessels, mainly coastal traders. How many were taken is not known, but the vessels being weak, vulnerable, and unarmed, it is likely that the actions were not very inspiring to Kidd's crew, who by this time had regained some of the mettle they had lacked prior to the sea-fight with the Portuguese. Eventually Kidd's path crossed that of a ship displaying English colours, called the *Thankfull*. Kidd tried the old ruse of flying French colours in the hope that the *Thankfull* would haul down the English flag and raise a French one, after which Kidd would raise his English colours and then attack. This practice is no different from that adopted today by twenty-first-century police forces attempting to entrap suspected criminals in "sting" operations. In the case of the *Thankfull*, the ruse didn't work, and she steadfastly maintained her English colours displayed from the masthead. Kidd refrained from ordering an attack, so eagerly anticipated by his crew, and the vessels continued on their way.

The *Adventure Galley* then sailed to the Laccadive Islands, presumably to careen once more or to carry out some urgently needed repairs to a vessel in a rapidly deteriorating condition in those tropical waters, where shipworm plays havoc with timbers below the waterline. With some rest and recuperation needed by the crew, the native islanders were soon disturbed from their otherwise tranquil existence by the customary looting, raping, and general mayhem that inevitably accompanied the presence of such unwelcome visitors. On this occasion, the natives managed to obtain a degree of satisfaction by slitting the cooper's throat!

Resuming the voyage, the *Adventure Galley* continued to cruise steadily south until they were close to the southernmost tip of the Indian continent off Cape Comorin. As far as can be ascertained, it was sometime in mid-October when they caught sight of a merchantman flying the colours of the East India Company, which turned out to be the *Loyal Captain*. Kidd hoisted his king's pennant and the captain of the merchantman came aboard. Emotions were running high by this time, as Kidd's crew saw a golden oppor-

The Taking of the Queddah Merchant

tunity of taking the *Loyal Captain* with little effort, the vessel being obviously unarmed. Kidd appears to have been hesitant to take a ship belonging to the East India Company, and this hesitancy would have been understandable. Firstly, there had been the armed confrontation with the *Sceptre*, also an East Indiaman, off the coast of Aden. Then they had taken a vessel flying English colours and kidnapped Thomas Parker, who with some of his men was still aboard. News of these two incidents had spread fast, as Kidd discovered when he entered first Carrawar, and then Calicut to take on water. After that had come the encounter with the *Thankfull*, also flying English colours, so unless a prospect was likely to contain a great deal of booty, it was better to refrain from attacking English shipping. At this point in the voyage, with his ship becoming increasingly unseaworthy, it appeared prudent to avoid incurring the wrath of the East India Company any further. If so inclined, the Company could raise a flotilla of armed vessels to hunt down the *Adventure Galley*, which more than likely would have come off worse in any such confrontation.

From the crew's point of view, they had thus far made a disastrous voyage. Many had perished from debilitating scurvy and disease, some had more gloriously died in combat. And for what? Precious little booty had been taken — a few gold coins and a few bags of pepper. Understandably they wanted much more, and they wanted it fast, regardless of the consequences. The men were becoming increasingly polarized between two extremes, those that were openly rebellious and unconcerned about the niceties of whether they were considered pirates or not, and those of a more sober disposition. The *Loyal Captain* represented booty, but sadly for those of a more mutinous inclination, that booty allegedly would have turned out to be sugar. Eventually the men listened to Kidd and desisted from taking the ship. Captain How of the *Loyal Captain* was permitted to continue on his way without further let or hindrance. Kidd had bullied and cajoled his rabble effectively, but sullen looks and mutterings of discontent were evident, and these were to reappear.

William Moore, the gunner, seems to have been the ringleader of a group of hotheaded malcontents who bandied about among them-

129

selves talk of replacing Kidd as their captain. At this point of the voyage Kidd would have been replaced, had there been anyone else on board the *Adventure Galley* with navigational skills. No one had, so they had to be content with Kidd, but only under duress. Matters came to a head on October 30 when they caught sight of a Dutch vessel, which was to escape their clutches. Ever since the incident with the *Loyal Captain*, William Moore had exhibited increasing hostility towards Kidd, and, from various depositions made later, it is also claimed that he had been ill. Moore was sulkily grinding a chisel when Kidd approached him. According to Hugh Parrott, a young deckhand, and other witnesses present on deck at the time, the dialogue and action between Moore and Kidd went something like this:

"Captain, I could have put you in the way to have taken the ship [he may have been referring to their recent encounter with the *Loyal Captain*], and have never been the worse for it."

This put Kidd into a towering passion and a heated shouting match commenced between the two men.

"You have brought us all to ruin," Moore yelled.

"Have I brought you to a ruin?" retorted Kidd. "I have not done an ill thing to ruin you. You are a saucy fellow to say such words." (Some witnesses claim that Kidd used the phrase "lousy dog.")

"If I am a lousy dog, you have made me so!"

Everyone agrees with what happened next. Kidd picked up an iron-hooped bucket and approached Moore. "Have I ruined you, you dog?" Kidd yelled, as he smashed Moore over the head with the bucket. As the gunner's mates rushed the stricken gunner below decks to attend to him, Kidd cried out "Damn him! He is a villain."

Moore died the next day from his wounds.

According to Hugh Parrott, the altercation between Moore and Kidd that led to the death of Moore had its origins in the squabbling that had ensued among the crew at the time they had come up with the *Loyal Captain*. Parrott claimed the following in his written testimony:

> My Commander [Kidd] fortuned to come up with
> this captain Hoar's [How's] ship, and some were

for taking her, and some were not; and afterwards there was a little sort of Mutiny, and some rose in Arms, the greatest Part, and they said they would take this Ship and the Commander was not for it; and so they resolved to go away in the Boat, and take her. Captain Kidd said, "If you desert my Ship, you shall never come aboard again, and I will force you into Bombay, and I will carrry you before some of the Council there;" Inasmuch my Commander stilled them again and they remained on Board ...

In the seventeenth century, ship's captains were very much a law unto themselves. In the face of possible mutiny, and in the case of Kidd a more probable mutiny, a captain had the right and, it may be argued, the duty to exert his authority. Hanging of potential troublemakers was not unknown in such circumstances. However, in the case of Kidd versus Moore, Kidd's temper got out of hand with the result that Moore received a mortal blow. In a cooler frame of mind, Kidd might have pondered upon arresting the troublemaker and appealing to his crew under the twelfth article of the Articles of Agreement that they had all signed. Kidd was fortunately well-built, strong, and burly; the crew were ill-disciplined and quarrelsome, even among themselves. If they had been united in purpose, Kidd might have been deposed there and then and likely finished up swinging upon his own yardarm. The mood of the men must have been decidedly ugly following Moore's death.

Four days after Moore's death, the *Adventure Galley* ventured into the East India Company's base at Tellicherry. Unfortunately for Kidd, the *Sceptre* was anchored in the harbour at the time and it did not take Captain Barlow very long to recognize his adversary of the Gulf of Aden. Shots from a shore battery were let loose upon the *Adventure Galley* and Kidd turned tail and ran, setting sail once more. Kidd's run of bad luck finally came to an end, as almost immediately they encountered the *Rupparell*, a small Moorish ketch of 200 tons with a mixed crew of Dutchmen and lascars. A few shots were fired at the *Rupparell* to force her to heave to and the captain was invited aboard the *Adventure Galley*. Kidd had been flying his French colours to give the other vessel the impression that he was French, and the captain of the *Rupparell* fell for the trick and produced a French pass. Kidd leapt to his feet crying, "My God I have catched you! You are a free prize." Kidd was acting within the law, or at least his own interpretation of his commission, which allowed him to take French ships.

The *Rupparell* was carrying little coin or gold, but it did carry a valuable cargo of drugs, cloth, sugar, and coral, all of which could be sold in a suitable market. Furthermore, according to some reports, she carried 30 bales of sugar-candy, tobacco, and myrrh, together with a couple of horses. The horses and some of the cloth were to be sold later to merchants, after which a distribution of the proceeds was made among the crew. Some of the crew of the *Rupparell* elected to join Kidd, including the Dutch pilot, boatswain, and gunner, and also the captain, who was allowed to retain his command.

In a later testimony given in the aftermath of the voyage, Samuel Bradley, who was Kidd's brother-in-law, declared that following the capture of the *Rupparell*, Kidd had wanted to restore the vessel to its rightful owners and send it on its way. This motion was put before the crew but was turned down by general consent. Perhaps the malcontents envisaged the possibility of taking the *Rupparell* for themselves and setting sail on their own account, or perhaps they were feeling increasingly uncomfortable with the by now apparent unseaworthiness of the *Adventure Galley*. Whatever the reason might have been, Kidd's motion was struck down in a true exhibition of pirate democracy.

The *Rupparell* was immediately renamed the *Maiden*, since she was the first ship that they had captured and retained, but this name did not last long, as she was subsequently renamed the *November*, in honour of the month in which she had been taken. However, in this record we shall retain the original name, the *Rupparell*. Both the *Adventure Galley* and the *Rupparell* sailed immediately for Caliquilon, a minor out-of-the-way port where the cargo was sold off to a renegade factor of the East India Company. With money in their pockets, Kidd's crew was now beginning to feel more kindly towards their captain. It was already well over a year since most of his crew had left New York, and they had felt that it was about time they had some reward to show for their efforts in the Indian Ocean, no matter how modest.

The *Adventure Galley*, with the assistance of the *Rupparell*, managed to take a couple of small trading vessels during the following weeks, but none carried sufficient booty for the effort to be considered worthwhile, even though supplies were augmented by looting the unfortunate ships. Finally, on January 30, 1698, they encountered the prize that was to make them infamous and lead to repercussions that were to echo around the globe. The *Queddah Merchant*, an ungainly vessel of Moorish construction, hove into sight around Cape Comorin, wallowing her way northwards to Surat. She was intercepted by the marauding vessels flying French colours. Given below are summaries from the statements entered into the official records:

> Statement dated 17th July, 1701 to the effect that it was the custom of Armenian merchants to join together to hire a ship for the conveyance of goods on trading missions together with associated bills of exchange and rupees. The merchants contracted the Queddah als Kary Merchant to go from Surat to Bengal and return to Surat. They took with them on the outward-bound voyage cotton goods and "with them agreate quantity of Rupees and bills of exchange to a very greate value". The ship arrived safely in Bengal. The merchants traded inland and exchanged or bought muslins, silks, callicoes, raw silk, opium, sugars, iron and saltpetre. The following are listed — 1200 bales of muslin, raw silk and callicoes, 1400 bags of brown sugar, 84 bales of raw silk, 80 chests of opium together with iron, saltpetre.

> In February 1698 on the coast of Malabar while returning, the Queddah encountered Kidd and was taken. Kidd threw overboard all bills of lading and

books belonging to the merchants and other papers relating to the ownership of the merchandise. The merchants together with the sailors from the Queddah were put ashore on the nearby coast, following which Kidd sailed to Cochin where he sold silk and opium to the value of £20,000 [English money] in gold bars and gold dust. The main merchant was Cogi Baba Sulthanam.

The *Queddah Merchant* was the only vessel of any real size that Kidd actually captured, or is known to have captured, during his short piratical career in the Indian Ocean. She was a large vessel by the standards of the time, being of an estimated 500 tons. Being a lightly armed merchantman, the *Queddah Merchant* is unlikely to have offered any resistance as Kidd's crew swarmed up her sides and boarded her with little observance of any delicacies. The value of the cargo being carried was later estimated as approximately $25 million in today's terms. A pretty good haul for Kidd and his men!

Kidd's own version of the events is terse and not very informative. His words, as taken down by Isaiah Addington, an official at Boston, when he was being subjected to a great deal of cross-examination following his return to North America are:

And that about the first day of February following upon the same coast, under French colours with a designe to decoy, met with Bengall merchantman belonging to Suratt of the burthen of 4 or 500 tuns, 10 guns and he commanded the master on board and a Frenchman, inhabitant of Suratt, and belonging to the French factory there, and gunner of said ship came on board as master, and when he came on board the Narrator [Kidd] caused the English colours to be hoysted, and the said master was surprised and said "you are all English", and asking which was the captain, whom when he saw said "here is a good prize", and delivered him the French

> passes and that with the said two prizes sailed for the
> port of St. Marie in Madagascar …

There is no mention in Kidd's account, as taken down by Addington, of the destruction of the papers that accompanied the merchandise on board the *Queddah Merchant*; neither is there any mention of the stripping of the Armenian merchants on board of every vestige of personal wealth, nor of the resale of goods on board. Even more surprising — there is no mention of the Armenian traders being set free from captivity unharmed. Surely Kidd would have wanted to portray an image of himself as being of a merciful disposition, and to have capitalized on it accordingly. Any self-respecting pirate, concerned about keeping his head on his shoulders, would have cut the throats of his victims and tossed their bodies overboard! After all, dead men tell no tales. The weakness of Kidd's narrative, and the release of the traders unharmed upon the shore, would indicate that Kidd seems to have been disinclined to unnecessary bloodshed, an interesting reflection on his character.

The leader of the Armenian traders, who suddenly found himself within Kidd's grasp, was Cogi Baba Sulthanam, and he attempted to buy off Kidd with an offer of 20,000 rupees for the release of his ship and its cargo. If he had the money about his person, then it soon changed hands with little ceremony. The *Adventure Galley* then headed the small flotilla back into Caliquilon, where some of the cargo of the *Queddah Merchant* was promptly sold for ready cash. It is likely that it was here that the Armenian prisoners were set free, most of the crew being retained to sail the captured merchantman.

During the rest of February, Kidd, in the *Adventure Galley*, with the *Queddah Merchant* in tow and accompanied by the *Rupparell*, cruised the Malabar coast in search of more prizes. They managed to take a small Portuguese vessel which yielded very little. Then they encountered a flotilla of ships which included the East India Company's ship the *Dorrill*, a ship that had very recently battled with Culliford in the Strait of Malacca. The small Portuguese vessel was abandoned as the *Adventure Galley* and her companions took immediate flight from the armed Indiaman. Kidd was not going to risk losing the booty he had accumulated thus far in any fierce-fought battle, and at this point of the game he had much to lose.

By now, the *Adventure Galley* was deteriorating rapidly. Her pumps had to be manned constantly, and furthermore, it would soon be time for the changing of the monsoon. The steady wind from the northeast had enabled Kidd to cruise safely along the coast with little risk of being driven on shore, but with a changing wind, and a leeshore wind into the bargain, the attendant risks would rise immeasurably. It was time to take his flotilla to a secure haven, count his profit and loss, and make necessary repairs whilst allowing the crew a little time for rest and relaxation. But perhaps there was still time for one last strike! This came in the form of a heavily laden East Indiaman, the *Sedgewick*.

For three days Kidd pursued the *Sedgewick*, but could not catch it. The winds failed, so the crew of the *Adventure Galley* took to the oars. The *Sedgewick* lowered her boats in turn and towed the ship out of range. It was a race, and it was won by the *Sedgewick*. For a pirate galley to be outrun by a heavily laden merchantman was a reflection upon the dire water-logged condition of the *Adventure Galley*. A last tidbit was found in the form of a small ketch from which water and food was taken, and now it really was time to seek that safe haven. Thomas Parker, who had been held captive for the previous five to six months on board the *Adventure Galley*, was given leave to depart, as Kidd no longer had need for a pilot on the Malabar coast.

St. Marie was the place to go for a pirate to effect repairs. There at the pirate base were traders only too anxious to retail rigging, canvas, ships stores, and equipment, food, clothing, and liquor in exchange for hard-won booty from dubious sources. Slaves and lascars took over the continual manning of the pumps on board the *Adventure Galley*, some shuffling around of the crews took place between the three ships, and then they were set for the long haul to Madagascar. The serious condition of the *Adventure Galley* is exemplified in Kidd's own words, during his later examination:

> With the said two prizes sailed for the port of St.
> Marie in Madagascar, and sailing thither the said

gally was so leaky they feared she would have sunk every hour, and it required eight men every two glasses to keep her free, and forced to woold [bind] her round with cables to keep her together.

It must have been a nerve-wracking experience for all those who found themselves on board such an unseaworthy vessel. The voyage took about six weeks, and it is doubtful that, had it not been for a favourable wind behind them, they would ever have reached their destination.

Kidd may not have been a pirate when he sailed from the Comoros towards the Babs a year earlier, but by the time he returned to the same region of the Indian Ocean, after cruising the Arabian Sea and the Malabar Coast, there is no doubt that he was. By sailing into the known pirate base of St. Marie, a place he had avoided on his northbound voyage, he had declared himself to be one of the "brethren of the seas." None of the vessels he had under his command was by then fit to engage a worthwhile adversary, and pirates could be expected at St. Marie. He had spent his time lurking around the coast of India preying upon harmless merchantmen, and when given to exhibiting some bravado, had the temerity to face off against ships flying English colours, from which he had then retreated. At no time did Kidd attempt to seek out any pirate vessel, let alone take the action he was specifically commanded to do under his commission. In fact it may be argued that in bypassing the pirate base at St. Marie when he sailed north from the Comoros, he displayed little or no intention to seek out and destroy pirates.

At which point on the voyage can it be said that Kidd first actively engaged in a piratical act? The intermingling with the Mocha fleet, and the raising of a red flag in its midst, is probably that point. That Kidd was unlucky enough to raise suspicion in the mind of Captain Barlow of the *Sceptre*, and to be chased off, does not alter the fact that if Kidd had succeeded in cutting out a suitable vessel, it would certainly have been boarded and plundered. Kidd may have had a couple of French passes in his possession, which might have given the illusion to some that he had kept to the terms of his commission, but his other actions indicate that he was no more than a common pirate. The temptations that abounded in the Indian Ocean, in the form of richly laden merchantmen, might have proved too great to resist, especially when under the provocation of a vociferous crew demanding a "good voyage." We will be gracious enough to believe that Kidd never contemplated any piratical action until he was at the Babs — at least for now. Later on, evidence will be presented to suggest that his intent, with the connivance of some of his backers, was otherwise and had been so even before his departure from London in the *Adventure Galley*.

Chapter 7

Robert Culliford and the Encounter at St. Marie

> *A tall, strong, heavy, nut-brown man;*
> *his tarry pigtail falling over the shoulders*
> *of his soiled blue coat; his hands ragged and*
> *scarred, with black, broken nails.*
> — *Treasure Island* (Stevenson)

The last chapter saw Kidd and his ragtag crew arriving at the pirate stronghold of St. Marie. The *Adventure Galley* had been woolded (bound) with cables during the voyage to prevent it from disintegrating, and the pumps had been fully manned with eight men every two glasses to keep the leaky ship afloat. Madagascar must have presented a welcome sight to Kidd and his crew, with the prospect of dry land under their feet. It is natural to ask the question: why didn't Kidd go to a nearer place than Madagascar, if his ship was in such dire straits? Why didn't he seek some secluded backwater along the Malabar coast or the Laccadive Islands to effect repairs, or at least somewhere he could transfer everything to the *Rupparell* and the *Queddah Merchant*, and then either abandon or burn the *Adventure Galley*? Kidd knew that he had been declared a pirate, his actions in the Arabian Sea and off the Indian coast were proof of that, but if he was caught by Indian authority in the form of the East India Company with the *Queddah Merchant* in tow, it would be like being caught with his hand in the proverbial cookie jar! Only by retreating from the Indian coast to a safe and secure base far away could Kidd hope to avoid the attentions of the Company. If he could return safely to North America he could count on the support of his friend Lord Bellomont, or so he thought. St. Marie provided Kidd with a virtual last hope, if he could make it, and there he would find friends who regularly traded between New York and Madagascar. To his chagrin, as the *Adventure Galley* limped into the pirate harbour, he was to find his old associate Robert Culliford already in port. Kidd had a bone to pick with Culliford, but since his leaky, unseaworthy ship was a priority, this was not the time for rancorous dispute.

Unfortunately, *The Pirates' Who's Who* is not very informative about the life and death of Robert Culliford, who is often referred to as "Cutlass Culliford." Tersely it records the following: "A Madagascar pirate. Little is known of him except that one day in the streets of London he recognised and denounced another pirate called Burgess."

Fortunately, however, tidbits of Culliford's life have emerged from the endeavours of more recent researchers since Gosse wrote his epic work. Despite these useful additions, Robert Culliford remains a rather shadowy figure, although it is virtually certain that he was Cornish and is believed to have been born in 1664 in East Looe.

Some six months earlier, before arriving at St. Marie, Kidd had encountered William Mason at Carrawar, and since the two of them had sailed with Culliford (sometimes written Cullover or Culliver), it is more than likely that they exchanged gossip regarding their mutual acquaintances. From Mason, who in the meantime had turned his hand to honest employment, Kidd would have learned that Culliford was still alive and likely to be in the region. Therefore it must have come as no surprise to Kidd to find Culliford already at St. Marie.

As far as can be determined, the connection between Kidd and Culliford went back to 1689, when they, together with Mason, were shipmates aboard a French privateer in the West Indies. The ship had a mixed Anglo-French crew, and on hearing that hostilities had been renewed between England and France, animosity broke out between the two factions. As a result, the Englishmen and their supporters jumped the Frenchmen, dumped them, and sailed the ship off to the English colony of Nevis. There they were given a warm welcome and the ship, of 20 guns, was given a new name, the *Blessed William*. It was then put into service under Captain Hewetson, who testified ineffectually on behalf of Kidd at his trial. A small flotilla headed by HMS *Lion*, with Captain Hewetson in overall command, attacked the island of Mariegalante, to the southeast of Guadeloupe, resulting in the French settlers being put to flight, and the town was looted and burned. Kidd and his men captured £2,000 of loot, and Hewetson later said of Kidd during his trial that he "fought as well as any man I ever saw."

The crew aboard the *Blessed William* did not appear to have relished the prospect of more fighting in the cause of national honour, even if they were likely to receive a share of any booty. They abandoned Kidd while he was on shore and absconded with both the ship and the £2,000 of captured loot. The leaders of this mutiny were William Mason, Samuel Burgess, and Robert Culliford, the first-named becoming the new commander. Under its new captain, the *Blessed William* captured a couple of Spanish vessels, raided and pillaged the odd town for more supplies and booty, and finally sailed off to New York, arriving in May 1690. The crew sold the cargo they had captured, which included a number of slaves, refitted their vessel, and set off with a commission from the governor to do some privateering in the Gulf of St. Lawrence. One of the six prizes they subsequently captured was renamed the *Jacob*, and after returning to New York they cashed in the proceeds of their enterprise, sold the *Blessed William*, and made plans to go buccaneering in the *Jacob*, a ship more appropriate for their purpose. They set sail for the Indian Ocean towards the end of December 1690.

Arriving in the balmy climate of the Indian Ocean, the *Jacob* cruised the coasts of India with little success. In the Nicobar Islands various arguments ensued and Mason, Culliford, and their adherents parted from the *Jacob* which, under the command of Henry Coates, sailed off to Madagascar, thence to the Red Sea where they made a "good voyage," after which they retired back to New York to enjoy a less exhausting lifestyle. There is some uncertainty as to the fate of Mason and Culliford immediately after their parting with the *Jacob*. One story has it that the two men also returned to New York and then subsequently returned to the Indian Ocean, taking passage to

Mangalore in India; another story is that the *Jacob* dropped them off there. Regardless of their exact movements, Mason and Culliford appear to have entered the service of the East India Company, Culliford acting as a gunner. Culliford's service with the East India Company lasted until 1696, at which time he was serving on board the *Josiah*. The crew mutinied, possessed the vessel and set off "on account" in the Bay of Bengal, making the Nicobar Islands their base. Unfortunately they were surprised while taking on water in the Nicobars and Culliford and his men, who had been on shore at the time, were marooned. As luck would have it, they did not have to wait long before they were picked up by a ship that hove to, also in order to take on fresh water. Before long a recalcitrant Culliford was making apologies to the officers of the East India Company in Bombay and begging for exoneration. This was forthcoming as the Company was in desperate need of skilled seamen, and before long Culliford found himself on board the frigate *Mocha*.

With a new ship under him, Culliford was not long in joining a group of disgruntled crewmates, and the inevitable result was yet another mutiny in June 1696 in which Culliford participated with apparent enthusiasm. The mutineers, led by Ralph Stout, killed the captain of the *Mocha*, now putting themselves well beyond the pale of the law, and set off once again to go "on account." In the process they renamed their vessel the *Resolution*, and it is by both names, the *Mocha* and *Resolution*, that Culliford's ship is known. In this text we will retain the original name of the *Mocha*. The *Mocha* joined up with another gang of pirates and cruised off the Indian Ocean coast of Siam. At the Nicobar Islands Culliford met up with a soulmate by the name of Dirk Chivers, also known as Shivers or Seivers. Chivers is reputed to have been the originator of the phrase "Shiver me timbers!"

Chivers came from Hamburg, and had set off to seek his fortune in the New World. He joined a ship called the *Portsmouth Adventure*, a vessel of 90 tons, which sailed to the Indies with intentions of cruising against the Moors. The *Portsmouth Adventure* became unseaworthy and Chivers and his shipmates transferred their allegiance to Captain Robert Glover, who commanded a vessel of 200 tons and 18 guns. This much larger and better-armed ship was called the *Resolution*, but this name should not be confused with the renamed vessel under Culliford. With a complement of 110 men, Glover and Chivers set their sights upon the feast of wealth they had heard of in the Red Sea. They took several Moorish vessels before retreating to the pirate base of St. Marie, where several of their crew died. After refitting they set sail again, this time for the west coast of India. Among the prizes they captured was the *Charming Mary* of 180 tons and 12 guns, the command of which fell to Chivers, who promptly renamed it the *Soldadoes*, by which it is more commonly known. Chivers and his men went "on account" and brought back to the pirate base at St. Marie a captured Moorish vessel of 400 tons.

In late 1696, Chivers in the *Soldadoes* fell in with Culliford in the *Mocha*, and together they set sail for the coast of India. Off Ceylon they took another Moorish ship of 200 tons and plundered her cargo of rice and stripped her of her rigging. They robbed a Portuguese ship of gold and silk to the value of £12,000 and then let her go. They then appear to have retreated towards the Strait of Malacca, capturing a total of four more ships, one of which was a Portuguese merchantman carrying 100 pounds weight in gold. After these successes they retired to the Maldives to count the loot and inflict their undesirable attentions upon the natives. The *Mocha* and the *Soldadoes* returned to the Strait of Malacca in the summer of 1697 and more successes were achieved. Having decided to extend their activities further east, they were sailing through the strait when a notable incident occurred between the *Mocha* and the East Indiaman the *Dorrill*, which Kidd was to encounter later off the coast of Malabar.

The story about Culliford and his encounter with the *Dorrill*, if true, sheds an interesting light upon his character. According to legend, Culliford hailed the *Dorrill* with the cry, "Gentlemen, we want not your ship, but only your money. Money we want and money we shall have." From this it might be construed that Culliford was averse to unnecessary bloodshed. However, the captain of the *Dorrill* was accepting no nonsense, no matter how blood-curdling the cries emanating from the pirate ship might be. He pressed on more sail and ran before the wind. The chase continued for three days until the *Mocha* managed to catch up with the less speedy merchantman. Battle ensued, in the process of which the mainmast of the *Mocha* was broken by a lucky cannonball. Culliford had to withdraw from the engagement, but then his luck turned, and retreating to lick his wounds he happened upon a couple of hapless Japanese vessels, followed by a Chinese ship of 300 tons. Battle-scarred though the *Mocha* might have been, the partially crippled ship, with its armaments and overwhelming number of men, was vastly superior to its prey, and with this last feat of arms proving successful, Culliford finally retreated to effect badly needed repairs. One suggestion is that he went to the mainland of what is now Burma, to a secluded cove near Cape Negrais. However, a possible alternative would be the Nicobar Islands, a place he knew well, which he had frequented often, and where there would be little chance of a surprise attack by an adversary. After this brief respite, the *Mocha* and its depleted crew retired to Madagascar and the pirate harbour of St. Marie, with its swaying coconut palms and wild fig trees. Here Culliford's tranquility was shattered by the sudden appearance of William Kidd, a former captain, and one whom he had treated shabbily some nine years earlier.

During the encounter between the *Mocha* and the *Dorrill* we have no knowledge of the whereabouts of Chivers in the *Soldadoes*. Certainly he would have entered the fray if he had been in the vicinity, however he could not have been too far away, because a few months later he and Culliford were to capture a grand prize in the form of a large merchantman, the *Great Mahomet*, and the taking of this vessel was effected with the enthusiastic participation of some of Kidd's crew.

The reports of the meeting between Kidd and Culliford at St. Marie contain a number of discrepancies. Some reports suggest outright hostility and suspicion, others extreme friendship and conviviality; the truth probably lies somewhere in between. In view of the circumstances in which Kidd and Culliford had parted nine years earlier in the West Indies, caution must have been uppermost in the minds of both men. However, Kidd had the leaky, unseaworthy *Adventure Galley* beneath him, with the *Rupparell*, not much of a fighting ship, in close attendance. The *Queddah Merchant*, a valuable ship with a rich cargo of merchandise, but not a fighting ship, was still far away from the shores of Madagascar. From Kidd's point of view, it was not the time to try to level scores with Culliford. From Culliford's standpoint, he would have known about Kidd's commission to combat piracy, but he also knew full well that Kidd had turned pirate himself. This was no time for either of them to start throwing stones at one another in the proverbial glass house.

Kidd's testimony as to what went on at St. Marie is extracted from the more detailed narrative of his voyage and is reproduced below. It should be noted that the original document is somewhat illegible:

> When I arrived there was a pyrate ship called the Moca Frigat at anchor, Robert Culliford, commander thereof, who with his men left the same at my coming in and ran into the woods, and I proposed to my men to take the same having sufficient power and authority to do so, but the mutinous crew told me if I offered the same they would rather fire two guns into me than one into the other [the *Mocha*] and thereupon 97 deserted and went into the Moca Frigat and sent into the woods for the said pirates and brought back Culliford and his men on board again. And all the time she staid in the said port which was for the space of 4 or 5 dayes, the said deserters sometimes in great numbers came on board the said gally [the *Adventure Galley*] and Adventure Prize [the *Queddah Merchant*] and carried away great guns, powder, shot, small armes, sails, anchors, cables, churgeon's chest, and what else they pleased, and threatened several times to murder me, for I was informed and advised to take care of myselfe what they designed in the night to effect, but was prevented by my locking myselfe in my cabin at night and securing myselfe with barracading the same with bales of goods and having about 40 small armes besides pistols ready

charged kept them out — their wickedness was so great after they had plundered and ransacked sufficiently they went four miles off to one Edward Welche's house where my chest was lodged, and broke it open and took out of it money, gold, forty pounds of plate, 370 pieces-of-eight, my journal and a great number of papers that belonged to me and the people of New Yorke that fitted us out.

That about the 10th [?] day of June the Moca Frigat went away being manned with about 180 [?] men and forty guns.

Joseph Palmer, one of Kidd's crew who is reputed to have deserted Kidd at St. Marie in order to join Culliford, was to turn King's Evidence at Kidd's trial, and this is what he said of the reception between Kidd and Culliford:

> Captain Culliford came aboard Kidd, and on the quarter deck, they made a tub of bomboo [water, limes and sugar], and there they drank to one another, and, says Captain Kidd, "Before I would do you any damage, I had rather my soul should broil in hell fire."

Palmer added that Kidd presented Culliford with four guns, and received £400 to £500 in return.

Robert Bradinham, who had acted as surgeon on the *Adventure Galley*, and who, like Palmer, deserted Kidd to join Culliford at St. Marie, testified in a similar vein, having also turned King's Evidence:

> In the beginning of May 1698, Culliford piloted Kidd into the harbour of Saint Maryes, and went aboard the Adventure Galley, where Kidd ordered a dividend of the goods which he hoisted out, and each man had three whole bales.

Are these testimonies believable? Frankly, no! On the one hand, Kidd gives the impression of hostility between himself and Culliford, whereas Palmer and Bradinham describe the converse. Certainly there may have been some mistrust, and a testy atmosphere may have prevailed, at least initially after Kidd's arrival. However, it was at least a month before the *Queddah Merchant* arrived at St. Marie, a period long enough for Kidd and Culliford to partake of the abundance of liquor available and smoke the proverbial peace pipe. After their arduous voyage, with the continual manning of the pumps, the crew of the *Adventure Galley* would have been more disposed to pleasure themselves on the womenfolk available and indulge themselves in a little debauchery, rather than take sides in a long-festering dispute, which as far as they were concerned had its origins in the distant past. It must also be remembered that by the time Kidd made his deposition he had been arraigned, and was under lock and key in the custody of Bellomont. Thus it may be concluded that the tale that Kidd told, of being threatened by his crew and dispossessed of his journal and papers, was intended to portray him to the authorities as being more victim than felon.

On the other hand, Palmer and Bradinham had both been prevailed upon to turn King's Evidence, and their statements might better reflect the image the lawyers for the Crown wished to present to the court, remembering that Kidd had no legal representation and had to defend himself as best he might from innuendo and deceit.

The deposition made by Kidd regarding the events at St. Marie is supported by those of his crew that were arrested once the law finally caught up with them. Specifically they are those of Abel Owen, a mariner of full age and ship's cook; Samuel Arry, late steward; English Smith; Humphrey Clay; and Hugh Parrott, all mariners of full age, whose testimonies were signed or accompanied by their mark (an *X*) to verify their acknowledgement of the truth of their statements. Other depositions available for scrutiny are brief and add little or nothing at all to determine more exactly what transpired at St. Marie. In any case, this truth would have been of little interest to the interrogators at the time the testimonies were taken, since they were only intent on establishing suspicion of piracy, and would have had no interest in sorting out internecine squabbles between the pirates themselves. The brevity of these later depositions is therefore quite understandable.

Kidd's testimony includes the following statement regarding the arrival of his vessel at St. Marie:

> ... and with much ado carried her [the *Adventure Galley*] into the said port of St. Marie where they arrived about the first day of April 1698 and about the 6th day of May the lesser prize [the *Rupparell*] was hauled into the careening island or key, the other prize [the *Queddah Merchant*] not being arrived, and ransacked and sunk by the mutinous men who threatened the Narrator [Kidd] and the men that would not joine with them to burn and sink the other [the *Adventure Galley*] that they might not go home and tell the news.

There is some discrepancy within the same testimony as Kidd stated that "the said deserters sometimes in great numbers came on board the said gally [the *Adventure Galley*] and Adventure Prize [the *Queddah Merchant*] and carried away great guns ..." and that this occurred within the four or five days while Culliford in his *Mocha* was in port.

It must have been obvious to all concerned that the condition of the *Adventure Galley* was beyond redemption. There was only one thing to do with her and that was to keep her afloat for as long as possible, and in the meantime strip her of everything that could be of any use. William Jenkins, a young apprentice who sailed with Kidd on the *Adventure Galley* from England, and who returned with him to New England, testified in his own examination at Boston, following his arrest:

> Captain Kidd and the men left behind, after the company deserted him for the Moco frigott, run the Adventure Galley on shoar in Madagascar.

> They stript her furnishings and set her on fire to
> get her iron worke.

There is some further discrepancy here. Jenkins positively asserts
that it was the *Adventure Galley* that was set on fire, when it had been
hauled onto the shore after the *Mocha* had sailed away. Kidd states that
the *Rupparell* was hauled into the careening yard and later ransacked
and sunk. If a vessel is lying on its side being careened, it is rather difficult to sink it. Better to burn it instead! Some doubt must exist,
therefore, as to which vessel was sunk, which was burned, or perhaps
even that both suffered the same fate. Regardless of these considerations, the *Rupparell* must have been questionable regarding her seaworthiness, and that is why she was hauled into the careening yard in
the first place. The fact that she was subsequently burned or sunk
would indicate that her condition was as irredeemable as that of the
Adventure Galley. This left Kidd with the *Queddah Merchant* which,
being of local construction, was most likely built from timbers more
suited to resist the voracious broma (shipworm), that feasted on the
hulls of ships built in northern waters. The burning of the *Rupparell*
and/or the *Adventure Galley* may well have been delayed until the
Queddah Merchant arrived at St. Marie, to ensure that Kidd had at
least one seaworthy vessel. Since the India merchantman was no fighting ship, Kidd really had no alternative but to join Culliford if he
wanted to continue his career in the Indian Ocean. This meant that
the two pirate captains would have entered into some serious deliber-
ations regarding the action they would take in their mutual best interests. By this time, we have no qualms in describing Kidd as a pirate!

Barry Clifford, a well-known searcher of wrecks who located the
remains of Sam Bellamy's *Whiddah*, which sank off Cape Cod in 1717
fully laden with booty, made a recent search for the remains of the
Adventure Galley in St. Marie harbour. His search was successful and
became the subject of a fascinating television documentary on
Discovery Channel titled "The Quest for Captain Kidd." Clifford's
work at the wreck site disclosed a sunken vessel constructed of English
oak and from which was recovered the following artifacts — one bat-
tered pewter tankard, one seven-pound sounding weight, some shards

of pottery, and the base from a square bottle. There was nothing else! If this was indeed the *Adventure Galley*, it had been completely and totally stripped of everything before it had sunk, or had been sunk, in the harbour. If the ship had sunk of its own accord, then surely there would have been something more valuable in the wreck than those few items recovered by Clifford and his diving team. The conclusion to be drawn is that neither the *Rupparell* nor the *Adventure Galley* were any longer of value to either Kidd or Culliford. If feelings were so high between these two men, why did Culliford leave Kidd with the *Queddah Merchant* when it eventually arrived at St. Marie? This was a ship carrying a valuable cargo, and Culliford could have taken it forcibly from Kidd, leaving Kidd and his few men truly high and dry. There are many questions, but precious few answers concerning this encounter between Kidd and Culliford at St. Marie, and the various testimonies that have come down to us over the centuries should therefore be viewed with considerable caution.

Culliford's own testimony, given in June 1700, states the following regarding the happenings at St. Marie:

> When Kidd came, 96 men deserted him for Collover [Culliford], which was at Madagascar in March 1698. Afterwards they plundered a French ship at Johanna on 8 June 1698, which had 11,000 peeces of eight, vallue £2000, and about 10 tonnes of wine and brandy, value £100. They rummidged her and let her goe …

Apart from the minor differences between the accounts of Kidd, Bradinham, and Culliford regarding the actual date of arrival of the *Adventure Galley* into St. Marie, there is also the date of the taking of the French ship by Culliford at Johanna. Kidd states that Culliford left St. Marie about June 10, and Johanna is approximately 600 to 700 nautical miles from St. Marie, necessitating almost a week of sailing time! The implications of all the discrepancies in the various testimonies is that a lot of lies were being told for almost as many reasons as there were people giving testimony.

Common sense suggests that, despite the various testimonies, Kidd and Culliford would have pooled their resources for their mutual well-being. Culliford, in his frigate the *Mocha*, had excellent fighting abilities; all he needed was more men. Kidd, in the ponderous *Queddah Merchant*, the sole vessel left to him, had a valuable cargo to rid himself of at the earliest opportunity. It consisted of numerous bales of muslin, silk, calico, bags of sugar, chests of opium, iron, and saltpetre. The problem was finding a market in order to dispose of these commodities in exchange for cash, preferably in the form of gold. The rest of the captured loot, in the form of gold, silver, jewels, and coin, had already found a repository in the pirates' pockets. It was not prudent to return to the Malabar coast in search of a market as the East India Company would be on the lookout for them. The obvious place was the Spice Islands, but the difficulty in making that venue safely was the presence of native pirates in the Strait of Malacca. Hence the plan was born that Culliford should take the better half of Kidd's crew, at least the fit fighting men. After a successful cruise, the two parties would rendezvous at a predetermined location, preferably a remote and secluded island where they could marshal their forces before sailing into the Dutch East Indies.

It was now June, and for four to five months the southwest trade winds were favourable for Kidd to make a smooth passage eastwards across the empty bosom of the Indian Ocean. For this he needed the sparsest of crews. In a few months, the eastward flow of trade would recommence from the Red Sea to India and ships would carry many returning pilgrims and merchants laden with personal riches. Culliford and Kidd would have been only too anxious to relieve them of any burden in this regard. Their crews would have been equally eager.

We are unaware of the details of any agreement to which Kidd and Culliford subscribed, and any articles of agreement drawn up between them would have adhered to the strictures that were common at the time. The only thing we can surmise is the rendezvous point, which was an island in the Nicobar group of islands, one that was lonely, secluded, and where there was a good high point to observe the approach of any potentially hostile ships.

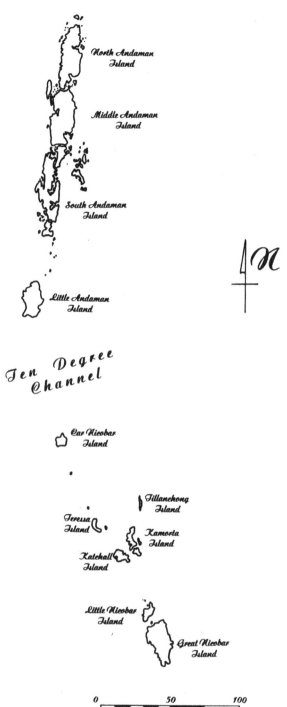

North Andaman
Island

Middle Andaman
Island

South Andaman
Island

Little Andaman
Island

Ten Degree
Channel

Car Nicobar
Island

Tillanchong
Island

Teressa
Island

Kamorta
Island

Katchall
Island

Little Nicobar
Island

Great Nicobar
Island

0   50   100

Scale   Miles

Map of the
Andaman and
Nicobar Islands.

We do not know where or when Culliford met up with his old partner, Dirk Chivers, who for all we know may have been party to the strange turn of events at St. Marie, but he did meet up with him.

Together they took up the chase and were highly successful. Subsequent depositions from pirates who participated in the hunt, namely Nicholas Turner and George Ogle (alias Jones), describe the taking of the *Great Mahomet* off Surat on September 23, 1698, and give the value of the treasure taken from this Turkish trader, of 500 tons and 19 guns with 400 people on board, as being £130,000. This is likely to have been a gross underestimate for obvious reasons, but even so it was truly a prize worth taking. This was in addition to the £2,000 they removed from the French trader at Johanna. The share of the booty amounted to £500 per man.

By Kidd's admission through his testimony, he lost 97 members of his crew to Culliford. Among these were Nicholas Churchill, James Howe, Darby Mullins, and Abel Owen, identified either by their names appearing on their own depositions to this effect, or because they were subsequently charged with counts of piracy against the *Great Mahomet*.

Culliford was later to give himself up to the British Navy when Thomas Warren, in a pink, the *Vine*, arrived at St. Marie in August 1699. Though initially committed to the Marshalsea on August 6, 1700, he was granted bail on the nineteenth, but subsequently re-arrested. Robert Culliford and Ralph Pattison were later transferred to Newgate, but Culliford's sailing career is unlikely to have ended when he was eventually granted a pardon and released in April 1702.

The departure of the *Mocha* from St. Marie in June 1698, believed to have been closely followed by Kidd in the *Queddah Merchant*, brings to a close that first part of Kidd's activities in the Indian Ocean that is mainly contained in the public record. There is a gap of at least five months in this self-same record where there is nothing to authenticate his presence anywhere. Kidd claims to have spent this period at St. Marie, waiting for the winds to change, in order to effect a rapid passage to the Cape of Good Hope with a diminished crew in his return to North America. However, a contemporary reports his presence in the

East Indies during this period, and this report is considered entirely credible.

Tracking Kidd's movements after St. Marie is dependent upon unravelling the Kidd-Palmer charts and identifying the island upon which he buried the treasure carried by *Queddah Merchant* before proceeding to the Dutch East Indies. For this, some appreciation of the rudiments of the art of navigation in the seventeenth century is necessary. The following chapters are a necessary digression in order to present a working hypothesis of what actually happened to the treasure, and who recovered it.

Chapter 8

Navigation in the Seventeenth Century

> *Now would I give a thousand furlongs*
> *of sea for an acre of barren ground;*
> *I would fain die a dry death.*
> — Gonzalo in *The Tempest* (Shakespeare)

Many a mariner, when beset by storm at sea, especially with the prospect of shipwreck, would doubtless echo the sentiments of Gonzalo. There must be few indeed who set foot upon a vessel bound for distant parts who did not ponder upon whether their lives might be lost before they saw land again. Many a wife has fondly embraced her husband, and many a girl her sweetheart, as he set out upon his various adventures. Many a woman has spent her time anxiously pacing her aptly named "widow's walk," before a joyous reunion after tiresome months and even years of separation. Often their menfolk spent more time at sea than they ever did at home. Tennyson, in his tragic poem "Enoch Arden," tells of how Enoch's wife waited for over 10 years for his return before finally remarrying. The unfortunate Enoch, meanwhile, had been marooned after being shipwrecked, and his homecoming held little joy. Doubtless this pathetic tragedy has been played out countless times over the ages with numerous variations.

The Greek writer Hesiod, in the eighth century BC, wrote about the dangers of voyaging in the following terms:

> For fifty days after the solstice, till the end of the har-
> vest, is the time for sailing; then you will not wreck

your ship, nor will the sea wash down your crew, unless Poseidon or Zeus wills their destruction. In that season winds are steady and ocean kind; with mind at rest launch your ship and stow your freight; but make all speed to return home, and await not the new wine and the rain of the vintage-time, when winter approaches, and the terrible south wind stirs the waves, in fellowship with the heavy autumnal rain of Zeus, and makes the sea cruel.

For many centuries seaborne traffic hugged the coastline because the means of navigating across stretches of open sea were non-existent. However, as shipbuilding techniques developed, and a realization dawned regarding the fixity of certain stars, man began to sail further and further afield. The discovery of the lodestone gave more heart to early navigators, but it was well over 2,000 years after Hesiod that navigation could be considered to be in any way reliable; it might have been an art, but a science it definitely was not. By comparison to the present day, navigation in Kidd's time was still very primitive. It is considered worthwhile to dwell on this subject for a chapter, and review, if briefly, the state of navigation in the seventeenth century. Many excellent books are available which discuss this subject in great detail, and the following is merely intended to assist the reader in understanding the uncertainties of establishing one's position at sea at the time Kidd carried out his exploits in the Indian Ocean. This rendering, therefore, should not be considered definitive.

There was general belief in the ancient world that the earth was flat; in some quarters this belief still persists! The history of astronomy, however, can be traced far back into antiquity, the motions of Jupiter and Saturn having been observed as long ago as 3062 BC, and the Chinese having recorded the simultaneous conjunction of Saturn, Jupiter, Mars, Mercury, and the moon in 2460 BC. At the time of Alexander the Great, the Babylonians possessed a history of making astronomical observations extending back 1,900 years. The belief gradually took hold among learned philosophers that Earth was spherical and not flat, and this viewpoint appears to have been held most tenaciously by the Egyptians and the Greeks. It was the Pharaoh Rameses II who unwittingly was to provide the stimulus for the first calculations regarding the size of Earth. In about 1300 BC, Rameses commissioned a detailed survey of the Nile valley, which extended more than 500 miles from Alexandria in the delta to Syene (modern-day Aswan) in the south. This detailed survey was later used by Erastosthenes (276–196 BC) to make the first attempt at computing Earth's diameter. A fellow Greek, Hipparchus (160–125 BC), first ascertained the true length of the year, discovered the equinoxes, and among other astronomical achievements, prepared a catalogue of the fixed stars, an important aid to early navigation.

Contrary to the conclusions of the early astronomers and mathematicians, Earth is not an exact sphere, the polar diameter being about 27 miles shorter than the equatorial diameter, a nicety of little consequence to navigators until recent times. For all practical purposes the equatorial diameter of Earth may be taken as 7,926.7 miles. A degree of arc along a meridian is, therefore, exactly the same length as a degree of arc along the equator. A degree of arc along a circle of latitude decreases in length towards the pole, where it becomes zero, the length of arc being proportional to the cosine of the latitude. As soon as it was realized that Earth was a sphere, the concept of nautical miles was developed; equivalent to a sixtieth part of a degree of latitude, a nautical mile is thus 6,080 feet. As far as early navigation was concerned, it was the concept of measuring distances in terms of nautical miles that was of greater importance than the equivalence in statute measurement, the circumference of Earth being 360 (degrees) x 60 (nautical miles per degree) to equal 21,600 nautical miles. When the scientists told the navigators this was equivalent to 25,000 statute miles, more or less, they were believed.

By the beginning of the seventeenth century most sea-going vessels carried a compass. This consisted of a magnetized needle attached to a card marked off in 32 points, and balanced upon a pivot mounted within a bowl. The needle required frequent remagnetiza-

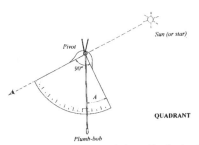

Sun (or star)

Pivot

90°

A

QUADRANT

Plumb-bob

While observer sights along top edge of quadrant his mate reads angle A.
Latitude equals A°

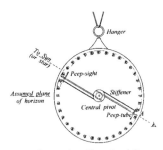

Hanger

To Sun (or star)

Peep-sight

Assumed plane of horizon

Stiffener

Central pivot

Peep-tube

Reading of scale at A = Latitude

The peep-tube would pass through the central pivot closer to the axis than shown

ASTROLABE

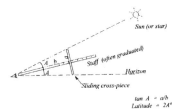

Sun (or star)

Staff (often graduated)

Horizon

A

b

a

A

Sliding cross-piece

$\tan A = a/b$
Latitude $= 2A°$

CROSS-STAFF

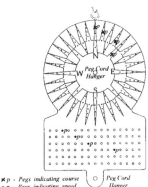

Peg Cord Hanger

W — E

N — S

✗ p - Pegs indicating course
● p - Pegs indicating speed

○ Peg Cord Hanger

In this example the course changed from NE to N. while the speed increased during the period

TRAVERSE BOARD

Sun

Adjustable slider on fixed scale

Sliding peep-sight

Horizon

A

B

Screen with slit

The observer views the horizon through the slit, then moves the slider until its shadow coincides with the slit. Latitude $= (A + B)°$

BACKSTAFF
(or DAVIS QUADRANT)

Sand

Sand

SAND-GLASS

Numerous types of sand-glass were in use with different capacities. That for timing the watch was for thirty minutes between bells

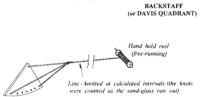

Hand held reel (free-running)

Line - knotted at calculated intervals (the knots were counted as the sand-glass ran out)

The chip - approx 12" per side and weighted along bottom edge with lead or iron inserts

CHIP-LOG

Principles of some Seventeenth Century Navigational Instruments.

Artist C.W. Jefferys — National Archives of Canada/CO73632

Champlain using the Astrolabe in Canada, 1613.

tion, and a lodestone was used for this purpose. The lodestone was first discovered in Magnesia, Asia Minor, from which the word *magnet* originates. Composed of ferric oxide (Fe_3O_4), or magnetite, it possesses an inherent magnetism, which can be imparted to needle-shaped pieces of iron brought into contact with it. When mounted upon a pivot, the magnetized iron needle oriented itself in a north-south direction, and this proved a great boon to early travellers both on land and sea. The dry-pivoted compass was first mentioned in 1269, and by 1380 the compass card had been invented. By the end of the sixteenth century the discrepancy between the geographic and magnetic poles had become understood, but published tables to facilitate correction were very unreliable. This discrepancy, known as the magnetic declination, i.e., the variation of the compass needle from the true meridian or line of longitude, was seriously effected by the presence of other iron in the immediate vicinity. The resultant magnetic deviation is unlikely to have been a major problem in the wooden ships of the age, unless objects containing significant amounts of iron were close to the compass mounting, or the mounting was built of iron. The bowl in which the compass needle was pivoted was dry, unlike that of a modern compass, and thus had a tendency to gyrate wildly in a rough sea.

The course and speed of a ship was generally recorded every hour or half-hour upon a traverse board. This consisted of a compass rose with holes into which pegs could be inserted. At the bottom of the board was a series of holes by which the speed of the ship could be recorded. Time was kept with a 30-minute sandglass and, by the mid-seventeenth century the chip log had been invented to measure the ship's speed and was in general use. The navigational requirements of a sea-going vessel were somewhat onerous, and required not only basic arithmetic skills of the navigator, but a strict attention by the watch to collect the basic data, which would enable the essential details of the ship's daily run to be recorded in the ship's logbook.

Traditionally, a ship's watch began at eight bells, i.e., at four, eight, and twelve o'clock. At the first turn of the glass a bell would be struck, at the second turn two bells, and so on until the four-hour watch had been completed. To ensure that the crew was rotated in an orderly manner, the watch between four and eight p.m. was split into two short dogwatches, each two hours long. At each bell, or two bells as the case may be, the ship's course would be recorded by a peg in the traverse board and its speed likewise, whether this was by estimate or by use of the chip log.

The chip log, when accurately calibrated, was a very reliable device. It consisted of a pie-shaped board, or "chip," about 12 inches per side, and ballasted in such a manner that it floated upright in the water. Attached to the chip was a line, knotted at intervals so that the ship's speed could be recorded in knots, or nautical miles per hour. A nautical mile is 6,080 feet and for a 30-second hourglass the knots were tied at intervals of 50.6 feet. Thus a sailor could count the knots slipping through his fingers while the glass ran after the chip had been thrown overboard, and the ship's speed thus estimated with a fair degree of accuracy.

Even though skilled mariners were well acquainted with the stars and used them for general guidance, the main method of estimating one's position at sea was by dead reckoning. This is the means whereby a ship's position was estimated without any reference to either sun or stars. By keeping an account of the daily distance the ship ran by means of the log, and the course steered by the compass, the daily position became a matter of simple trigonometry. However, allowances had to be made for drift, leeway, and other uncertainties, and it would have been irresponsible on the part of any navigator to place total reliance on estimating his position by means of dead reckoning alone. When better and more precise instruments became available, accompanied by appropriate tables, the practice of dead reckoning was soon abandoned. Until that time, the art of navigating a sea-going vessel on a long voyage was exceedingly onerous; allowances had to be made for magnetic declination, magnetic variation, leeway, wind, and current before a single entry could be made to the ship's daily journal regarding course and speed. In addition, there was the troublesome task of determining latitude and longitude in fixing the ship's position.

Latitude determinations were dependent upon observation of either the sun or the North Star, or Polaris, when in the northern hemisphere. One of the earliest devices for measuring latitude was the astrolabe, which was a disc, often of brass, marked off in degrees around the circumference. It was suspended by a ring at its top edge, and had a moveable arm with a sight through which the navigator could view the North Star. When his eye, the sight, and the star were in line, the angle of inclination could be read, which gave the latitude. A similar device was the quadrant. These were simple and effective, but not very accurate, especially when the ship was wallowing in a rough sea on a cloud-ridden night.

An improvement came in the form of the cross-staff, which consisted of a stick with a sliding cross-piece mounted at right angles.

This aid to navigation was first described by Levi ben Gerson, a Jewish astronomer, in 1330, but received little attention at the time. The observer could eye the North Star along the length of the stick and adjust the cross-piece by sliding it up and down until the upper end touched the star, and the lower end was coincident with the horizon. Theoretically, the altitude of the North Star is the latitude, supposedly being directly overhead at the North Pole. However, the star wandered as much as 3.6 degrees from Earth's axis during the seventeenth century, which necessitated the use of tables computed by astronomers to make the required adjustments. Latitude could also be measured by making observations on the sun using the same technique, but this was difficult and dangerous. John Davis (1550–1605), one of the foremost early English navigators, who wrote a book on the subject in 1595, made sighting of the sun easier and less dangerous by his development of the backstaff. This instrument enabled the observer to keep his back to the sun by sighting the horizon away from the sun and moving the cross-piece until a shadow was cast upon the sight.

Davis improved his backstaff and developed what is known as the Davis Quadrant, a predecessor of the modern sextant. The observer stood with his back to the sun, sighted along the horizontal staff, and moved a lens mounted on a small quadrant attached to the staff until the image of the sun struck a slit in the screen at the far end of the staff. Then, in order to achieve greater accuracy, the peep sight was moved down the larger arc until the bright spot of the sun focused by the lens lay exactly upon the horizon. The Davis Quadrant was one of the most reliable devices of the age for determining latitude, being accurate to within one-sixth of a degree. Since a degree of latitude is equivalent to 60 nautical miles, it is obvious that greater precision was desirable. Determination of position by sightings made on the sun required the use of tables of declination, since only twice a year is the sun directly over the equator. Tables of declination were readily available in the seventeenth century.

Although the determination of latitude had been satisfactorily accomplished by the end of the seventeenth century, at least to acceptable limits of accuracy, that of longitude remained unresolved, and would remain that way until the invention of the chronometer by John Harrison in the mid-eighteenth century. The concept of longitude had been in existence since it was first appreciated that Earth was a sphere, but with no exact way of measuring it, and with no reference meridian, the problem was intractable. Numerous ships were wrecked or lost at sea because of the inability of navigators to determine their longitude to a satisfactory degree of exactness. This inability was overcome to a large extent by calculating the ship's departure, i.e., the distance travelled due east or west since the last determination of latitude, by means of dead reckoning. The departure in terms of nautical miles, divided by the cosine of the latitude, gave a reasonable estimate of the change in longitude. This was only accurate if the course was direct east or west, i.e., along a parallel of latitude. Otherwise, mean values had to be taken which placed a heavy burden upon the judgement of the navigator involved.

An excellent example of the abilities of seventeenth-century navigators to determine the departure of their vessels to an acceptable level of accuracy is provided by the journal, or logbook, of HMS *Falcon*, which sailed from the West Indies to England in 1688. Apart from the wind direction, the course, and the miles travelled each day, the journal records the latitude and the longitude (or departure), and the bearing of the last observed headland. In this connection, the "longitude" represented the daily shift as the ship sailed eastwards. Of interest is the entry when, off the Lizard, after 38 days out of sight of land, the daily shifts in longitude are summed. This summation amounted to 64°30'. The actual difference in longitude between Samana Bay, Hispanola, the ship's point of departure, and the Lizard is 64°09'. Thus the error by the navigator on board the *Falcon* was a mere 0.55 percent. This is truly astonishing when performed in a period renowned for its supposed inability to measure longitude with any degree of precision. Thus, despite the lack of a reliable means of determining a fix in longitude, a skilled navigator could determine his position with remarkable accuracy under the right conditions.

The Lizard appears to have been a reference meridian for many of the English navigators of the late seventeenth century. Sir John Narbrough (1640–88), a noted mariner of the age, made constant reference to his longitude from the Lizard during his voyage to the South Seas in 1669–71. His account of the voyage in HMS *Sweepstakes* includes the following entries:

September 29, 1669 — About 12 a clock at noon I stood to the south westward as near as I could; the Lizard bore north of me ... Taking my departure from the Lizard, I intend to keep my daily account of the difference of my longitude from that meridian.

December 24, 1669 [off the east coast of South America] — I observed a considerable difference within the 48 hours, betwixt my dead account, as we call it, which is kept by the log, and the observations I made these two days, when the sun was on the meridian; for I find myself more south by 12 miles, than the log allows; I can't perceive any variation, and the log is well kept, and the half minute glass good.

December 15, 1670 [off the west coast of South America] — The mouth of the harbour of Baldavia [modern-day Valdivia] on the coasts of Chili in the S.Sea lies at 39d 56m S.Lat. In Longitude West from the Lizard 70d 19m. According to the account made by my sailing from the meridian of the Lizard, according to my daily computation of my ships way; for I don't look upon the account of plain sailing fit for observations at sea, but the best is by Mercator, sailing according to the circle of the globe, which I ever made use of, and keep my account of easting and westing by longitude, the best and truest sailing, to give exact description of the globe: I have set down the meridian distance, whereby such navigators as know better, may have that to give them the knowledge of the distance of places, according to their understanding. Most of our modern seamen sail, and keep their account of the ships way by the plain chart, though they sail near the poles; a great error! for they can't tell how to find their way home again, for want of understanding the true difference of the meridians, according to their miles of longitude in the several latitudes. I wish all navigators would sail by Mercator's chart.

June 10, 1671 — At 6 a clock in the afternoon the Lizard north of us about 3 leagues; I make my difference of longitude from Cape Blanco to the Lizard in England, to be 60d 45m 5 tenths.

On the outward voyage, Narbrough computed the difference in longitude between the Lizard and Cape Blanco to be 61°56'. The true difference measured from modern charts is 60°35'30". Thus his computational errors were approximately 2 percent on the outward, and 0.25 percent on the homeward-bound voyages. The sailing distance between Cape Blanco and England is little less than 8,000 miles, and Narbrough's navigational ability, using the crude instruments of his day, can only be judged a credit to his dedication in ensuring accurate readings at all times, and his wisdom in using Mercator's projections.

Chapter 10 is devoted to William Dampier, the celebrated English navigator who, during his early years, sailed with buccaneers and pirates. One of his voyages, after he had abandoned his former way of life, was to New Holland (Australia) on a voyage of discovery in HMS *Roebuck*. While crossing the Indian Ocean from the Cape of Good Hope in 1699, he made constant reference to his longitude east of the Cape. The following are extracts from his journal:

June 19th ... when we had run six hundred leagues we were at 34°17' south latitude, and longitude from the Cape 39°24' east.

> July 25th ... being at 26°14' south latitude and longitude from the Cape of Good Hope 85°52' we saw more seaweed ...

> August 7th ... I call'd the mouth of this sound, Shark's Bay, lying at 25° south latitude, and according to our reckoning 87° longitude from the Cape of Good Hope ...

It will become apparent later why there is great significance to the established practice in the seventeenth century of recording a ship's departure as a shift of longitude from a particular point of reference, usually from where the ship began its voyage. Interpretation of the Kidd-Palmer charts, to be discussed in the next chapter, depends on appreciation of this fundamental practice of seventeenth-century navigation.

In Chapter 5 mention was made of how Commodore Warren, escorting a number of East Indiamen, could not find St. Helena, and, while drifting rather aimlessly in the South Atlantic, encountered Kidd. Obviously Warren's navigational skills, or those in charge of the navigation of his ship at the time, were considerably inferior to those navigating the *Sweepstakes*, the *Falcon* or the *Roebuck*. We have no certain knowledge regarding the skills possessed by Kidd himself, but bearing in mind his lengthy voyage from New York in the *Adventure Galley*, his rounding of the Cape of Good Hope, and his landfall on Madagascar, all accomplished without undue incident (except for meeting up with Warren), it must be concluded that Kidd possessed superb qualities as a navigator. Aided by compass, chip log, and backstaff or quadrant alone, and with little in the way of charts or maps to assist him, Kidd, like many of his age, set out on a perilous voyage and arrived at his destination, despite all the hazards. What is equally important to bear in mind is that his crew must have been sufficiently competent and reliable to record meticulously both course and speed to enable him to make the necessary computations using dead reckoning with any degree of certainty. There are few today who would attempt to repeat such a venture armed only with the rude and primitive instruments of that period.

A brief mention must be made of maps and charts, which, in the seventeenth century, varied enormously in accuracy. The Dutch had been leaders in European map-making, and the Blaeu family of Amsterdam were renowned for their pioneering work in establishing order into the art. However, the Arabs produced better charts, at least as far as the northern regions of the Indian Ocean were concerned. The caliph of Baghdad, in 827, made determinations of latitude and measured an arc of the meridian, and from these endeavours sprang a tradition of producing high quality maps of the region. Vasco da Gama, after he penetrated the Indian Ocean in 1498, made a statement to the effect that Arabian charts were far superior to anything similarly available in the Mediterranean.

Chapter 9

The Kidd-Palmer Charts

*Yes, sir, this is the spot, to be sure; and very
prettily drawed out. Who might have done that I wonder?
The pirates were too ignorant, I reckon. Ay, here it is:
'Capt Kidd's Anchorage'*
— Long John Silver in *Treasure Island* (Stevenson)

The prospect of finding buried treasure possesses a peculiar fascination, one that draws many people to purchase metal detectors, and to
spend their leisure hours plodding along beaches or across fields in the
hopes of finding something of value. Sometimes they are successful
and, as the newspapers testify, a crock of ancient coins or an equally
ancient sword comes to light every now and again. Pirate treasure
maps have a similar appeal, though there is little evidence that pirates
resorted to disclosing on paper the locations where they may have
buried their ill-gotten gains, if they did bury anything of value. But
the appeal, and along with it a measure of hope, is that perhaps that
old map with the "X" marked on it does after all represent a certain
desert island, where some rum-sodden pirate actually did cache his
loot, but was prevented by an appointment with the hangman's noose
from effecting its recovery. Such maps, where "X" marks the spot, are
the very stuff of films and youthful fiction, but nevertheless they hold
their own emotional attraction to a great body of people.

This book admits to having, as one of its purposes, the objective
of determining what happened to the treasure that Kidd claimed to
have "lodged in the Indies," the premise being that his claim possessed substance. Since that claim was made, a great deal of effort,

and many a fortune, has been squandered on seeking his treasure. Naturally, there are those who prefer to scoff at the notion that Kidd would ever have buried anything at all.

In the decade prior to the outbreak of World War II a number of charts were discovered that hinted at the possibility that Kidd had indeed left a trail behind him, and that this trail would lead to where he had buried his ill-gotten gains in that far-off place he spoke of before he was hanged. The existence of these charts first became public in 1935 and, as might be expected, fuelled a frenzy of speculation. The charts were reported to have been X-rayed, photographed in infrared light, microscopically examined, and likely would have been subjected to radiocarbon dating and possibly DNA analysis, if they hadn't vanished as quickly, and as mysteriously, as they did in 1957. The legacy of these charts, and their enigmatic history, has spawned much theorizing on the part of armchair treasure hunters, and for the more adventurous, led to expeditions into far off lands. One such party finished up as nonpaying guests of the Vietnamese government! There has been no inkling that Kidd's treasure has ever been found. But then, if it had, the fact is unlikely to have been publicized.

There are two main reference sources relating to the discovery of the Kidd-Palmer charts, as they have become known. The earlier of these is the well-known book by Harold T.Wilkins titled *Captain Kidd and his Skeleton Island*, published by Cassell & Co, London (1935). The second is that by George Edmunds, *Kidd — The Search for His Treasure*, published by Pentland Press, Durham (1996). The book by Edmunds is entirely devoted to the charts, and to the various interpretations that may be deduced from their examination, whereas the book by Wilkins gives a less exact account set against a backdrop of Kidd's activities. As might be expected, there are some variations, generally of a minor nature, regarding the factual details of these two accounts: how the charts were found, the furniture in which they were discovered, the chronological order in which they appeared, and other incidentals. Edmunds's account is considered the more precise of the two. Wilkins wrote shortly after the charts had been discovered by Hubert Palmer, who understandably was keen to maintain a certain amount of secrecy about the information the charts divulged. As far as is known, Wilkins never had full access to examine the charts at his own leisure.

It is due to the tenacity and persistence of George Edmunds in doggedly researching the background to the Kidd-Palmer charts over many decades that the public has access to a remarkable book devoted solely to these intriguing charts. Edmunds has granted his kind permission to reproduce herein excerpts from his book that relate to the finding of the charts, and to the equally fascinating way in which the charts subsequently disappeared. Whether the charts will reappear at some future date, enabling them to be examined in greater detail is, of course, a question that only time will answer.

In his book *Kidd — The Search for His Treasure*, Edmunds gives the following account regarding the discovery of the charts by Hubert Palmer:

> The story starts in Eastbourne in 1929. Guy and Hubert Palmer lived there in retirement, both wealthy bachelors with a deep interest in the sea and maritime history.
>
> Their collections included seafaring relics associated with famous ships and with Drake, Nelson and many other distinguished sailors. Hubert Palmer was a recognised authority on piracy, his collection of books and relics in his museum being probably unique and without rival anywhere in the world. He was very careful to accept into his collection only those items that had passed his rigorous tests to prove genuineness. The bureau he bought in 1929 was to receive the same intensive testing. It came from London and was a heavy seventeenth-century oak bureau bearing a much worn brass plate inscribed with the words 'Captain William Kidd, Adventure Galley 1669'.
>
> Knowing that furniture of the period often contained secret compartments, Palmer subjected the

bureau to his usual intensive examination and found three hiding places that had been unknown to previous owners: all were empty.

One day whilst using the bureau, one of the runners supporting the lid broke off. Carved upon it he noticed the barely decipherable words: 'William Kidd, his chest'. There was also impressed upon one end, in wax, the insignia of a foul anchor. Guessing the runner to be hollow, he carefully broke the seal. Inside there was a brass tube, and tightly rolled around this was a small piece of parchment-vellum, yellow with age. He called his brother and, unrolling their find, they discovered they had before them (although they did not know it at the time) the first of the Kidd charts. It showed in red and black ink the outline of an island with an 'X' in the middle. At the top were the words 'CHINA SEA,' and at the bottom 'W. K. 1669'. There was a compass north bearing and along the bottom, 'of me Sarah-W'.

Although 1669 appears on the chart, it was obviously drawn at least twenty-three years later, after Kidd had married Mrs. Sarah Oort. This suggests that Kidd visited the island in 1669.

Subsequent scientific testing by experts confirmed that the wax, ink and parchment were of seventeenth-century origin. Further examination revealed nothing more, leaving Palmer with a mystery and wondering if there were any other Kidd relics in existence that might provide a clue to the map.

He now concentrated in particular on Kidd relics, hoping that perhaps he might find more clues to his mystery drawing. A thorough examination of Kidd relics already in his possession revealed nothing, so he started to advertise, without of course revealing his real reason. It was the start of a long search.

Towards the end of 1931, Palmer bought an old oak sea chest from his antique dealer friend, who also supplied a "pedigree" as follows:

> Oak sea chest, 26 1/4 inches long, 13 inches wide and 16 inches deep, left by Captain William Kidd to his boatswain Ned Ward, with a threat that Kidd would haunt him forever if he broke the chest open after he was dead and gone. This chest was sold to Captain Thomas Masterman Hardy (of the famous warship HMS Victory, later Vice-Admiral Sir Thomas Masterman Hardy, author) by the great grand-son of Ward, the boatswain to Kidd. This chest came from the (late) Miss Pamela Hardy, great-niece of Captain Masterman Hardy. It was bequeathed to her by her father, John Hardy, brother of the said Captain T. M. Hardy. On the lid is a Black Flag, carved with date 1699. There is in it a cutlass also carved. Under the Black Flag is deeply carved the words 'Capn Kidd his chest'.

Palmer gave the chest his usual thorough examination; he noticed that some nails on the bottom were really cleverly disguised screws. Removing these released a false bottom inside the chest which lifted out.

Secured by rusty nails to the false bottom was a slim book on the title page of which were the words: Carolus Redux or a sermon preach'd on May 29, 1662 being the Anniversary Day of His Majesties

Return, By Danial Cudmore Minister at Tiverton in Devon, London.

Behind the book Palmer discovered a piece of ancient parchment. It was another map, but to his great disappointment it was more or less the same as that which he had discovered in the bureau, but with no reference to the China Sea, and told him nothing new. Scientific tests once again proved this map to be of seventeenth-century origin.

In 1932, Palmer was introduced to a Captain Dan Morgan of Bristol by Mr Hill Cutler, his antique dealer friend. Cutler was, on behalf of Palmer, on the lookout for Kidd relics. He had received the following letter from Morgan:

> Respected Sir,
>
> As you seem keen for pirate stuff i have dug something out of my attik wich may sute you it is a bit more Kidd stuff and hope you will like it i have been told Kidd was a kind gent and was murdered but when you see this thing i think you will say he was only a Bloody pirate and deserved all he got i will try and hoble down end of the week sir so heres to 15 men on the dead mans chest and dont forgit the rum ile hav som you bet after the deal.
>
> your obedant servant.
> D. Morgan.

Morgan claimed descent from the famous buccaneer Sir Henry Morgan. He explained that he had a sea chest that once belonged to Kidd, saying that one of his ancestors had been head gaoler at Newgate Prison at the time of Kidd's trial, who after Kidd's death had 'removed' the chest. It had remained in his family ever since. Morgan carried on:

> My old dad told me when I was a boy that this was the same box that was brought in at the trial of Captain Kidd and used as evidence against him. The lawyers froze onto the skull on the box, which they said proved Kidd was a pirate. It was Kidd's chest and used by him.

The chest had ornamental brass hinges, a plate engraved with the monogram "K," and the skull and crossbones. Inside the chest was a plaster skull fixed to a bible, also in plaster, this item most probably used for the swearing in of pirate crews. The skull and bible were attached to a false bottom to the chest — something like a shallow tray about 1/2 inch from the real bottom; there was no attempt at concealment. When you lifted the skull out, the false bottom came as well.

After checking for the usual hidden compartments and finding none, Palmer turned his attention to a small mirror on the inside of the false bottom. On removing the beading and mirror a cloth was revealed. Carefully cutting this away he found a shallow well, inside which was parchment. To his great delight it proved to be the same island depicted in the previous maps but with a difference. This chart showed hills, a lagoon, reefs, four conspicuous looking "dots" and a cross. A red zig-zag line joined the cross and the dots. A compass north and compass bearing with distance were also shown. Palmer was elated; it looked as though Kidd really had buried a treasure. He had the chart checked and once again its authenticity was proved.

In 1934 a small box believed to have been Mrs Kidd's workbox was located. It belonged to a retired naval officer living in Jersey and had previously belonged to his brother who had lived in America. It was a small box 12 1/2 inches long, 7 1/2 inches wide and 7 inches deep, bound and decorated with ornamental brasswork, with a brass plate on the top with the words "William and Sarah Kidd, their box" engraved on it.

Careful measuring tests led Palmer to believe that the box was hiding a secret compartment. He withdrew four nails from the beading around the edge of the bottom of the box. This released the beading, revealing a narrow cavity. Probing inside he withdrew what appeared to be an old piece of leather binding. This turned out to be the backing of an oblong piece of yellow parchment. He realized straight away that this was 'the' chart — the key to all the others. The search was over.

Larger and more detailed than the "skull chest" chart, there were additional directions around the margin but, most important of all, the latitude and longitude of the island was given. Palmer could hardly contain his excitement. He quickly had the chart examined by the experts who verified its seventeenth-century origin. The writing around the edge was compared with known specimens of Kidd's in the Public Record Office and it was declared that it could well have been Kidd's writing.

Some three or four years after Palmer had found the final 'key' chart, he purchased a very old oak framed mirror. It was about 15 inches square with a

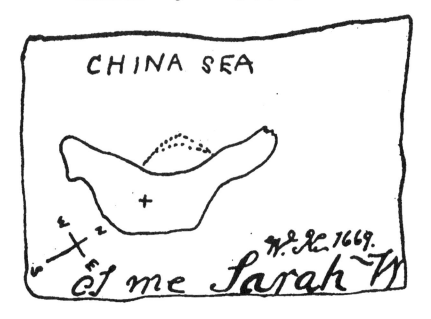

The First Kidd-Palmer Chart, found 1929.
An identical chart was found in 1931.
Actual chart size 4.75 by 3.1 in. (12 by 8 cm).

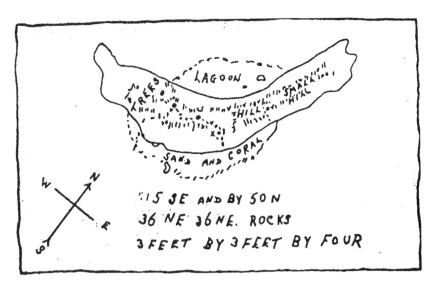

The Third Kidd-Palmer Chart, found 1932.
The dashed line linking the dots and the spot marked "x" in the south-cen-
tre of the island is understood to have been marked in red on the original.
Actual chart size 5.55 by 3.35 in. (14 by 8.5 cm).

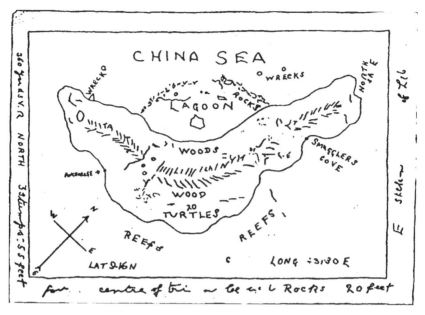

The Fourth Kidd-Palmer Chart, found 1934.
Actual chart size 8.3 by 5.8 in. (21 by 14.7 cm).

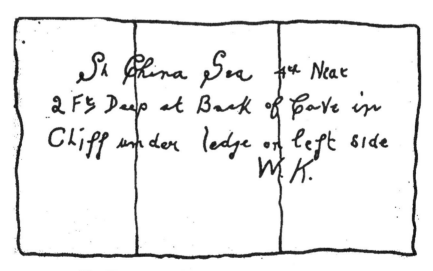

The Yunnan Parchment, found 1937 or 1938.
Actual size 7.5 by 4.2 in. (19 by 10.5 cm).

skull and crossbones and had the initials 'W K' carved on the frame. The mirror was thought to have been salvaged from a wreck near Eastbourne.

Palmer was not happy about its supposed history and viewed it with some suspicion. However, the 'W K,' for obvious reasons, intrigued him and he gave the mirror his usual close examination. He discovered a very small arrow carved on the front of the frame. After removing the back of the mirror he found a concealed shallow cavity: the arrow on the front had been pointing to this. Inside was a piece of folded parchment with a piece of thin wood as backing, and marked upon the wood, as though pricked out with the point of a pin, were the words 'Yunnan Island'. The parchment contained three lines of writing: 'Sh China Sea 4th NE at 2ft Deep at Back of Cave in Cliff under ledge on left side'. Underneath were the initials in block capitals ' W K'.

The foregoing makes mention of the fact that Hubert Palmer sought expert advice to determine whether the charts he had found were, or were not, authentic. And what would have been more natural? One does not need a great deal of imagination to visualize an excited Palmer scurrying off in search of reliable authentication. Where did he go? One source that he consulted was the British Museum, an institution whose opinion would have been the most credible of all and whose experts would have been not only impartial in the advice they gave, but, more importantly, completely uninterested in benefiting from Palmer's find. Wilkins makes no mention of any attempt by Palmer to verify the charts as being genuine. This lapse is understandable, as Palmer would have wished to maintain a certain amount of discretion on such a subject, especially when the subject was likely to become a focal point in the book that Wilkins was writing.

Almost 40 years later Rupert Furneaux was researching his own book, *Money Pit — The Mystery of Oak Island*, when, attracted by the similarity in shape of the island depicted on the Kidd-Palmer charts to that of Oak Island, off the coast of Nova Scotia, he approached the British Museum in an endeavour to re-authenticate the same charts. Though Hubert Palmer had died in the interim, the charts had been bequeathed to Palmer's former housekeeper, Mrs. Dick. Furneaux relates in his book that while the charts were in Mrs. Dick's possession they were examined by R.A.Skelton, then Superintendent of the Map Room, who was a renowned authority on cartography. He tells how the maps were concluded to be genuine seventeenth century, conforming in type, ink, parchment, and style of writing to others of that period, and also stating that the charts were photographed using methods which included infrared photography. Furneaux claims that this authentication of the charts was reaffirmed by Skelton in 1965. Furneaux's book was finally published in 1972.

Furneaux's claims appear to be rather sweeping. There is a letter on file from Skelton to Furneaux dated June 1965 in which Skelton states categorically that he had only seen one of the original charts some 14 to 15 years earlier. This was the fourth chart found in Mrs. Kidd's workbox. Skelton states that the map was "drawn on the back of a perfectly genuine will, apparently in the early eighteenth century, and gave latitudes and longitudes which locate it [the island] somewhere in the China Sea." If Skelton is correct in his opinion regarding the age of the will as being early eighteenth century, there is obviously some uncertainty regarding the authenticity of the chart, if it was indeed prepared by Kidd. He was hanged in May 1701!

Under such circumstances it is difficult not to accept the fact that the Kidd-Palmer charts were probably genuine. And yet a lingering doubt remains! Why were all the maps found by the same person within a few years of each other, to be exact, over the five year period between 1929 and 1934? And why, two years after he is supposed to have re-authenticated the maps, did Skelton retire from his employment with the British Museum? Skelton would have been 61 years old at the time, a young age to retire for someone who was in good health, at the pinnacle of his chosen profession, and with all the resources of the British Museum behind him. Skelton had joined the British Museum in 1931 and, apart from the war years of 1939 to 1945, his service was unbroken up to his retirement in 1967.

Edmunds writes further regarding the history of the charts following Palmer's death in 1949 at the age of 85 years:

> He left his huge collection of pirate relics and books to Mrs Elizabeth Dick, his companion and nurse for eleven years. When Mr Palmer's will was declared, Mrs Dick gained world wide publicity. Interviews with newspapers and magazines in this country [Britain], in France and in America were followed by newsreel and television appearances.
>
> Within a few days she had received more than 1,000 letters and had to engage two secretaries to answer them. Many contained proposals of marriage for this gray-haired lady. More contained offers to buy the treasure maps.
>
> At that time, Mrs Dick, to whom the relics and curios meant as much as they did to Palmer, said she would never part with them. But a year later, alone in a large eighteen-room Victorian house, heavy taxation and rates forced her to change her mind. She decided that all the relics had to go and so an auction sale was arranged over two days at the house.

This auction was held on July 20 and 21, 1950. Mrs. Dick only put up one of the charts and which one is uncertain. However, the chart was withdrawn from the sale since the highest bid was a mere £25, and less than its reserve price. Edmunds continues:

> Mrs Dick died in July 1965, but the charts had been sold [by her] in 1957. Apparently a Maurice Taylor of Toronto, Canada, had contacted Mrs Dick in June of that year. He was acting for [and part of] a

syndicate of Canadian and American sponsors who wished to purchase the charts.

In December of the same year, one of the syndicate, a Mr Alex Freeman of Winnipeg, arrived and finalised the deal. The four charts, Yunnan Island parchment and various photographs of them were handed over to a representative of the solicitors acting for the syndicate.

For the next couple of years there was some minor correspondence between the various interested groups on both sides of the Atlantic, the result being that Maurice Taylor bought out the other members of his syndicate and became sole owner of the charts. He is stated to have held the opinion that the charts possessed great commercial value, but nothing else was heard of Mr. Taylor or his charts after 1959. The charts vanished as quickly as they had appeared 30 years earlier, and with them went Mr. Taylor.

In the process of following up all available evidence connected with Kidd, which included examining data relating to the Kidd-Palmer charts in the hope of gaining useful information, I made a visit to the British Library, now the repository of maps, books, manuscripts, etc. that had previously been housed in the British Museum. It proved an interesting visit with curious implications.

On approaching the enquiry desk in the library's Maps Reading Room and making my purpose known, the attractive young lady behind the desk smiled indulgently and said, "We get an awful lot of enquiries about these." She then extracted a plastic envelope from a ring binder which was ready to hand. The envelope was stuffed with various oddments. There was little order, if any, to the miscellaneous assemblage the envelope contained. There were photocopies of extracts from various pirate books relating to Kidd (most of it well known), an odd original letter from Furneaux and others, a copy of a British Library letter of more recent date concluding that the maps could not have been seventeenth century, but were more likely twentieth century, and so forth. There was little information of value in this strange assortment and a total lack of the detailed records implied by Furneaux. The overall impression gained by this visit to one of the inner sanctums of the prestigious British Library was that the Kidd-Palmer charts were an embarrassment. The lack of order and security on the contents of this file suggested that the sooner they were stolen by larcenous researchers or hopeful treasure seekers, the better, as far as the library was concerned. If the British Museum had indeed examined, photographed, and X-rayed the charts after Palmer's discoveries, as had often been reported, then why wasn't there some semblance of order and security in the file? This left a nagging doubt in the mind of this particular researcher, which was strengthened as further realizations dawned. The charts took on the aspect of a mighty hoax, which at the time would have had its usefulness. That time had now seemingly past.

Despite the dismay that ensued in drawing an apparent blank in the search for clues as to what might have happened to the treasure of Captain William Kidd, a glimmer of hope shone through the shambles of the Kidd-Palmer file. The British Library letter within the file, addressed to an enquirer, closed with the suggestion that the finger of suspicion ought to be directed at the finder of the charts, Hubert Palmer, who possibly possessed his own copy of Robert Louis Stevenson's *Treasure Island*.

The suggestion that the person who prepared the Kidd-Palmer charts was familiar with R.L. Stevenson's classic tale *Treasure Island* is very plausible. The book was first published in 1882 and the map that illustrated the first edition is, of course, one of the most famous cartographic creations of all time. However, none of the Kidd-Palmer charts bear any resemblance to the one included in that first edition of *Treasure Island*, which as one observer puts it, is "shaped, you might say, like a fat dragon standing up." Incidentally, a first edition of *Treasure Island* sold for $7,200 at a June 2001 sale by Sotheby's in New York.

To support a link with Stevenson's fictional fantasy one only has to look at the letter from Captain Dan Morgan reproduced earlier. This was purportedly received by Palmer in 1932, shortly before he bought the old sea chest that is supposed to have been owned by Kidd while he was incarcerated in Newgate Prison. Can anyone honestly accept this letter as genuine? Morgan's spelling is one thing, but apart from that, the closing phrase "so heres to 15 men on the dead mans chest and dont forgit the rum ile hav som you bet after the deal" is laughable, and a childish imitation of words from Stevenson's *Treasure Island.*

Stevenson's island is named Skeleton Island, and the fourth Kidd-Palmer chart has a word written in the right-hand margin which could be construed as "skeleton" or an acceptable facsimile. When Long John Silver first looks at the map of Skeleton Island he remarks, "Ay, here it is: 'Capt. Kidd's Anchorage' — just the name my shipmate called it." The fourth Kidd-Palmer chart also has "Anchorage" marked upon it. It also has a "Smuggler's Cove" — strangely enough, Skeleton Island had a "Rum Cove," rum being a commodity long associated with smugglers of contraband. An even stranger coincidence is that the superintendent of the Map Room of the British Museum, during the period when Furneaux was investigating the authenticity of the Kidd-Palmer charts, was Mr. R.A. Skelton. He had joined the staff of the museum during the period when the Kidd-Palmer charts were being discovered.

Raleigh Ashlin "Peter" Skelton was a remarkable man. He was born in Plymouth, England on December 21, 1906. After graduating from Cambridge University in modern languages in 1929, he spent two years teaching before entering the British Museum as an assistant keeper in the Department of Printed Books. His early work brought him into contact with old atlases and accounts of voyages of exploration, and this was to prove a foundation for his later devotion to cartography, especially as this related to old maps.

Skelton's period with the British Museum was broken by military service during World War II, when he served with the Royal Artillery in the Middle East and Italy. He ended the war in Austria with the Monuments, Arts, and Archives branch of the Allied High Commission, and was demobilized with the rank of major. On returning to the British Museum, he was seconded to the map room, became superintendent in 1950, and was appointed deputy keeper in 1953. From then on, Skelton made numerous contributions to his chosen field, sat on many committees, and was one of the most respected authorities on the subject of old maps. After his inexplicable decision to retire in 1967 he worked as hard as ever, and his enthusiasm for his work remained unabated until his untimely death, caused by a tragic car accident in December 1970. This occurred in Farnham, Surrey, where a two-lane highway narrows to a single lane to pass under a bridge.

Skelton is described as being tall, slim, walking with a military stride that belied his age, and with no more than the slightest suspicion of a scholar's stoop. He was fond of outdoor exercise, gardening and, it is reported, cherished his membership of the local cricket club. With his death Britain lost not only one of the finest cartographic experts of modern times, but also a man of great integrity who was scrupulous in all his affairs, particularly those relating to his profession. The question to be asked is — how would a man of Skelton's undoubted probity and rectitude behave when asked to compromise himself? Let us ask ourselves the question in another way. Suppose when Furneaux asked Skelton to re-authenticate the Kidd-Palmer charts in 1965, the latter soon realized they were bogus, and not only that they were bogus, but that he could tell who had drawn them in the first instance. What if the faking of the charts had been done within what was now his own department, long before he had assumed his present senior position? Skelton is likely to have asked a lot of questions, not only of his superiors, but also of himself!

For obvious reasons a forger cannot flaunt his talents nor his skills in deluding others. He cannot append his signature as an artist does to a painting, and as a consequence, the pleasure he derives is solitary. But forgers are very often arrogant and frequently leave their mark. In the case of the Kidd-Palmer charts, the fourth one found by Palmer in 1934 appears as if it might disclose such a mark. Careful scrutiny of the hachures towards the west end of the island reveals the initials "TA."

Who was TA? We don't know. But what if Skelton knew? Furthermore, Skelton joined the British Museum in 1931, and his name could have inspired the forger to have incorporated upon that fourth and final chart, discovered in 1934, elements reminiscent of

Stevenson's *Treasure Island*. When Skelton realized this he would have been understandably infuriated. Who could blame him?

The History of the British Museum Library, written by P.R. Harris (1998), The *Dictionary of National Biography*, and various obituaries all make the bald statement that Skelton retired, but we know none of the reasons for this apparent early retirement. If Skelton had determined, at least to his own satisfaction, that the British Museum was involved in covering up some incident of the past, one that an older generation had cause to feel embarrassed about and anxious to mask, then it is possible that Skelton may have felt his principles compromised and decided to depart with little ceremony, despite his long and faithful service of 36 years.

If the common man counterfeits money, copies old masters, or otherwise engages in activities declared unlawful by the government for purposes of deception and fraud, he is locked away in prison for a long time, where he is supposed to dwell upon his sins and show repentance for his crimes. But when government agents engage in the same illegal activities in pursuit of "national interests," these agents are applauded for their prudence and foresight, and often their bravery. Everyone knows that nation spies upon nation, that governments forge passports and papers, that they counterfeit currency in order to undermine the economic well-being of an enemy, whether declared or merely potential. When caught or found out, these perpetrators face censure, sometimes ignominy and shame, but rarely are they incarcerated in a prison cell. The exception might be when one is caught by the declared enemy, in which case he often faces the firing squad.

An exciting book, followed by a film of the same name, appeared shortly after the end of World War II called *The Man Who Never Was*. It was a vivid portrayal of how the British deluded the Germans into believing that the Allies, after the successful North Africa campaign, would attack the underbelly of Europe by invading either Sardinia or the Balkans. A suitable body was found, dressed in a Royal Marines uniform, and set afloat from a submarine off the Spanish coast. Strapped to the wrist of the corpse was a briefcase containing forged documents relating to the proposed assault. The body washed ashore on the chosen beach, as calculated by the boffins, and, as had been expected, was picked up by the Spanish authorities. The briefcase and contents were immediately handed over to representatives of the German government. Ostensibly neutral, Spain was indebted to Germany for assistance in squashing anti-fascist resistance during the Spanish Civil War. The Germans swallowed the bait and relocated many divisions into Sardinia and the Balkans, leaving Sicily less defended. Thousands of Allied casualties were avoided by this brilliant piece of wartime deception. There is an old maxim that if one wishes to hide the real truth, it is prudent to create another truth for people to believe. This maxim is considered to apply equally to the Kidd-Palmer charts as it did to *The Man Who Never Was*, despite the vast difference in the implications and consequences of the deceit.

The Kidd-Palmer charts were discovered by Hubert Palmer, a retired solicitor and wealthy bachelor indulging his passion for collecting pirate relics, in itself a perfectly innocent and lawful hobby, however eccentric it might appear. Palmer amassed a large collection of artifacts, quite a few of which were likely bogus. However, his discovery within the space of five years of four charts depicting the same island and a mysterious parchment carrying a cryptic message, all of which were hidden in secret compartments in articles of furniture bought at auction, is suggestive of a well-planned conspiracy. The equally mysterious manner of the disappearance of the charts is similarly suggestive that the planners had achieved their objective — the Kidd-Palmer charts having accomplished all that the fraudsters had intended when they set out to bait Palmer's "trap."

Knowing Palmer's reputation as a discriminating but ardent collector of pirate relics, it would have been a simple task to filter items onto the auction block in those areas of the country where Palmer's agents were known to be on the lookout for items appearing to be of piratical origin. Once the first map had been found and authenticated, Palmer's appetite would have been suitably whetted, and, it may be assumed, his agents instructed to observe a keen watch for future items. As one map after another was discovered, the trail that led away from where the real treasure lay became increasingly well trodden. As Long John Silver truthfully remarked when he first saw the map of Skeleton Island, "Who might have done that I wonder? The pirates were too ignorant, I reckon."

During the period when Palmer held the charts he never once attempted to benefit from their possession. He never offered them for sale to other collectors and, apart from a few intimates, they were not shown to anyone. On the few occasions when he did permit strangers to view them, as in the case when Wilkins was writing his book, Palmer jealously masked from view the information on the charts which he thought might enable the island to be identified. It can be concluded, therefore, without any doubt whatsoever, that Palmer was an honest, if rather eccentric, man, firm in his belief that he now possessed important information on the whereabouts of Kidd's buried treasure. If anything, Palmer is more victim than culprit, despite hints to the contrary.

We now come to the fascinating question of who might have deemed it necessary to go to the trouble of forging the Kidd-Palmer charts, and why.

The British Museum Library has been one of Great Britain's prime repositories of valuable manuscripts accumulated over the ages. The museum was founded in 1753 as a direct result of the decision of Sir Hans Sloane, physician and President of the Royal Society, to offer to the nation his large collections of books, manuscripts, drawings, artifacts, and specimens that he had amassed during his lifetime. From that date the British Museum gradually grew in stature into one of the most prestigious institutions of its kind. Numerous collections were acquired, or were donated, with the result that it now contains priceless and irreplaceable treasures.

During the latter part of the nineteenth century, Edward J.L. Scott, holding the post of keeper in the Department of Manuscripts, consistently bemoaned the state of his department and had recommended that detailed cataloguing be carried out, in order to create some order out of the chaotic state that prevailed in referencing the numerous papers, manuscripts, and documents in his charge. This mammoth task was commenced in 1898 and, though the task was not to be completed until 1922, a substantial inroad had been made by 1904, the year of Scott's retirement. He was succeeded by G.F.

Warner, who in turn was followed by J.P. Gilson in 1911. Gilson had first joined the British Museum as an assistant in the Department of Manuscripts in 1894, and after his promotion to keeper was to remain with the museum until 1929, when he died following an operation for appendicitis at the age of 61 years. Gilson had spent virtually his whole working life in the service of the British Museum.

The *Dictionary of National Biography* notes that Gilson possessed "a notable gift of silence, but one which could never be taken for misanthropy." One is not quite sure what to make of this statement, but it suggests that if there was a secret to be kept then J.P. Gilson was the man to keep it. The thesis is therefore advanced that papers, letters, or other documents came to light during the cataloguing process that Scott had so ardently requested which might have been considered to reflect a bad light upon past government. We know that the Harley papers, held by the Department of Manuscripts, contain much of the information relating to Kidd, his arrest and trial in particular. What if those same papers held other information, information disclosing beyond any doubt whatsoever that Kidd's treasure had been recovered by noblemen shortly after he was hanged? An interesting question! One that cannot be answered with any degree of certainty.

During the 1920s, the spectre of Indian independence from Britain was looming even larger, accompanied by violent and non-violent demonstrations. The last thing the British government of the time would have wanted was the exposure of political dirty linen, especially any dragged up from centuries earlier to the effect that the Mogul's treasure had found its way into the pockets of English noblemen. The authorities would have been acutely aware of the dilemma which confronted them and understandably reticent about public disclosure. Today, after 50 years of Indian independence, the British government need have little regard for either the delicacy of that historical dilemma or the niceties of international relations. Any further timidity in this respect can be safely dismissed.

The plan to produce the Kidd-Palmer charts "in the national interest" was skilfully executed. Accompanying it would have been an intensive "laundering" of the archives to ensure that no evidence remained where stigma might arise concerning the real where-abouts of the treasure that Kidd "lodged in the Indies," and who recovered it and when. As Robert Ritchie notes in his book *Captain Kidd and the War Against the Pirates*, there is an abundance of information in the archives relating to Kidd's outward-bound voyage and to his capture and trial, but there is desperate little relating to the 10-month interval between June 1698 and April 1699, the period when he is most likely to have buried his treasure.

One final comment may be made about the Kidd-Palmer charts. The observant reader will have noticed that the first chart to be found carried the date 1669, and was found in an oak bureau bearing a brass plate inscribed "Captain William Kidd, Adventure Galley, 1669." It is doubtful that Kidd ever sailed at such an early stage in his career on a vessel that carried the same name as the one he later commanded on his fateful voyage. It is equally unlikely that in 1669, in his early twenties, he would have possessed much treasure, let alone any inclination to bury it. What seems more likely, if one accepts the thesis that the Kidd-Palmer charts are a forgery, is that someone, during the preparation of the bureau, which required a brass plate to be affixed, incorrectly inscribed the date as 1669 instead of 1699. This further bit of unintentional misinformation would have served the purpose of muddying the waters even more, especially for future treasure seekers.

The forger, whoever "TA" was, would have felt very smug if he ever chanced upon an article titled "The Mystery of Captain Kidd's Treasure," which appeared in *Wide World* magazine in October 1958. It was written by Anthony D. Howlett, a dedicated researcher who had expended much time and effort in the examination of the Kidd-Palmer charts, to which he had gained access in the early 1950s. It reads as follows:

> First of all I verified all the details of the discoveries from Palmer's own records and photographs and made numerous enquiries and checks of my own. I very thoroughly examined the charts themselves, together with enlarged photographs of them, taken

by infra-red and ultra-violet light. In addition, I perused and checked written opinions of the British Museum, of eminent handwriting experts, cartographers and other leading authorities, deliberately seeking flaws. I was forced, nevertheless, to recognise the fact that the evidence indicated that the charts were genuine.

In spite of this opinion, which is founded upon Howlett's appraisal of Palmer's files, there is enough evidence, circumstantial though it may be, to suggest otherwise. This evidence has been outlined and it would be prudent therefore to exhibit serious reservations about the authenticity of the charts. The initial authentication attributed to the British Museum, the lack of confirmatory evidence in its files, followed by a later suggestion by them that the charts are bogus, are all cause to believe that they were indeed forged; at best some may be replicas. As the British Library Maps Department now correctly asserts, the charts smack of *Treasure Island*, particularly the fourth one. The forger might just as well have included such topographical features on this chart as "The Spy-glass" or "Mizzenmast Hill." Despite all this, there is nothing that precludes the possibility that the island represented upon the Kidd-Palmer charts is the real island, the one upon which Kidd actually did bury his treasure! The only difference is that the treasure was recovered over 200 years before the charts were drawn!

Chapter 10

Treasure Island

They sailed away for a year and a day,
To the land where the Bong-tree grows.
— The Owl and The Pussy-Cat (Lear)

The publicity that surrounded the Kidd-Palmer charts in the aftermath of World War II resulted in a wild goose chase into isolated corners of the globe to search for Kidd's treasure. Edmunds, in his book *Kidd — the Search for his Treasure*, documents many of the expeditions that were launched by hopeful treasure seekers. For a detailed description I urge the reader to consult Edmunds's work.

A lot of emphasis was placed upon the fact that the term "China Sea" was prominent on the maps, and as a result, several of the expeditions ventured into Far Eastern waters. Others, convinced that this was a ruse intended to deceive, focused their hopes elsewhere, mainly towards the West Indies and North America. These latter regions had been frequented by Kidd prior to receiving his commission to seek out pirates and, also, had been his last stopping point before his final return to New York. It was surmised, therefore, that these locations were more promising than the Far East. An unusual interpretation of the words *China Sea* was to associate the French word *chêne* with *china* and thus, it was reasoned, Kidd had buried his hoard of treasure on Oak Island in Nova Scotia, *chêne* being French for *oak*. Everyone who was convinced of the authenticity of the Kidd-Palmer charts and was prepared to undertake the financial risks and other perils of the search seemed to be only too willing to put their hard-earned money, and their lives, at hazard in these various ventures. Apart from the known expeditions that have been mounted to seek the treasure, there are likely to have been just as many that have gone unrecorded. The Kidd-Palmer charts have generated worldwide interest, and there is little sign so far of any abatement in the enthusiasm and conviction that the Kidd treasure still awaits discovery.

The Palmer brothers themselves appear to have been totally convinced of the veracity of the charts they had discovered. They planned an expedition to the Sequeiras, an island group in the Philippine Sea which appears and disappears above sea level with bewildering frequency, but World War II intervened. One well-publicized expedition began in 1951, apparently to search for the treasure somewhere north of Borneo. However the motor yacht, which was going to sail from England, was wrecked in the English Channel four days after departing from Gosport, Hampshire, and although plans for a further expedition followed hard upon its heels, this also had to be abandoned. As far as is known, these ventures were targetting islands in the South China Sea.

Though Furneaux had made an argument supporting the theory that Oak Island, Nova Scotia had been a repository for the Kidd treasure, he was not totally convinced of his own theory. Instead he led an expedition to an island in the Turks and Caicos group which, in shape, bore a resemblance to that depicted on the Kidd-Palmer charts. It was a total disaster. Since there was some media participation in this expedition, later comment in the press was particularly cutting, with headlines such as: "Dead men tell no tales — neither it seems do their charts," and "A work which ended up drenched in calamity." However, undeterred, Furneaux returned to the same island a year or two later to pursue his search. The second expedition was equally fruitless and Furneaux died a few years later, still convinced that he had the right island and that with sufficient funding and enough time he would have found Kidd's treasure. Unfortunately he had neither the money nor the time to realize his ambitions.

A man named Marshall claimed to have solved the mystery of the Kidd-Palmer charts, and in 1980 set off with a financial backer. No one knows where they went, and once the backer's money ran out they had to return home. Edmunds gives the opinion that Marshall's island was Bonaire, one of the Lesser Antilles. While on the island, Marshall expended much effort in plotting the locations of tree stumps, in the firm belief that their positions would help him locate the exact spot where the treasure was buried. Undeterred, Marshall organized a second expedition and, surprisingly, found investors with ready ears and ready pockets anxious for a piece of the action. The second expedition was spent mapping more boulders and tree stumps, but they did manage to find a cave, in which Marshall asserted the treasure lay. Unfortunately more sophisticated equipment was required to penetrate the back of the cave than that which they had available, and a third expedition was planned. As the necessary funds began to accumulate, police arrived on the scene eager to question Marshall about some of his fundraising methods, at which point he promptly disappeared. Where he went no one seems to know — perhaps back to his island in search of the elusive treasure!

The last documented search for Kidd's treasure seems to have begun in 1978, or thereabouts, with a man named Richard Knight. Knight was convinced that the Kidd treasure was buried on an island off the coast of Vietnam. He identified it as Hon Tre Lon (now Hon Doc), which was once known as Grand Pirate Island. Permits to hunt for buried treasure were not easily obtainable in Vietnam, especially from authorities who remembered only too vividly the horrors of the Vietnam War. A number of subterfuges were necessary, including that of illegal entry aboard a Malaysian fishing vessel. He claims to have found a number of chests filled with coins, figurines, gold bars, and other valuables. The story goes that he removed the treasure and reburied it in Malaysia, fearing that he might become a target for modern-day pirates. Subsequently, in 1983, he mounted a second expedition to Hon Tre Lon, and this time he and his accomplices were arrested and detained by the Vietnamese authorities for a total period of 14 months. Edmunds tells the saga of Knight's adventures with ironic humour and, even if the adventures are not factually correct, there is no denying that they make an entertaining story.

There is little point in relating any more of the various ventures that have been mounted to seek Kidd's treasure, even if the records can be considered accurate. The only purpose this would have is to confirm the wide-flung nature of the search and the grip it has held on certain people. Hopeful treasure-seekers often subconsciously select "facts" to suit their particular theory. If they really believed in the authenticity of the charts, then they should accept all the "facts" without reservation and not select ones for their own purpose. In this author's opinion, the charts are bogus, but that does not necessarily mean they are fictitious. The hoax is not considered pointless; the island could be a real island, but the information on the charts needs to be carefully studied and only ignored or discarded after careful deliberation. If the object in preparing the charts was to deflect interest away from what really happened to the treasure, i.e., when it had been recovered and by whom, it can be concluded that the Kidd-Palmer charts should be regarded in a serious light, but with caution, otherwise it would have been totally irresponsible to forge them in the first instance. The elaborate way in which the charts were placed on the market and found their way into Palmer's possession is a sufficient testimony.

The most vital clue to the location of the real "Treasure Island" is the reference to latitude and longitude given on the fourth and final Kidd-Palmer chart. There is no dispute about the latitude, it is plainly given as 9-16N, which is interpreted as 9°16' North. The reference to longitude, on the other hand, is open to a number of interpretations; variously it might be +31.30E, 431.30E or 43.30E. As may be seen from careful inspection of the chart, there is what appears to be a broken "4" preceding the given figures. Knowing that mariners of the seventeenth century had no means of identifying their longitude position from a reference meridian such as Greenwich, which is common today, they would track their voyage by reference to their last point of departure. Examples of this have been given from the voyages of Narbrough and Dampier in Chapter 8. Thus, it is reasoned, the longitude quoted on the Kidd-Palmer charts must be from Kidd's last point of departure, which was the pirate base on St. Marie island. St. Marie is at longitude 49°52'E relative to Greenwich. Thus, taking either 31°30'E or 43°30'E as the most acceptable of the various interpretations given on the charts, Kidd's island would, by this argument, be located on the longitude of either of the following:

(a) $49°52'E + 31°30' = 81°22'E$, which is close to Mullativu on the northeast coast of Ceylon. This location is highly unlikely for a number of reasons, the most important being the highly frequented nature of these waters at the time and the close proximity of trading posts and factories of the East India Company and rival concerns. A relatively large vessel, like the *Queddah Merchant*, would have soon attracted a great deal of unwelcome attention. It is also likely that the region would have been fairly densely populated.

(b) $49°52'E + 43°30' = 93°22'E$, which is slightly north, by a few sea miles, of Car Nicobar Island in the Nicobars. The island is isolated and off the beaten track of vessels plying between India and the East Indies, and in view of the uncertain accuracy of navigation by the practice of dead reckoning, this island warrants detailed examination.

Let us take a closer look at Car Nicobar Island. In the following discourse, some reference will have to be made to the third and fourth Kidd-Palmer charts, and for brevity these will be referred to as KP3 and KP4. The other two charts contain little useful information and are not, therefore, discussed. The reader may wish to make reference to the various plates depicting Car Nicobar in this chapter and the Kidd-Pamer charts in the previous chapter.

A general similarity of shape will be observed between Car Nicobar and the island portrayed on both KP3 and KP4. Admittedly, Car Nicobar is somewhat stouter, but features such as the lagoon on the north side of the island, and the reefs skirting the south shore both exist. The fact that the words "CHINA SEA" are given on KP4 presents no difficulty in explanation. Car Nicobar, though strictly lying within the Bay of Bengal, lies close to the Indian Ocean shore of present-day Thailand, and just as India was once considered to be part of the Orient, so the lower Indo-Chinese mainland and its isthmus with

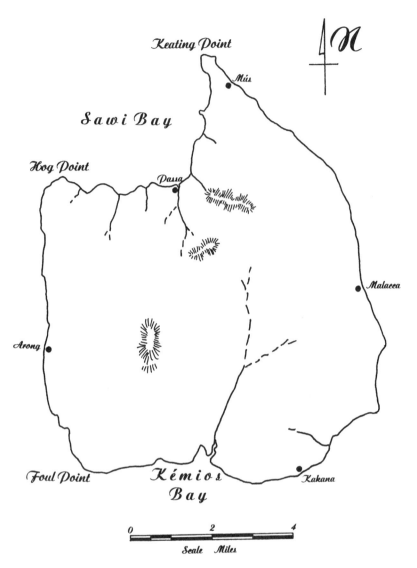

Car Nicobar Island.
Showing topographical detail taken from the 1886–87 survey.

the Malay Peninsula was often referred to as China. In the seventeenth century there was not the strictness of precise geographical definition for such regions as we use today. Thus, Car Nicobar can be considered to be within the China Sea.

There are two main anchorages on Car Nicobar Island where ships can lie close inshore, namely Sawi Bay in the north and

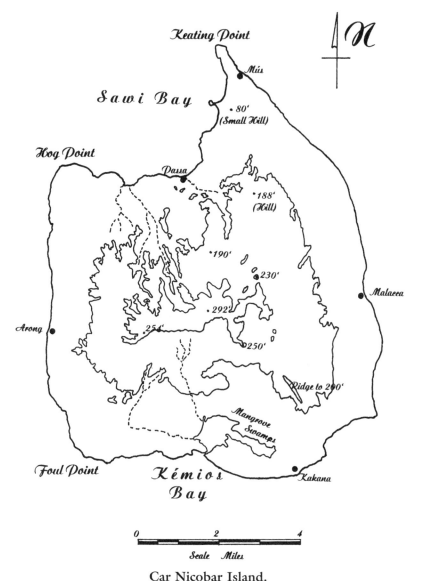

Car Nicobar Island.
Showing topographical detail taken from the 1943–44 survey.

Kémios Bay in the south; elsewhere ships have to lay further off. As the island is surrounded by coral reefs, Sawi Bay and Kémios Bay are the only secure anchorages for large vessels, and both are vulnerable to the changing monsoons. When the southwest monsoon prevails, Sawi Bay is the better anchorage, and likewise Kémios Bay during the northeast monsoon. The latter is the cen-

tre for present-day export of coconuts. The Admiralty Sailing
Directions say this about the two bays:

> Sawi Bay, on the north-western side of the island,
> affords anchorage in a depth of 12 fathoms, over
> rock, coral, and a thin surface of sand, about three-
> quarters of a mile northward of Sawi village, and in
> 7 fathoms water off Observation spot point [on the
> east side of the bay] there is good landing for boats
> at low water.

> Kémios Bay, on the southern side of Car Nicobar,
> affords anchorage during the North-east monsoon,
> when the landing is good. Trading vessels anchor in
> depths of from 10 to 12 fathoms, about midway
> between the two villages situated on the shore of
> the bay, which is a convenient position for shipping
> coconuts. The tidal streams in Kémios Bay are reg-
> ular and strong; the flood stream sets east-south-
> east about 3 knots at springs, the ebb in the oppo-
> site direction.

By reference to KP3, it may be inferred that the lagoon on the
north side of the island can be associated with Sawi Bay, while the
"Anchorage" marked on KP4 is synonymous with Kémios. It is of
value to note also that on KP3, the red zig-zag route reported on
the original which connects various dots, and which terminates
with an *X*, can be considered as originating at Kémios.

With regard to the aspect of Car Nicobar to the north compass
point, it is of value to measure the angle between due north and the
line connecting the extremities of the two promontories on either
side of Sawi Bay. On KP3 the angle is 50°, on KP4 it is 47°30',
whereas in fact it is 50°30'. Since the annual change in magnetic
declination, or variation between true north and compass north, is
negligible, it can be deduced that the general aspect of Car Nicobar
compares very favourably with that of the island shown on KP3 and

KP4. If there is one thing that can be relied upon, it is the direction of the compass point on both KP3 and KP4.

Car Nicobar is the northernmost island of the Nicobars, which forms the southern extremity of the Andaman and Nicobar chain, and stretches out into the Indian Ocean from the Burmese mainland. The islands represent the peaks of a submarine ridge created by volcanic activity along a line of tectonic weakness in the earth's crust. This volcanism resulted in an upwarping of the marine sedimentary rocks and, as a consequence, the surface rocks of Car Nicobar are of shale, sandstone, and limestone, with some coral fringing around the central upper land mass, where reports have suggested outcrops of volcanic rocks can be found either at surface or at shallow depth. On some of the Andaman Islands, north of the Nicobars, deposits of coal can be found.

Car Nicobar is an island of low physical relief, averaging about eight miles long in a north-south direction, and somewhat less west to east. The high point at the centre of the island rises to 292 feet above sea level, and is located upon a central ridge about three miles long. Though the upper regions of the island are mostly grassland, the lower regions are densely covered with trees and forest growth, or would have been 300 years ago. The high point would not have been a distinctive feature as seen from a vessel lying close inshore, measuring a little more than 1° above the horizontal, but it would be easily discernible from far out at sea.

Of great interest are the two hills shown on KP3, one of which is marked "hill," the other "small hill." That marked "hill" may represent the highest topographical feature, as just discussed, but this feature would be masked by intervening ground and tree growth from a ship anchored in Sawi Bay. However, there is an isolated peak of slightly less elevation, rising to 230 feet above sea level, which is located about a mile northeast of the central peak, the sighting of which would not be affected by intervening ground or vegetation. This is believed to represent the "hill" marked on KP3. On the eastern promontory to Sawi Bay there is another isolated peak or knoll, which, though it only rises to a height of 80 feet above sea level, is located close inshore, a matter of about a quarter-mile from the shoreline. It is clearly visible, the top representing an angle of 3° from the horizontal for an observer within the bay, and this is believed to be the "small hill" represented on KP3.

Modern-day charts, e.g., "Admiralty Chart 84 — Little Andaman to Great Nicobar," show three shore-based beacons and one lightship on the north side of the island. This number of navigational aids in such close proximity to one another suggests that entry into the lagoon of Sawi Bay can be tricky. In this context it is interesting to note that KP4 shows a number of wrecks around the reef encircling the lagoon. KP3, on the other hand, shows no wrecks in the proximity of Sawi Bay, suggesting the creation of KP4 post-dated the drawing of KP3.

For a shipboard observer, viewing the hinterland of the island from the secure anchorage of Sawi Bay, one of the most prominent aspects of the island is a 100-foot-high ridge to the immediate southeast which juts out towards the bay. Since this ridge drops off abruptly towards the shore, it can be expected that its steeper slopes would be scarred by bare rock outcrops showing through the vegetation cover. Today the native village of Passa nestles around the termination of this ridge at the shoreline, where there is a good-sized beach about 200 yards long. Elsewhere the bay is fringed with jagged coral, as is most of the island.

The aforesaid ridge has a number of high points or knolls along its spine, and the closest of these to the beach is about 515 yards or paces. Standing atop the nearest knoll, there is a level expanse of ground to the immediate northeast at a slightly lower elevation. Was this where Kidd buried his treasure? The notation on KP3 indicates:

515 SE and 50 N
36 NE 36 NE Rocks
3 feet by 3 feet by four

This cryptic clue could be interpreted as:

Walk 515 paces southeast from beach (to top of knoll)
Take 50 paces north, then 36 paces northeast to first rock,

Take another 36 paces northeast to second rock,
Treasure in hole 3 feet square at four foot depth.

One more fascinating similarity can be found between KP3 and Car Nicobar. The red zig-zag line on the original map commences on the south shore at the anchorage now identified as Kémios. This zig-zag line extends first north then east and finally terminates in an "X." Does X mark the spot? The southeast quarter of Car Nicobar is dominated by an extensive mangrove swamp, but directly northeast of Kémios, visible from the bay across the swamp, there is a ridge of high ground that juts out from the central land mass towards the southeast. This ridge reaches a height of slightly more than 200 feet above sea level, and its west-facing slope is so steep that bare rock would be seen. It represents the most significant landmark in the immediate vicinity of Kémios Bay. To get to this ridge one first has to go due north from Kémios village, along some higher ground forming the western limits of the mangrove swamp, then bear east, the land steadily rising. In this manner, one may skirt the swamp in an arc in order to arrive at point X. The total route is about six miles long, and the four conspicuous dots on KP3 can be identified with the local high points, three of them along this route. Whether a cave exists beneath the ridge is not known, but it is highly likely since there is much limestone on the island, and possibly some coral at higher elevations. The Yunnan parchment may have some relevance after all.

The cryptic clue written on KP3, and the zig-zag route also marked thereon, indicate two potential locations where treasure could have been buried on Car Nicobar. Whether Kidd made two caches is unknown, but he most surely made one of them.

One final comment may be made regarding KP3 and KP4. The former has the inscription "trees" towards its western extremity, whereas the latter carries the word "wood" in the centre of the island. The word "trees" suggests distinctive tall trees that do not present an obstacle to penetration, whereas "wood" or "woods" implies a mass of tangled forest undergrowth. Car Nicobar has always possessed a large number of coconut palms, and groves of such palms usually present no hindrance to pedestrians — though they aren't without danger, as 150 people were killed in 2001 by falling coconuts! The northwest promontory to Sawi Bay is low-lying and relatively flat, its situation being ideal for supporting dense groves of coconut palms. This part of the island is denoted by "trees" on KP3. Before modern-day expansion of coconut production, the island would have supported a dense forest undergrowth on the rising ground away from the immediate shoreline, and this would have encircled the higher central grassland region. This forested area is likely the "wood" or "woods" denoted on KP4.

In all major respects the island of Car Nicobar fits that depicted on the Kidd-Palmer charts. There are small things for which no explanation can be given. These are:

- The apparent valley cutting through the central ridge on the island marked on KP4. There is indeed a canyon on Car Nicobar in this region, but it does not dissect the ridge.
- The word "turtles" on KP4. The presence of turtles on many islands in the Indian Ocean is not peculiar to any one island and is well documented, though turtles are now far fewer in number. On the chart the word is considered irrelevant by the author, but others are known to place some importance on it, believing it to be a cryptic clue.

The first detailed contour mapping of the Nicobar Islands was carried out during World War II, using aerial photographic mapping techniques. The purpose of the survey was to aid in the selection of airfield sites in the war against Japan. Prior to this date, the most recent survey of the islands had been conducted in 1886–87 by the Indian Survey. If, as may be surmised, the Kidd-Palmer charts were prepared in the interwar years, then it is obvious only the 1886–87 survey maps could have been referenced by the forger.

The plates in this book include two maps of Car Nicobar showing topographical details taken from these two surveys. These may be compared to both KP3 and KP4. It may be noted that the 1886–87 series of maps contain the following caution: "The interiors of the island are mostly covered with dense forest and are not surveyed in detail." As a result, higher areas, like the hills and ranges, are shown using hachures. Only the highest points are indicated.

The three high points shown on the 1886–87 map are indicated without any spot elevation, and the map gives no evidence of either the central east–west trending ridge, which is the backbone of the island, or the highest point on the island, which is close to dead centre, as shown on the later 1943–44 survey. In fact the southward-flowing stream shown to discharge into the sea at Kémios does not exist. The conclusion that can be reached by comparing the 1886–87 survey with the detailed survey of 1943–44 is that the former is highly unreliable. Both KP3 and KP4 show a crescent-shaped island with a well defined central range running from tip to tip. Such a range can be inferred from the sparse mapping of 1886–87, erroneous though such a conclusion might be. There is, therefore, the merest hint that the forger was possibly perpetuating an earlier error when he drew KP4, which is concluded to be a hoax for the reasons outlined in Chapter 9. If this is correct, then it is possible that KP3 might be a replica of an original, and out of the four Kidd-Palmer charts it is KP3 that gives the impression of being the most reliable.

From every point of view, Car Nicobar fits the information provided upon the Kidd-Palmer charts. The only criticism that may be levelled at such a statement is that the crescent shape of the island shown on the Kidd-Palmer charts is at variance with the more rounded shape of Car Nicobar. This may be so, but at the end of the seventeenth century, any mariner would have lacked the technical abilities to draw the island with any degree of accuracy, especially when viewed from offshore. Even the 1886–87 survey, carried out using contemporary mapping procedures, made fundamental errors when compared to the aerial mapping techniques of 1943–44. Car Nicobar is an island with low relief, and the skyline, when viewed from the open sea, could well have given the impression of a long central ridge running its entire length. The important point is that the detail of Sawi Bay is excellent despite such a shortcoming, and it may be concluded that this was the pirate harbour in the Nicobars, or at least one of them, the other being Kémios, when the northeast monsoon was blowing.

The first reliable reference to the Nicobar Islands is in the writings of I'Tsing, a Chinese Buddist monk, in 627 AD. He describes the islands as being "the land of the naked people." Later references to the islands were made by Arab writers of the ninth century, in which the inhabitants of the Nicobars were called "Lankabalus." Ptolemy made mention of the islands much earlier than these, and a legend was established that the natives possessed tails. As with Herodotus, who was quoted in an earlier chapter, certain descriptions of life in antiquity must be treated with some caution.

The Andaman Islands, belonging to the same chain as the Nicobars, are more numerous, possess more natural resources, and are today far more populated. Ancient Arab traders first came to the Andamans and initiated a trade in iron and other commodities in exchange for ambergris and coconut. Marco Polo is reported to have visited the islands in 1290 and made the observation that the local inhabitants "are most cruel generation and eat anybody they can catch if not of their own race." Other Europeans who ventured that way were Friar Ordoric in 1322, who referred to the inhabitants as "dog-faced," and Nicolo Conti in 1440, who called the islands "the Islands of Gold."

The history of the Andaman and Nicobar Islands following the golden age of piracy is one of colonization and attempts at converting the natives to Christianity, the latter being first attempted in 1688. Austrians and Danes made various efforts to establish permanent settlements in the islands, but eventually gave up and abandoned their schemes. The British, through the East India Company, became interested in seeking suitable harbours where storm-stricken ships could ride out the monsoons, and so official British interest began in 1777 when a vessel was dispatched to reconnoitre the islands for this purpose. The first survey was very favourable, and later surveys followed, but it was not until 1789 that the British formally decided to take control of some of the islands.

Colonization by the British began through active settlement by the new arrivals, who cleared land, planted crops and fruit trees, and generally started to make themselves at home. Some problems were experienced with the indigenous peoples, who were not favourably disposed to the newcomers. In 1845 the islands became a centre for the establishment of various penal colonies. Those found guilty of the crimes of mutiny, rebellion, sedition, and similar offences in India soon found themselves being transported to a tropical paradise.

The British left the settlements in the islands to their own devices by not pursuing further colonization, nor establishing elaborate government control. The malarial climate, lack of moral restraint, little religious custom, and difficulty of transportation throughout the islands severely restricted development and exploitation of the natural resources, what little there were. The colonial yoke was one of the lightest, with no interference by the British to constrain or subdue the native islanders, who were permitted to carry on with their centuries-old lifestyle and traditions. The authorities did concern themselves with various aspects of external trade that may have had a disquieting influence, like gun-running, smuggling of liquor, and inter-tribal warfare agitated by traders. They may have held certain misgivings regarding some of the customs of the indigenous natives, and the following gems are taken from *The Andaman and Nicobar Islands*, published by the Superintendent of Government Printing, Calcutta 1908:

> The religion of the Nicobarese is an undisguised animism, and the whole of their very frequent and elaborate ceremonies and festivals are aimed at exorcising and scaring spirits. Fear of spirits and ghosts is the guide to all ceremonies ...

> Evil spirits, especially those that cause sickness or are likely to damage a new hut, can be caught by the menluana (shaman) and imprisoned in special cages which are placed on special rafts and towed out to sea.

> In the north, elaborate feasts and ceremonies are held to confine the spirits and ghosts to the elpanum

[public ground] and cemetery, and to keep them away from the coconut plantations during the trading season.

On Car Nicobar there is a serious wrestling over a corpse on its way to the grave; one party being for the burial and the other against it. This goes on till the corpse falls to the ground and several of the carriers injured. It is then sometimes just thrown into the grave with the sacrifice of all the deceased's livestock.

In 1922 another report was made, this time to the Royal Geographical Society, by H.S. Montgomerie, vividly describing the culture of the Nicobarese. Montgomerie describes the profusion of coconut trees in the islands in the following delightful terms:

Though the Nicobarese have strong individualistic views as to the ownership of coconuts, due weight is given to the claim of those of the rest of the family who have helped to grow them. A kindly custom allows anyone going from one place to another to cut down nuts he needs to eat or drink on the spot, and it would be thought churlish to refuse. This custom is the more valuable since in many places good drinking water is very scarce. It would, however, be thought in the worst taste to carry one away without payment or to help yourself in the neighbourhood of your own dwelling, where it is supposed you have coconuts of your own. It is also etiquette, should the owner be present, to ask him from which tree he wishes you to help yourself.

Montgomerie also describes the way the Nicobarese count their coconuts. He writes:

They seem to think of nuts in pairs as we think of pairs of boots or so many brace of pheasants. The nuts are usually carried in pairs for the sake of convenience, and I think that if you got a man to carry one nut for you he would promptly get another and loop the two together for his convenience.

The Nicobar Islands certainly sound enchanting, but this enchantment is disappearing. The last century saw a vast increase in the total population of the islands, rising from 24,700 in 1901 to 280,700 in 1991. Because of the intensive development of coconut production, most of this population increase has been on Car Nicobar, where the 1991 census recorded 6,831 people, i.e., 152 people per square kilometre. This contrasts with population densities of between 12 and 52 people per square kilometre on other islands. Most of this increase is due to immigration from the mainland and Hindus now represent almost 70 percent of the population. However, there is still a surprising number of approximately 25 percent who profess the Christian faith, so perhaps the efforts of the early European missionaries were not entirely in vain.

One of the first Englishmen to visit the Nicobar Islands was William Dampier, the celebrated buccaneer-turned-navigator, who by good luck or good management managed to evade the hangman's noose. His visit was unplanned and happened while he was escaping from a pirate ship. It is generally understood that he had become increasingly disenchanted with his profession, and his desperation must have been great for him to have selected such an isolated spot as the Nicobars! This unscheduled visit took place in 1688, several years before the region began to be frequented by Robert Culliford, and, as we surmise, a decade before the visit by William Kidd in the summer of 1698. As there is evidence suggesting that Kidd and Dampier were not unknown to one another, we will now turn our attentions to examine the life of Dampier. He was a most remarkable individual who has been described as one of the most noteworthy of all the buccaneers, and who, under the most inauspicious circumstances, viz. sailing with pirates, managed to make valuable contributions to navigational science, botany, and zoology that are still as treasured today as they were 300 years ago.

Chapter 11

William Dampier — Buccaneer

> *What is most conspicuous in Dampier's writings*
> *is his modesty and self-effacement …*
> *one of the hallmarks of a gentleman.*
> — Sir Albert Gray

William Dampier was a member of that strange band of Englishmen who roamed the world during the latter part of the seventeenth century in pursuit of high adventure. He occupies a unique position among the adventurers of his day, as he was one of the few who diligently recorded his observations. When those around him were single-mindedly occupied in brawling, plundering, raping, and garnering wealth, he, with his notebook, was busily engaged in making maps and charts, observing winds, tides, and currents, and assiduously drawing and describing everything novel that he encountered during his years of wandering, no matter where fate led him around the globe. In order to keep his papers safe from the weather, he would roll them up inside bamboo canes and seal the ends with wax. He was an earlier Charles Darwin, but one who lacked the power and discipline of a scientific education.

Dampier and Kidd were contemporaries, with the former being some six or seven years junior. How well they knew one another, or what state of friendship existed between them, is unknown, except that they had not only served, but fought alongside one another aboard the *Royal Prince*, after the outbreak of the Second Anglo-Dutch War in 1672. The *Royal Prince*, a first-rater of 1,400 tons and 100 guns, had been built at Chatham in 1670 to replace its namesake, lost during hostilities with the Dutch some four years earlier. It is claimed that the engagements of May 28 and June 4, 1673, were hotly contested and it would be expected that Dampier and Kidd, who both survived these actions, would at least have a common bond. We know considerably more of Dampier's early life than that of Kidd's, but their paths might well have crossed elsewhere in those early years in either the West or East Indies. It is more certain, however, that after Kidd's trial and public execution, Dampier would have become fully aware of Kidd's later questionable career. During the legal proceedings against Kidd in 1700–01, Dampier was away voyaging in eastern waters around New Holland (Australia), a voyage that ended disastrously with Dampier and his crew being shipwrecked upon Ascension Island during their return voyage, from which they were rescued on April 3, 1701. It is possible, therefore, that Dampier might have viewed, with above average interest, the hanging of Kidd at Execution Dock, and "there but for the Grace of God go I," might have been a phrase which entered his head. Dampier has been variously described as a buccaneer, a pirate, a circumnavigator, a captain of the navy, and a hydrographer. Certainly he led a checkered career and penetrated regions that were far off the beaten track; for example, he was the first European to record in any detail his impressions of the Nicobar Islands and their inhabitants. It is thought fit, therefore, to examine his fascinating career.

William Dampier was born in 1652 at East Coker, near Yeovil, Somerset, the son of a tenant-farmer, and lost both his parents before he reached the age of 16. He went to sea as a young boy, his first voyage being to Newfoundland, and after a short spell at home he joined an East Indiaman bound for Bantam in Java, returning in time to participate in the aforementioned engagements against the Dutch. In 1674 he accepted an offer to go to Jamaica as an assistant manager on a plantation, but soon tired of this landlocked existence and engaged himself upon a coastal trading vessel. About the beginning of August 1675 he shipped on board a ketch bound for the Bay of Campeachy (Mexico) with a cargo of rum and sugar to be exchanged for logwood. This voyage turned his enquiring mind to the science of hydrography and pilotage, and his account of this voyage has been described as one of "minuteness and accuracy." The brief time Dampier spent with the logwood cutters of Campeachy was hard and unremitting, but interspersed with periods when much rum punch was consumed. While homeward bound, the ketch blundered onto almost every shoal, reef, or island that lay in its path, and some that did not, and Dampier was appalled at the captain's ineptness in the art of navigation. His recollections of the rollicking times spent at Campeachy determined him to return there, and this he did in 1676. Though life was harsh, the earnings could be high if one could dissociate oneself from the excesses rampant in that environment. Dampier writes the following of his companions:

> The logwood cutters inhabit the creek of the east and west lagones, where they erect their huts, which are slightly built, but well thatched with palmeto leaves; they are hard working fellows, but when invited aboard a ship will drink very hard, and spend all their money in strong liquor.

Despite the pleasures of a hard-working, hard-drinking life in the jungles of Central America, Dampier appears to have restrained himself and returned two years later to England with a tidy sum of money. The ensuing year he occupied himself with intentions of setting up as a trader on his own account, and married a woman named Judith, about whom we know nothing more.

In the spring of 1679, Dampier sailed again for the West Indies, but he was not to return home for over 12 years. While on the Mosquito Coast (Nicaragua) he was tempted to throw in his lot with a party of buccaneers or, as he describes them, privateers. They were to have some amazing adventures. They crossed the isthmus of Panama, sacked Santa Marta, seized a number of Spanish ships, and ransacked, plundered, looted, and burned their way as far south as the island of Juan Fernandez, off the coast of Chile. They attacked Arica in January 1681, but were repulsed with great loss of life, and this setback caused the hitherto successful band to break up. About 50 of them, including Dampier, went north, and after many hardships recrossed the isthmus of Panama and came across a French ship cruising on account. With this new band of pirates, Dampier sailed for another year before finally ending up in Virginia in July 1682.

In August 1683, Dampier joined a vessel commanded by one named Cook, who had been a shipmate during their predations off the west coast of South America. The intention was to go on account in the Pacific, but when they set sail they decided their vessel was too small, and altered course towards West Africa in search of a larger ship better suited to their purpose. This they found at Sierra Leone, a Danish ship mounting 36 guns, which they promptly took and renamed the *Batchelor's Delight*. With this sturdier fighting vessel, Cook and his crew resumed their original plan. They rounded Cape Horn, a treacherous undertaking, and reacquainted themselves with Juan Fernandez, where they picked up a Mosquito Indian who had been marooned there by Dampier and his friends some three years earlier. They then set about the ultimate object of their voyage by sacking the coast of South America once again. During this free-roving period of rapine and looting, Cook, the captain, died, and was succeeded by Edward Davis, of which more will be said later. At times the pirate fleet amounted to as many as 10 sail, with nearly 1,000 men, mainly English and French, who could be put against the "enemy." In 1685 the pirate fleet broke up and Dampier, who had previously sailed under Davis, elected to sail in the *Cygnet* under Captain Swan, who was intent on savaging the Spanish Manila fleet as it lay into Acapulco. Finding they were too late for the Manila fleet, and other pickings on the coast being poor, the crew of the *Cygnet* decided to seek further plunder on the other side of the Pacific. Dampier records in his diary that "Many were well pleased with the voyage, but some thought, such was their ignorance, that he [Swan] would carry them out of the world."

The *Cygnet* set out across the Pacific on March 30, 1686, and reached Guam on May 20. It was a voyage of great hardship. The *Dictionary of National Biography* quotes Dampier in the following account:

It was well for Captain Swan, that we got sight of it before our provision was spent, of which we had but enough for three days more; for as I was informed, the men had contrived first to kill Captain Swan and eat him when the victuals was gone, and after him all of us who were accessory in promoting the undertaking of this voyage. This made Captain Swan say to me after our arrival at Guam, "Ah! Dampier, you would have made them but a poor meal;" for I was as lean as the captain was lusty and fleshy.

After a short stay of twelve days, Swan and his men pushed off towards the Philippines where they remained for six months, indulging themselves in excesses of drunkenness and pleasures of the flesh. In Dampier's own words "which disorderly actions deterred me from going aboard, for I ever did abhor drunkenness." However, he did reboard the vessel, after which the crew, desirous of some action, mutinied, leaving Swan and 36 of his more loyal followers ashore. Though Dampier expostulated against this marooning of Swan, his endeavours were fruitless and he continued with them "knowing that the further we went, the more knowledge and experience I should get, which was the main thing that I regarded." For the next 18 months they cruised from China to New Holland (Australia) under a new commander, Captain Read. During this period, Dampier appears to have become disillusioned with the occupation of buccaneering and resolved to make an escape. At last his opportunity came in May 1688. In a later version of his monumental *Voyages*, first published after his return in 1691, he describes the circumstances of his escape, which he managed to effect when the *Cygnet* arrived in the Nicobar Islands:

I had, till this time, made no open show of going ashore here: but now, the water being fill'd, and the ship in a readiness to sail, I desired Captain Read to set me ashore on this island. He, supposing that I could not go ashore in a place less frequented by ships than this, gave me leave: which probably he would have refused to have done, if he thought I should have gotten from hence in any short time; for fear of my giving an account of him to the English or Dutch. I soon got up my chest and bedding, and immediately got some to row me ashore; for fear lest his mind should change again.

The canoa that brought me ashore, landed me on a small sandy bay, where there were two houses, but no person in them. For the inhabitants were removed to some other house, probably, for fear of us; because the ship was close by: and yet both men and women came aboard the ship without any sign of fear. When our ship's canoa was going aboard again, they met the owner of the houses coming ashore in his boat. He made a great many signs to them to fetch me off again: but they would not understand him. Then he came to me, and offered his boat to carry me off; but I refused it. Then he made signs for me to go up into the house, and, according as I did understand him by his signs, and a few Malayan words that he used, he intimated that somewhat would come out of the woods in the night, when I was asleep, and kill me, meaning probably some wild beast. Then I carried my chest and cloaths up into the house.

I had not been ashore an hour before Captain Read and one John Damarel, with three or four armed men more, came to fetch me aboard again. They need not have sent an armed posse for me; for had they but sent the cabbin-boy ashore for me, I would not have denied going aboard. For tho' I could have hid my self in the woods, yet they would have abused, or have killed some of the natives, purposely to incense them against me. I told them therefore that I was ready to go with them, and went aboard with all my things.

When I came aboard I found the ship in an uproar; for there were three men more, who taking courage by my example, desired leave also to accompany me. One of them was the surgeon Mr Coppinger, the other was Mr Robert Hall, and one named Ambrose; I have forgot his sirname. These men had always harboured the same designs as I had. The two last were not much opposed; but Captain Read and his crew would not part with the surgeon. At last the surgeon leapt into the canoa, and taking up my gun, swore he would go ashore, and that if any man did oppose it, he would shoot him: But John Oliver, who was then quarter-master, leapt into the canoa, taking hold of him, took away the gun, and with the help of two or three more, they dragged him again into the ship.

Then Mr Hall and Ambrose and I were again sent ashore; and one of the men that had rowed us ashore stole an ax, and gave it to us, knowing it was a good commodity with the Indians. It was now dark, therefore we lighted a candle, and I being the oldest stander in our new country, conducted them into one of the houses, where we did presently hang up our hammocks. We had scarce done this before the canoa came ashore again, and brought the four Malayan men belonging to Achin, (which we took in the proe we took off of Sumatra) and the Portuguese that came to our ship out of the Siam jonk at Pulo Condore: The crew having no occasion for these, being leaving the Malayan parts, where the Portuguese Spark served as an interpreter; and not fearing now that the Achinese could be serviceable to us in bringing us over to their country, forty leagues off: nor imagining that we durst make such an attempt, as indeed it was a bold one. Now we were men enough to defend our selves against the natives of this island, if they should prove our enemies: though if none of these men had come ashore to me, I should not have feared any danger: nay, perhaps less, because I should have been cautious of giving any offence to the natives. And I am of the opinion, that there are no people in the world so barbarous as to kill a single person that falls accidentally into their hands, or comes to live among them; except they have been injured, by some outrage or violence commited against them. Yet even then, or afterwards, if a man could but preserve his life from their first rage, and come to treat with them, (which is the hardest thing, because their way is usually to abscond, and rushing suddenly upon their enemy to kill him at unawares) one might, by some slight, insinuate one's self into their favours again; especially by shewing some toy or knack that they did never see before: which any European, that has seen the world, might soon contrive to amuse them withal: as might be done, generally even with a little fire struck with a flint and steel.

Dampier continues:

As for these Nicobar people, I found them affable enough, and therefore I did not fear them; but I did not much care whether I had gotten any more company or no.

But however I was very well satisfied, and the rather, because we were now men enough to row our selves over to the island Sumatra; and accordingly we presently consulted how to purchase a canoa of the natives.

It was a fine clear moon-light night, in which we were left ashore. Therefore we walked on the sandy bay to watch when the ship would weigh and be gone, not thinking our selves secure in our new-gotten liberty till then. About eleven or twelve a-clock we saw her under sail, and then we returned to our chamber, and so to sleep. This was the 6th of May.

The next morning betimes, our landlord, with four or five of his friends, came to see his new guests, and was somewhat surprized to see so many of us, for he knew of no more but my self. Yet he seemed to be very well pleased, and entertain'd us with a large calabash of toddy, which he brought with him. Before he went away again, (for wheresoever we came they left their houses to us, but whether out of fear or superstition I know not) we bought a canoa of him for an ax, and we did presently put our chests and cloaths in it, designing to go to the south-end of the island, and lye there till the monsoon shifted, which we expected every day.

When our things were stowed away, we with the Achinese entered with joy into our new frigot, and launched off from the shore. We were no sooner off, but our canoa overset, bottom upwards. We preserved our lives well enough by swimming, and dragg'd also our chests and cloaths ashore; but all our things were wet. I had nothing of value but my journal and some drafts of land of my own taking, which I much prized, and which I had hitherto carefully preserved. Mr Hall had also such another cargo of books and drafts, which were now like to perish. But we presently opened our chests and took out our books, which, with much ado, we did afterwards dry; but some of our drafts that lay loose in our chests were spoiled.

We lay here afterwards three days, making great fires to dry our books. The Achineses in the meantime fixt our canoa, with outlagers on each side; and they also cut a good mast for her, and made a substantial sail with mats.

The canoa being now very well fixt, and our books and cloaths dry, we launched out a second time, and rowed towards the east-side of the island, leaving many islands to the north of us. The Indians of the island accompanied us with eight or ten canoas against our desire; for we thought that these men would make provision dearer at that side of the island we were going to, by giving an account what rates we gave for it at the place from whence we came, which was owing to the ship's being there; for the ship's crew were not so thrifty in bargaining (as they seldom are) as single persons, or a few men might be apt to be, who would keep to one bargain.

Therefore to hinder them from going with us, Mr Hall scared one canoa's crew by firing a shot over them. They all leapt over-board, and cried out, but seeing us row away, they got into their canoa again and came after us.

The firing of that gun made all the inhabitants of the island to be our enemies. For presently after this we put ashore at the bay where were four houses, and a great many canoas: But they all went away, and came near us no more for several days. We had then a great loaf of melory [a breadfruit] which was our constant food; and if we had a mind to coco-nuts, or toddy, our Malayans of Achin would climb the trees, and fetch as many nuts as we would have, and a good pot of toddy every morning. Thus we lived till our melory was almost spent; being still in hopes that the natives would come to us, and sell it as they had formerly done. But they came not to us; nay, they opposed us where-ever we came, and often shaking their lances at us, made all the shew of hatred that they could invent.

At last, when we saw that they stood in opposition to us, we resolved to use force to get some of their food, if we could not get it other ways. With this resolution we went into our canoa to a small bay on the north-part of the island; because it was smooth water there and good landing; but on the other side, the wind being yet on that quarter, we could not land without jeopardy of oversetting our canoa, and wetting our arms, and then we must have lain at the mercy of our enemies, who stood 2 or 300 men in every bay, where they saw us coming, to keep us off.

When we set out, we rowed directly to the north-end, and presently were followed by seven or eight of their canoas. They keeping at a distance, rowed away faster than we did, and got to the bay before us; and there, with about 20 more canoas full of men, they all landed, and stood to hinder us from landing. But we rowed in, within a hundred yards of them. Then we lay still, and I took my gun, and presented at them; at which they all fell down flat on the ground. But I turn'd my self about, and to shew that we did not intend to harm them, I fired my gun off towards the sea; so that they might see the shot graze on the water. As soon as my gun was loaded again, we rowed gently in; at which some of them withdrew. The rest standing up, did still cut and hew the air, making signs of their hatred; till I once more frighted them with my gun, and discharged it as before. The more of them sneak'd away, leaving only five or six men on the bay. Then we rowed in again, and Mr Hall taking his sword in his hand, leapt ashore; and I stood ready with my gun to fire at the Indians, if they had injured him: But they did not stir, till he came to them and saluted them.

He shook them by the hand, and by such signs of friendship as he made, the peace was concluded, ratified and confirmed by all that were present: And others that were gone, were again call'd back, and they all very joyfully accepted of a peace. This became universal over all the island, to the great joy of the inhabitants. There was no ringing of bells nor bon-fires made, for that is not the custom here; but glad-ness appeared in their countenances, for now they could go out and fish again, without fear of being taken. This peace was not more welcome to them than to us; and now the inhabitants brought their melory again to us; which we bought for old rags, and small strips of cloath, about as broad as the palm of one's hand. I did not see above five or six hens, for they have but few on the island. At some places we saw some small hogs, which we could have bought of them reasonably; but we could not offend our Achinese friends, who were Mahometans.

We stayed here two or three days and then rowed toward the south-end of the island, keeping on the east-side, and we were kindly received by the natives where-ever we came. When we arrived at the south-end of the island, we fitted our selves with melory and water. We bought three or four loaves of melory, and about twelve large coco-nut-shells, that had all the kernel taken out, yet were preserved whole, except only a small hole at one end; and all these held for us about three gallons and a half of water. We bought also two or three bamboes, that held about four or five gallons more: this was our sea-store.

We now designed to go for Achin, a town on the N.W. end of the island Sumatra, distant from hence about 40 leagues, bearing south-south-east. We only waited for the western monsoon, which we had expected for a great while, and now it seemed to be at hand; for the clouds began to hang their heads to the eastward, and at last moved gently that way; and though the wind was still at east, yet this was an infallible sign that the western monsoon wind was nigh.

It was the 15th day of May 1688 about four a clock in the afternoon, when we left Nicobar Island, directing our course towards Achin, being eight men of us in company, viz three English, four Malayans, who were born at Achin, and the mungrel Portuguese.

Dampier had finally effected his escape from Captain Read in the Nicobars, but there is an interesting postscript to the subsequent voyaging of the *Cygnet*. After many adventures, it reached Madagascar and there sank at its anchorage.

In a 1705 edition of *Dampier's Voyages*, which was included in *Collection of Voyages and Travels: Consisting of above Four Hundred of the Most Authentick Writers*, to which reference has already been made, Dampier gives the following impressions of the Nicobarese:

The 5th of May we anchored in a small bay at the N.W. end of the Isle of Nicobar, properly so called, in eight fathoms of water. Its length is twelve leagues, the breadth three or four, at 7 degrees 30 minutes N. latitude. It produces great plenty of cocoes and mellories, a fruit of the bigness of the bread-fruit of Guam which the natives boil with water in covered jars. The inhabitants here are strait limbed, long visaged, with black eyes, and well proportioned noses; their hair is lank and black, their complexion of a copper colour. The women have no eye-brows, I suppose they pulled them out, because the men did not like them. The men wear only a sash around their middle; and the women nothing but a petticoat from the waist to the knees. Their language had some words of Malayan and Portuguese in it. Their habitations were built upon posts near to the sea side; but I could find no settled government among them. Their canoes were flat on one side with outlayers like those of Guam.

The voyage to Sumatra was a desperate undertaking. Relying solely upon Dampier's pocket compass, and his skills as a navigator, the open boat was no match for the elements. Beset by tropical storms almost as soon as they departed, their native canoe was in constant danger of being overwhelmed by heavy seas for the four days it took them to make a landfall. Dampier reflects upon this episode of his life in the following terms:

> I had been in many imminent dangers before now, but the worst of them all was but a play-game by comparison with this. I must confess that I was in great conflicts of mind at this time. Other dangers came not upon me with such a leisurely and dreadful solemnity … I made very sad reflections on my former life, and looked back with horror and detestation on actions which before I disliked, but now I trembled at the remembrance of.

He continues:

> Three days after our arrival here, our Portuguese died of a fever. What became of our Malayans I know not; Ambrose lived not long after, Mr Hall also was so weak, that I did not think he would recover. I was the best; but still very sick of a fever, and little likely to live.

For the following two years, Dampier occupied himself working with a local trader in eastern waters, making voyages to various parts including Tonkin and Madras. Finally, he arrived at Fort York, an outpost of the East India Company at Bencoolen on the southwest coast of Sumatra, where he was engaged as a master-gunner somewhat against his will. At last he managed to escape his detention by smuggling aboard the *Defence*, an East Indiaman, and after further seaborne trials and tribulations, finally arrived back in England at The Downs on September 16,1691. Thus ended his first circumnavigation of the globe, taking him a period of over 12 years. This circumnavigation had not been intended, and had begun much like one takes a saunter on a summer's evening and, after finding oneself halfway round the block, there seems little reason not to continue!

Following his return to London, Dampier busily engaged himself on writing an account of his travels. This was to become one of the most famous accounts of exploration of the age, and was eventually published in 1697. During this period, he seems to have become acquainted with Jonathan Swift, the renowned author of *Gulliver's Travels* and other notable works. Swift has been credited with polishing up *Dampier's Voyages*, as there is reference in Swift's introduction to *Gulliver's Travels* to "correct the style, as my Cousin Dampier did by my advice, in his book called *A Voyage Round the World*." This is, however, by no means certain, and more will be said about this in the next chapter. When his book was finally published, it propelled Dampier into virtual stardom. While he was engaged upon its writing he made a number of short voyages from London, which are believed to have been of a trading nature, possibly to eke out his finances, and it was during this period that Kidd sailed into port in his ship, the *Antigua*, in August 1695. It is highly likely that the two renewed old friendships and discussed the old days and past acquaintances in the interim until Kidd set sail in the *Adventure Galley* the following February.

There is an interesting comment on the social graces of Dampier, given by the noted diarist of the time, John Evelyn. On August 6, 1698, Evelyn dined with Samuel Pepys and Dampier, and he records:

> I dined with Mr Pepys, where was Captain Dampier, who had been a famous buccaneer ... He was now going abroad again by the King's encouragement, who furnished a ship of 290 tons. He seemed a more modest man than one would imag-

ine by relation of the crew he had assorted with. He brought a map of his observations of the course of the winds in the South Seas, and assured us that the maps hitherto extant were all false as to the Pacific Sea, which he makes on the south of the line, that on the north end running by the coast of Peru being extremely tempestuous.

Sir Albert Gray, in his introduction to a 1927 edition of the *Voyages*, which carried the title *A New Voyage Round the World* (Argonaut Press), observes of this evening spent between Pepys, Evelyn, and Dampier:

> It would seem that Evelyn expected to meet a swashbuckler and found a modest and courteous gentleman, with perhaps much to tell of his life's adventures, but for the moment chiefly concerned with his objection to calling an ocean pacific unless it is so. How pleasant it would have been for any person, however eminent, to have made a fourth at that dinner!

Following the first edition of *Dampier's Voyages* there were several revised printings, and Dampier was requested to provide greater details regarding various aspects of his travels, such details being inserted into the later editions. It was not until 1709 that all of his work appeared in print, as his further travels created great interest from an eager public. In 1729, 14 years after his death, Dampier's travels were finally compiled into four volumes. As John Masefield (1878–1967), the well known poet, writer, and ex-mariner, notes in his introduction to a 1906 reprint of *Dampier's Voyages*:

> When one considers his busy life of action, one is surprised that Dampier should have found time to write the three books of his voyages by which he is remembered today. But when one considers that the man's

literary life was spent among pirates, lumbermen, and drunken and ignorant sailors, one is surprised that he ever wrote a word. It is pathetic to think of him, writing up his journal, describing a bunch of flowers, or a rare fish, in the intervals between looting a wineshop and sacking a village.

Dampier dedicated the first (1697) printing of his *Voyages* to Charles Montague, president of the Royal Society, and Montague reciprocated this kindness by introducing Dampier to various notables of the day, and in numerous other ways. One of the men to whom Dampier was introduced was Edward Russell (1653–1727), Earl of Orford and First Lord of the Admiralty. The two men must have discussed a great number of matters relating to maritime affairs, and possibly to William Kidd in particular, as Russell was one of Kidd's backers.

One of the matters that concerned Russell, and upon which Dampier's advice was requested, was connected with a proposed voyage of exploration to New Holland (Australia) and the islands of the East Indies that lay directly to the north. Dampier was invited to command this expedition. Another matter was the serious effects of piracy, which was rampant in the Indian Ocean. Dampier's advice on this was also eagerly sought, and he was accordingly called before a meeting of the Council of Trade and Plantations, in September 1698, to formally answer a number of questions. John Masefield, on the fourth page of his 13-page introduction to his edited version of *Dampier's Voyages*, quotes the following from Dampier's own record of these proceedings:

> On September 22nd he attended the Council to advise them about the fitting out of a squadron against the pirates "to the east of the Cape of Good Hope." On the 26th he was asked *"how long a ship might be, running from England to Madagascar at this time of year?"* In answer to this question and to others of the same nature, he writes:

Sept. 27, 1698.

... to the best of my judgement it might be done in three months and a half. (2) *How long a ship might be in passing from Madagascar to the Red Sea?* I could not answer this without consulting my papers, and I now inform you that since, according to the best of my information, on the coast of Madagascar the winds are at NE and NNE from the end of January to the end of May (which is right against them) the voyage could not be performed in less than two months. (3) *How long a ship might be in passing from the Red Sea to Cape Comorin?* This depends upon the setting in of the western monsoon. In the Red Sea this falls out in May, when you may pass in a month, but you cannot bridge that way earlier. Thus if a ship leave England in November she may reach Madagascar by the middle of February and the Red Sea about the middle of April. She must then wait about a month for the monsoon, and about the middle of June she will reach Cape Comorin, a week or two sooner or later according to the setting in of the monsoon."

— Will Dampier.

It seems strange that the council would bother to ask Dampier the kind of questions that could have been answered by the captain of any East Indiaman found wandering the London streets or docksides, or any clerk of the East India Company itself. Furthermore, why should Masefield record this apparent trivia so early in his introduction? Masefield may have smelt a rat, but likely could not put his finger upon it!

After Kidd attacked the Mocha fleet in the Gulf of Aden in August 1697, it had taken five months for the news to trickle back to London. A similar period of time would have elapsed for details of the capture of the *Queddah Merchant* to also become public knowledge. Since the *Queddah Merchant* had been taken in late January, or early February 1698, the concern of the Council of Trade and Plantations in September 1698 would have been perfectly natural. However, why request information from Dampier regarding the specific routing from England to Madagascar to the Red Sea and then to Cape Comorin? This is an unusual route for any honest merchant vessel, but it is exactly the same route that Kidd followed, though there is no direct reference to Kidd in the question-answer session that Dampier attended. The conclusion that may be drawn is that a member of the council had personal knowledge of the route that Kidd had intended to take, before he set sail from England. That person can only have been Edward Russell, one of Kidd's backers. He, out of all the members of the consortium, would have been the most likely to have discussed maritime affairs with Kidd during the planning of the voyage, and as such would have been intimate with the proposed itinerary, and in fact it is known that he met with Kidd in the company of Henry Sidney. Therefore, it can be concluded that Russell was fully aware of the fact that Kidd meant to go first to the Red Sea, after making landfall in Madagascar, and thence to cruise the coast of India. By implication, Russell and at least one other member of the consortium knew that they were aiding and abetting piracy in the guise of privateering.

It is known that Russell was fully aware of the circumstances whereby Kidd in the *Adventure Galley* had lost the better part of his crew to the captain of the *Duchess* at Sheerness shortly after sailing from London. In fact, Russell had played a pivotal role in sorting out the mess that Kidd had landed himself in. However, for Russell to volunteer the information before the council that he was more interested in the sailing time between New York and Madagascar "at this time of year," instead of London to Madagascar, would have disclosed the fact he had more of a personal interest in Kidd's voyage than in combatting piracy in the Indian Ocean. What appears to have been uppermost in Russell's mind are the answers to the questions — Where is Kidd? How much booty has he got? When and where will he appear? How much will I get? By including the full text of Dampier's submission to the Council of Trade and Plantations in his edited version of the *Voyages*, Masefield has provided a vital piece of information, and one which suggests that the voyage of the *Adventure Galley* had a rather different agenda from that outlined in Kidd's commission.

Other questions naturally arise from this incident. How much did Dampier know of Kidd's real intentions before Kidd embarked? Did Dampier detect an undercurrent that the purpose of the council (or at least one member) was to quiz him on the likely whereabouts of Kidd? Did Dampier give his responses in writing to prevent any suggestion that he, himself, might have colluded with Kidd? Unfortunately these hypothetical questions cannot be answered.

Dampier's appointment to command the voyage of exploration to New Holland was soon forthcoming, and it would be expected that Russell played a part in securing this. At the time, the Whig lords were coming under increasing attack from the Tories, their long-time adversaries, because of what was fast becoming known as the "Kidd Affair." Russell was one of those Whig lords singled out for pillory by the Tories, as he was known to be one of Kidd's backers. The curious incident retold by Masefield can thus be regarded in a rather different light. Dampier, being highly respected because of his achievements, was an old shipmate of Kidd. In the event of Kidd's apprehension with the possibility of a public trial, Dampier might be prevailed upon to testify on behalf of Kidd, and this might have damning repercussions. Therefore, get rid of Dampier as fast as possible, and send him to the other side of the world, ensuring a long absence, before an ugly situation got uglier and there was even more political fallout. Dampier sailed on HMS *Roebuck* from The Downs three months later.

Dampier's voyage to New Holland in the *Roebuck* is well documented. It was not a particularly happy voyage in many respects, and Dampier did not excel as a commander. He had difficulty with his men, and though he may have been an excellent navigator, with numerous other talents of a pseudo-scientific nature that contributed greatly to such an expedition, he seems to have lacked the qualities required in exercising command. The *Roebuck* departed on January 14, 1699, and sighted the west coast of New Holland some six months later. For a year they cruised the northern coast of the island continent and around the islands of Timor, New Guinea and others lying to the east of the Dutch strongholds of Batavia and Amboyna. The condition of the ship deteriorated badly and Dampier took her into Batavia for refit, where she lay for three months. Eventually they sailed for England on October 17, 1700, and the *Roebuck* arrived at the Cape of Good Hope on December 30. During the homeward-bound leg of the voyage from the Cape, the ship sprang several severe leaks, her timbers were rotting, and the hull was covered with barnacles. The pumps were in constant use, both day and night. Dampier managed to reach Ascension Island on February 21, 1701. and three days later the ship sank at anchor. Dampier and his crew found water, and food in the form of goats and turtles. They lived in reasonable comfort before being res-cued by a squadron of East Indiamen and naval vessels who were bound for the West Indies. Dampier returned to London, sailing up the Thames about the time that Kidd was being hanged at Execution Dock. If he did not witness this gruesome fate of one of his old shipmates, then he would most certainly have seen Kidd's iron-caged corpse dangling from the gibbet on Tilbury Point.

Various charges were brought against Dampier about his inept handling of the command of the *Roebuck*, and the court issued the following pronouncement: "Captain Dampier is not a fit person to be employed as commander of any of His Majesty's ships." Nevertheless, within the year, Dampier had another command under his charge. *The London Gazette* of April 3, 1703, issued the following news item: "Captain William Dampier, being prepared to depart on another voy-age ... had the honour to kiss His Majesty's hand."

Dampier was given command of the *St. George*, (26 guns and 126 men) and the *Cinque Ports*, (16 guns and 63 men), and the two ships sailed for the South Seas from Kinsale, Ireland on September 11, 1703. The voyage was as fruitless, in many ways, as that of the *Roebuck*, due to the indiscipline of the men and Dampier's inability to control them. Dampier wrote no account of the voyage, but others did, in very hostile terms. Petty squabbles between Dampier and his officers were described and he was accused of cowardice. The latter is difficult to believe in view of his early history of rampaging with buccaneers in various quarters of the globe. Perhaps, now that he was in command, Dampier was more acutely aware of the responsibilities he had towards his men, rather than concerned about his own personal safety. There were many mutinies and desertions among the two crews, one of which was to become famous in the annals of literature. Alexander Selkirk, master of the *Cinque Ports*, was to be marooned on Juan Fernandez for some four years before being rescued, ironically by Dampier on a subsequent voyage, and this was to inspire Daniel Defoe to write his classic tale, *Robinson Crusoe*.

Off Juan Fernandez, Dampier attacked a French ship but was beaten off, and an attack on the Spanish Manila fleet resulted in much loss of life. After these failures, there was a great deal of incrimination, with the result that the *St. George* and the *Cinque Ports* parted company, leaving Dampier with only 30 men to sail the *St. George* back to England. Eventually the *St. George* was abandoned on the coast of Peru. The untiring Dampier, together with the nucleus of men left to him, managed to take a small Spanish ship and sailed across the Pacific. They finished up being imprisoned by the Dutch in the East Indies. In 1707, Dampier and the survivors finally arrived back home, no richer than when they had left Kinsale four years earlier, and with Dampier's reputation much diminished by the whole episode. Thus ended, somewhat ignominiously, Dampier's second circumnavigation of the world.

Though Dampier suffered a considerable loss of prestige as a commander, his reputation as a navigator was little compromised. A year later he was appointed pilot to an expedition sailing under the command of Captain Woodes Rogers. This privateering venture consisted of two vessels, the *Duke* and the *Duchess*. The ships sailed from England in August 1708, doubled Cape Horn, rescued Selkirk from his solitary confinement on Juan Fernandez, captured one of the Manila ships, crossed the Pacific and arrived back in London in October 1711, bringing with them plunder to a value of almost £200,000. Thus ended Dampier's third circumnavigation, on a far happier note than the previous venture. However, as usual, there was a fly in the ointment, and the prize money from this voyage was not paid out until 1719, four years after Dampier's death in March 1715.

There is nothing on record to inform us of how Dampier spent his final four years, except that he lived in London in the parish of St. Stephen, Coleman Street. His will describes Dampier as "diseased and weak of body, but of sound and perfect mind." Nothing is mentioned in his will of his wife Judith, who must be presumed to have predeceased him, though there is evidence that she was living in 1703. It must be assumed that in these twilight years he reverted to writing, retouching up his *Voyages*.

Dampier's name does not seem to be much celebrated in the British Isles. However, in Australia his name is bestowed upon a group of offshore islands known as the Dampier Archipelago, and there is a town in Western Australia named in his honour. There is also a district in New South Wales bearing his name. Outside of Australia his name is celebrated on maps of the East Indies by the Dampier Strait, which lies to the northwest of Papua New Guinea. His contribution to navigational and botanical science deserves no less respect.

William Dampier.
An Australian stamp (1963–65) issued in his honour. In the background is a likeness of HMS Roebuck.

Chapter 12

Captain Charles Johnson

Whose heart hath ne'er within him burned,
As home his footsteps he hath turn'd
From wandering on a foreign strand?
— "Lay of the Last Minstrel" (Scott)

In May 1724, a small book bound in dull leather binding appeared in the shop of Charles Rivington, a bookseller located in close proximity to St. Paul's Cathedral. We have no idea what the shop looked like in reality, but we can imagine it to be small, cramped, and badly lit, the sole illumination filtering through the irregular panes of helix glass fronting onto the street. In short a sort of "Curiosity Shop" that predated Dickens.

The book carried the rather pretentious title *A General History of the Robberies and Murders of the Most Notorious Pyrates*, by Captain Charles Johnson. It was an immediate best-seller. Though Rivington dealt mainly with religious books, tracts, and pamphlets, he must have wished for other such books as the *General History*. Within a few months the first edition had been entirely sold out and a second printing instantly followed. The popularity of the book remained undiminished and a third edition was published in 1725, and a fourth in 1726. The latter was enlarged considerably with the inclusion of a dozen more lives of renowned pirates, and was published in two volumes. Some years later, in 1734, another book appeared that not only included all Captain Johnson's previous work, but also that of a Captain Alexander Smith, who wrote *A General History of the Lives and Adventures of the Most Famous Highwaymen, Murderers, Pirates,*

Street-robbers and Thief-takers, and which had been published earlier in 1714. The composite work was ascribed to Johnson and carried the unwieldy title by today's standards of *A General History of the Lives and Adventures of the most famous Highwaymen, Murderers, Street Robbers, etc, to which is added a genuine account of the Voyages and Plunders of the most notorious Pyrates, interspersed with several diverting Tales and pleasant Songs, and adorned with the Heads of the most remarkable Villains in copper.*

These published works, in this unusual and fascinating genre, have been translated into a number of European languages, recompiled countless times in numerous republications, and have formed the basis of many plays, films, documentaries, and works of fiction. The foundation for this vast outpouring of literary and artistic endeavour, at least where it relates to pirates, springs from Captain Johnson's original work, which is indisputably considered by all to be the ultimate reference source. But who was he? Who was the man that almost 300 years ago created this masterpiece?

The *Dictionary of National Biography* lists two entries for Charles Johnson. The first is for Captain Charles Johnson, who flourished 1724–36, and was the author of the *General History,* as it will be referred to hitherto for the sake of brevity. The comment is made that the writer's name was most likely assumed. The entry then details the various editions and changes in content that ensued in the 12 years following first publication. The second entry is for Charles Johnson (1679–1748), who was a dramatist. He wrote a total of 19 plays, including one that bore the title *The Successful Pyrate,* which appeared in 1713. He tackled a variety of plots, acted in many of his own works, and was not immune from indulging in a little plagiarism from time to time. Following the premiere of *The Successful Pyrate,* he wrote *The Victim* (1714), *The Cobbler of Preston* (1716), *The Masquerade* (1719), and *Love in a Forest* (1723). These productions preceded the appearance of the *General History* in 1724. Though many have suggested he may have written the *General History,* there is nothing about this particular Charles Johnson that suggests he possessed either the travelling experience or knowledge of nautical affairs so evident in the narrative of the *General History*. In fact all the evidence suggests he never strayed very far from the London stage.

The authorship of the *General History* has attracted a great deal of scholarly debate. At one time, the consensus of opinion was that Daniel Defoe was the author. Defoe, who is best known for his *Life and Surprising Adventures of Robinson Crusoe* (1719), wrote many works of fiction under a variety of nom-de-plumes, some of which were on piratical themes. These included *The King of the Pirates* (1719), *The Life, Adventures and Pyracies of the Famous Captain Singleton* (1720), and *An Account of the Conduct and Proceedings of the Late John Gow* (1725). The wealth of piratical pseudo-fiction arising from his pen is highly suggestive that he may well have been the genius behind Captain Johnson's remarkable work. This unwarranted assumption has led to Johnson's work being ascribed to Defoe to the extent that it is now generally listed under his name in catalogue lists, and has been republished carrying Defoe's name as author.

The literary world appears to have been quite happy about attributing authorship of the *General History* to Defoe until 1988, when, as David Cordingley notes in his introduction to one of the more recent republications of the *General History*, scholars began to point out numerous inconsistencies between Captain Johnson's work and that of Defoe. Cordingley summarizes the present debate on this issue by concluding that the attractive idea that Defoe wrote the *General History* must be abandoned, and that the search for its authorship must be made elsewhere.

All would not appear lost however. The reader is encouraged to scrutinize the text of the *General History* for himself, or herself, as the case may be, and, it is hoped, will endorse the following comments, which are believed to represent clues relating to the contentious issue of authorship:

- The writer obviously had an excellent background in classical history, as Johnson's introduction to the book describes many piratical actions in the Mediterranean during Roman times.

• Approximately 30 percent of the book is devoted to the lives of two pirates that frequented the Guinea coast of Africa, namely Bartholomew Roberts and Howel Davis. The lives, as retold, give full and detailed accounts of how the Guinea pirates were captured, how they were tried, how they were hanged, and the last words they spoke before the hangman stretched their necks at Cape Coast Castle. With this demonstration of detail it is obvious that the writer must either have been present, or have had an informant who witnessed these proceedings. Also, within these accounts there is a wealth of factual detail of geographic and botanic interest relating to the islands within the Gulf of Guinea and upon the coast of Brazil.

• Though Dampier, who was perhaps the most notable of all pirates, was recently deceased (1715), and Kidd had been hanged over 20 years earlier (1701), these two were studiously omitted from the first edition of the *General History*. It is not surprising that Dampier was omitted because he had in later years achieved a degree of scholarship and an honourable position in maritime circles, but to omit Kidd from this rogues' gallery is difficult to credit. Kidd, as we have seen, had been hanged with great publicity at Execution Dock. His hanging was necessary as a public gesture to the Mogul of India in order to recement the bonds of trade and commerce that he had unwittingly ruptured by his actions, thereby restoring the fortunes (and profits) of the East India Company. Kidd's omission from the first edition of the *General History* is perhaps indicative of a degree of sympathy by the writer towards Kidd, or even that he knew him personally. If Johnson himself had experienced a degree of misfortune from a seemingly unjust and often hypocritical system, he could have felt partisan to the unfortunate man. However, Johnson rectified this omission in the enlarged version of the *General History*, which by 1726 had attained even greater popularity.

- The *General History* included two women pirates in its first edition, namely Mary Read and Anne Bonny. Neither were particularly bloodthirsty. In fact their menfolk did much of the dirty work of attacking vulnerable vessels, slitting throats, and making off with the loot. Why include them? A close reading of the two chapters concerned suggests a woman's hand. There are far too many details included in the text of these two chapters that are unessential to the thrust of the book, but they are details that are likely to fascinate female curiosity.

- The lives of the pirates in the first edition, with the exception of Avery, generally reach the heights of their infamies between 1716 and 1723, the year before publication.

There is thus a dichotomy. It is inconceivable that an educated European woman would be present at the hanging of pirates on the coast of West Africa. It is even more inconceivable that a woman would admit to writing such a work as the *General History* in the early part of the eighteenth century. In fact the mores of that society suggest that a woman would be a virtual outcast if she wrote anything that was published! Almost 100 years were to pass, if not more, before aspiring women writers could cast nom-de-plumes aside and embark upon recognized and respected careers on a par with their male counterparts. The thesis is advanced that Captain Charles Johnson, author of the *General History*, was two people, Captain Charles ——— being a well-travelled adventurer, well-versed in nautical matters and familiar with piracy in general, if not personally known to certain pirates. The other, ——— Johnson, was a member of the female sex with a literary bent.

There is another clue to authorship. The second edition of the *General History*, printed in 1724, contains a preface which has been reproduced in a number of later impressions. The editor comments as follows:

The gentleman who has taken the pains to make these observations is Mr Atkins, a surgeon, an ingenious man in his own profession and one who is not tied down by any narrow considerations from doing a service to the public, and has been pleased generously to communicate them for the good of others. ...

There have been some other pirates besides those whose histories are here related, such as are hereafter named, and their adventures are as extravagant and full of mischief as those who are the subject of this book. The author has already begun to digest them into method and as soon as he receives some material to make them (which he shortly expects from the West Indies) if the public gives him encouragement he intends to venture upon a second volume.

A footnote to this preface makes a statement to the effect that the aforementioned Mr. Atkins was John Atkins (1685–1757), naval surgeon to the *Weymouth* and *Swallow* in their cruise against the Guinea Coast pirates in 1721. John Atkins was indeed a naval surgeon and entered the navy after completing his training. He saw active service in 1703 in the Mediterranean, and later elsewhere against the French. In 1721 he participated in a celebrated and successful voyage against the Guinea pirates, and interestingly enough, was present at Cape Coast Castle when the pirate crews of Bartholomew Roberts and Howel Davis were publicly hanged. After this satisfactory outcome the *Weymouth* and *Swallow* voyaged to Brazil and the West Indies, returning to England in April 1723. John Atkins was paid off and, being unsuccessful in getting another ship, he resorted to writing. He published a noteworthy book titled *The Navy Surgeon* (1732), which is a general treatise on surgery. He also wrote an account of the voyage of the *Weymouth* and *Swallow*, which appeared in 1735 under the title *A Voyage to Guinea, Brazil and the West Indies*. It is interesting to note that the text to this voyage includes a passing reference to the *General History* in the following context:

> In October 1721 we understood everywhere that the
> pyrates under the command of Roberts, had been
> plundering the ships down the whole coast ... by a
> joint consent of George Lowther the second mate,
> and some of the sailors, proceeded to sea; the effect
> of which, see in the History of the Pyrates.

Despite John Atkins's indisputable connection with the *General History*, as admitted by the editor of the second edition produced soon after the first, his own writing abilities, and the fact that the *General History* contains vivid and detailed accounts of fauna, flora, and the geography of the places he visited, which are included in the chapters dealing with the lives of Bartholomew Roberts and Howel Davis as mentioned earlier, John Atkins cannot be considered to be the enigmatic and elusive Captain Charles ———. There was simply inadequate time for him to write or co-author the *General History*, following his return to England, before it was published by Rivington in 1724. However, John Atkins did have a father whose name was Charles, who was far wider travelled, who had once held the rank of captain in the navy, and furthermore had also attained the rank of captain in the militia of the East India Company. The father's history, imperfect though it is, makes far more interesting reading than the more sober son, John. And it is to Charles Atkins that we must look for participation in the co-authorship of the *General History*, although John was more than likely an active participant in the various republications.

Charles Atkins was the son of Sir Jonathan Atkins, whose brother-in-law was Charles Howard (1629–85), the first Earl of Carlisle. Barbados, previously known as the Carlisle Islands, constituted part of his domains, and Sir Jonathan Atkins was appointed to the position of governor of Barbados. Presumably then, as now, people liked to keep sinecures within the family. Sir Jonathan was to return from his West Indian paradise in 1681 full of wrath and indignation, and this parental ire was directed at his son Charles. We can only surmise the reason for Sir Jonathan's anger by a letter written from Dublin by Charles Atkins and addressed to his uncle, the earl. The letter is dated December 10, 1681. It reads:

My Lord,

I was very much ashamed that the speedy commands of my father after his arrival in England admitted me not to discharge my duty to my best and onliest patron, or at least with a line or two to have kissed your Lordship's hands, which I humbly beg you now to accept though in a manner from a banished man, whose misfortunes cannot well be greater than my own, and as it hath been my good fortune upon all occasions to receive continual favour and relief from your Lordship I cannot but sue and beg the continuance as lying only in your hands to restore me to myself again for I can never hope for my father's favour unless your Lordship will be pleased to intercede for me and I hope by my future carriage I shall deserve this great favour amongst many more already received by,

Your Lordship's most humble servant and nephew
Charles Atkins

We will never likely know what Charles had done to merit the wrath of his father, and to force him to face the prospect of banishment. The correspondence of the earl, Sir Jonathan, and of Charles himself, is silent on this subject. Did the young jackanapes get into debt through gambling, cards, cock-fighting, or what? Hardly pursuits that would warrant ejection from the family fold! In any event these activities were enthusiastically pursued by all classes. Did any wild escapade of the youthful Charles give him trouble with the law? There was little enough law to bother about in those days, and more than likely, the lordly influence of the earl could have craved some indulgence on the part of the authorities towards his irresponsible nephew, if that was the case. No, Charles's infraction, whatever it was, had to be more serious than any of these. It could well have had its origin some years earlier when Charles committed an act of cowardice, which at best might be considered weak and irresponsible. It was to lead to his being cashiered from the navy or, if not actually cashiered as we know it today, he was denied any further commission.

The incident in question took place in the Mediterranean in the autumn of 1676, when Charles Atkins, holding the rank of captain, was in command of HMS *Quaker*, a naval ketch of 85 tons. Despite orders to the contrary, Captain Charles Atkins had on board a private shipment of bullion, the shipment of which was being made for his own profit. The ketch was captured by corsairs, and without any resistance Atkins permitted his vessel to be taken into Algiers. This action was to spark another Mediterranean war between England and the Moors. As a result of his craven behaviour, his father Sir Jonathan cut him off without a penny. For the next few years he drifted, borrowing money wherever he could (with no intention of paying it back), consorting with villains (of high as well as low rank) and, in general, he may be considered to have been a wastrel little better than those with whom he consorted. He has been described as "depraved" and one "who loved wine and women." During the years 1678–79 he became involved in court proceedings as a witness to a charge of murder against an unfortunate man carrying the same name as himself, a certain Samuel Atkins. His behaviour throughout was totally reprehensible and unbecoming in a man such as he, especially one who had received a good education and who came from a good family. One can only sympathize with Sir Jonathan for having been saddled with such a son, who would surely turn his father's hair white! With an entire litany of misdemeanours to his credit it would be presumptuous to identify any single event that might have provoked Sir Jonathan to banish his miscreant son. Wherever the rogue went could never have been too far for the long-suffering parent!

Where Charles went after he wrote the letter to his uncle from Dublin in 1681 we do not know, but we do catch our next sight of him in April 1700. On the sixteenth he writes a note from on board the *Martha*, an East Indiaman, berthed at Gravesend but bound for the Persian Gulf. The intervening years, 19 in total, had seen him master skills in the art of medicine and surgery; he had been appointed to the post of surgeon at the East India Company's factory at Gombroon, his intended destination. The likelihood is that this position was not the first he had held, neither was the *Martha* the first ship in which he had sailed.

From Gombroon Charles wrote a number of letters to James Petiver in 1701 and 1703; Petiver was a noted English botanist. The letters relate to certain botanical specimens that were being shipped back to England. He also undertook various expeditions into the hinterland of Persia, presumably trading missions on behalf of the East India Company. It was not too long, however, before Charles ran afoul of authority at Gombroon, and thereafter his career appears to have become rather tarnished despite its bright start. The impression gained from the subsequent records of the company is that Charles was impetuous, independent, wilful towards his superiors, and possessed a penchant for argument, which at certain times led to brawling to settle the disputes in which he became embroiled.

Charles was transferred to Fort St. George (Madras) in May 1703. The surgeon's post at Gombroon may have held certain privileges that would ensure a blind eye would be turned to many minor infractions, but nevertheless transferred he was, and he didn't last long at Fort St. George! In August 1704 he was transferred again, this time to Fort St. David, near Pondicherry, further south along the coast. He had no better luck there, because within six months he had been dismissed from that post also. The record gives the date of his discharge as February 1, 1705. No reasons are given regarding this succession of dismissals from the various factories of the East India Company where Atkins managed to secure employment.

We pick up his track once more in the records of the East India Company at Fort York, in Sumatra. The records tell us that he served as a lieutenant in the militia, and became captain of the garrison's forces in 1707, serving in that rank until 1709. He was also surgeon to this frontier post in addition to holding military rank.

An East Indiaman under Full Sail.
Many ships that carried specific cargoes, such as tea, were designed for high speed on the open seas. They could cover almost 400 miles per day under ideal conditions.

He appears to have been as quarrelsome as ever, despite the position he held, because there is mention of a court case in March 1711, and an order in council dated January 5, 1713, to the effect that he be shipped back to England for assaulting a Mr. Thomas Kingsley. Perhaps we should not judge Charles too harshly, as there is further reference that Kingsley be "suspended for neglecting the accounts, insolence to superiors, and embezzling the company's goods and cash." Shortly after this illuminating aspect of Kingsley's character, for which one is forgiven for feeling sympathy for Charles, there is the bold statement "Lieutenant Atkins broke for assaulting one of the council, he with his wife gone to Batavia." The date is September 10, 1713. The assault on Kingsley, whatever its merits, had lost Charles his post and his captaincy.

Tensions could be high among the inmates of a factory at times. In the outlying factories there might have been as few as eight men cooped up with one another for years at a time. Once the daily chores had been completed there was little to do. Excessive drinking became a curse and local women inevitably became a necessary adjunct to factory life, a life that was highly spartan. Tropical diseases frequently laid waste these outposts of commerce, often with dire results. At Fort York, built in 1685, after one such outbreak, a report proclaimed: "All our servants are sick and dead ... we have no living to bury the dead." A later governor was to write in 1712, "Our fort indeed stands in a swamp which can't be very wholesome. But the country all about and even within half a musquett shot of us is as pleasant as you can imagine." Under these sort of living conditions, with fever and pestilence in constant attendance, is it any wonder that Charles Atkins lost his temper on occasions, and had a native "wife"?

We do not know the matrimonial details of Charles Atkins, or whether he had a loyal and devoted wife back in England who suffered stoically the enforced separations from her roving and erratic husband. But a son, John, was born in 1685, four years after the estrangement between Charles and his father. It is possible that Charles maintained a clandestine home in England, and made periodic return visits; it is equally possible that parental wrath diminished slowly over the passing years. After being dismissed from the East India Company's factory at Fort St. David in 1705, it is likely that the opportunity was taken to return to England and a new post obtained at Fort York where he reappeared in 1707.

By 1718, the now thoroughly well-travelled Charles had returned to England, probably for good, as he must have been at least 60 years of age. This time we find him involved in a legal dispute at the Vice-Chancellor's court at Oxford. The legal action seems to have been rather a minor affair (the documents are written in an illegible hand) and relate to some material, presumably fabric of some sort, which retailed at a halfpenny per yard! Charles Atkins appears to have been fond of wrangling, whether in the courts or out, and this gives the impression that he was a man who at times could be very obdurate in his convictions.

Those who have read Jonathan Swift's masterpiece *Gulliver's Travels* with more than a cursory eye cannot but have been impressed by the wealth of biographical detail that Swift provides regarding his hero Lemuel Gulliver. It is not necessary to dwell on these details, but one can be forgiven for wondering whether Swift did not use an actual living person as the archetype of his hero. After the first printing of *Gulliver's Travels* Swift was apparently angry that much of the nautical description of Gulliver's voyages had been edited out of his original manuscript. Furthermore, the four voyages of Gulliver to Lilliput, Brobdingnag, Laputa, and other regions, and finally to the country of the Houyhnhnms, spans the period from May 1699 when Gulliver sets out on his first voyage, to his return from his fourth and final voyage in December 1715. This period approximately spans that spent by Charles Atkins in his various roamings around the East where the greater part of *Gulliver's Travels* is set, though it must not be imagined, however fertile the imagination, that Charles encountered little people no bigger than his thumb, giants who could hold him in the palm of their hands, or horses that talked! His travels, and the embellishments that strange adventures inspired, could well have given Swift the stimulus to set his satirical masterpiece against such a backdrop.

Of some relevance to the thesis that Captain Charles Atkins was the archetype of Swift's Lemuel Gulliver is the "Letter from Capt

Gulliver, to his Cousin Sympson" which is reproduced in the preface to most reproductions of *Gulliver's Travels*. We cannot be sure whose words they really are and whether it might be Atkins or Swift writing, or a combination of the two. In this letter there is reference to Dampier in the following context:

> I hope, you will be ready to own publickly, whenever you shall be called to it, that by your great and frequent urgency, you prevailed upon me to publish a very loose and uncorrect account of my travels; with direction to hire some young men of either university to put them in order, and correct the style, as my Cousin Dampier did by my advice, in his book called, A Voyage Round the World.

Here we have a hint that either Swift knew Dampier, or Atkins did, or both. Definitely at the time Dampier was writing the account of his own epic travels, Swift was in London, and so also Atkins might have been, but for certain so was Kidd. To what extent that they knew one another, or had spent some in each others' company, is uncertain.

We must now move on to consider the mysterious woman that is believed to have co-authored the *General History* with Captain Charles Atkins. The fatal attractions of a well-travelled rake, like Atkins might have been, would certainly have held a fascination for any modest gentlewoman of the age. After all, is it not the desperadoes of derring-do, whatever the deficiencies of their characters, that win the hearts of most women, even today? Three hundred years ago, the passions, emotions, and allurements of the fairer sex towards their baser menfolk would have evoked the same spell. The primitive nature of this sexuality is testified so many times in history that it would be banal, as well as futile, to dwell on this issue. If the reader does not accept this premise, read one of the daily tabloids!

Not a great deal is known of the woman that dominated so much of Jonathan Swift's life. Though Swift wrote poetry about her, sent her long letters when he was in London and she in Ireland, and was heavily dependent upon her in the management of his household, Stella Johnson remains a rather enigmatic creature. The best portrait of her is that by Swift himself in his tribute to her titled *On the Death of Esther Johnson*. This character portrait of her life was commenced by Swift on the evening of her death, January 28, 1728. Though she was baptized under the name Esther, or possibly Hester, she has always been known as Stella, a name apparently give to her by Swift, and one by which she is best known in literary circles. Whether Swift actually married Stella has been a contentious issue in literary debates over the centuries, and one that does not concern us here. Also, no satisfactory conclusion has been reached about her parentage, though it is virtually certain she was illegitimate. Swift writes about her as follows:

> She was born at Richmond, in Surrey, on the thirteenth day of March, in the year 1681. Her father was a younger brother of a good family in Nottinghamshire, her mother of a lower degree; and indeed she had little to boast of her birth. I knew her from six years old, and had some share in her education, by directing what books she should read, and perpetually instructing her in the principles of honour and virtue; from which she never swerved in any one action or moment of her life. She was sickly from her childhood until about the age of fifteen; but then grew into perfect health, and was looked upon as one of the most beautiful, graceful, and agreeable young women in London, only a little too fat.* Her hair was blacker than a raven, and every feature of her face in perfection.

*NOTE: Swift appears to be too critical. A contemporary portrait of Stella as a young lady shows she had a waistline to be envied.

Swift continues:

> She was well versed in the Greek and Roman story, and was not unskilled in that of France and England.

She spoke French perfectly, but forgot much of it by neglect and sickness. She had read carefully all the best books of travel, which serve to open and enlarge the mind. She understood the Platonic and Epicurean philosophy, and judged well of the defects of the latter … She had a true taste of wit and good sense, both in poetry and prose, and was a perfect critic of style; neither was it easy to find a more proper or impartial judge, whose advice an author might better rely on, if he intended to send a thing into the world, provided it was on a subject that came within the compass of her knowledge.

Swift first encountered Stella, who was to have such an influence on his life, at the home of Sir William Temple (1628–99) located at Moor Park, Farnham, Surrey. Swift had entered the service of Sir William, to whom he is said to have been distantly related, towards the end of 1689, when Stella would have actually been eight years old, rather than six as quoted by Swift himself — a mistake perhaps the result of a fading memory, and one haunted by the spectre of tragedy resulting from his loss. Swift, born in 1667, would have been some 14 years older than the girl who was to steal his heart. The Temple household contained various members of the Temple family and relations through marriage, and these interrelations have occupied the attentions of biographers, scholars, and researchers. But whatever these interrelations may or may not have been, Stella's position in the Temple household was indisputably privileged. This is at variance with that of her "mother," Bridget Johnson, who was a servant and whose name appears on Stella's baptismal certificate with Edward Johnson, the "father."

The mysterious parentage of Stella, and the equally elusive relationship of the Temples with their extended families are of little interest. But Stella grew up within the household under the tutorship of Swift, and the guardianship of Sir William Temple, immersed in a cultured and learned atmosphere, an atmosphere portrayed so vividly in Swift's own description of her education.

Here we have, therefore, a well educated, cultured, and refined woman, whose lifelong companion was a giant in the literary world of the day. Listening to the experiences of the real-life Gulliver, his travels, adventures, hardships he encountered, and the vagabonds and villains with whom he consorted could well have inspired her to venture upon the writing of the *General History* with that self-same person. There is much that is attractive about this thesis. With Swift lurking in the background to guide her pen, can there be any doubt of a successful outcome where the intriguing subject matter is so well written?

It was the fashion of the age to often publish under a nom-de-plume. During his lifetime Swift only once put his name to any of his own works, and that was one of his least, *A Project for the Advancement of Religion*. The cunning nom-de-plume adopted by Captain Charles Atkins and Stella Johnson to mask their joint authorship of the *General History* displays a wry sense of humour.

Now we come to the all-important question — the connection with Captain Kidd. The *General History* states quite categorically that Kidd visited Amboyna in the Spice Islands. In fact Amboyna is mentioned twice after Kidd and Culliford made their surprise encounter at Madagascar. The following excerpt is given in terms which suggest some detailed knowledge of events following this surprise meeting:

> Soon after which, the greatest part of the company left him [Kidd], some going on board, Captain Culliford and others absconding in the country, so that he had not above forty men left. He put to sea and happened to touch at Amboyna, one of the Dutch spice islands, where he was told, that the news of his actions had reached England, and that he was there declared a pirate. The truth on it is, his piracies so alarmed our merchants, that some motions were made in parliament, to enquire into the commission that was given him, and the persons who fitted him out …. In the mean time it was

> thought advisable, in order to stop the course of
> these piracies, to publish a proclamation, offering
> the King's pardon to all such pirates as should vol-
> untarily surrender themselves, whatever piracies
> they had been guilty of at any time, before the last
> day of April 1699. ... In which proclamation, Avery
> and Kidd were excepted by name. When Kidd left
> Amboyna he knew nothing of this proclamation, for
> certainly had he notice of his being excepted in it,
> he could not have been so infatuated, to run him-
> self into the very jaws of danger.

Numerous writers on Kidd have ignored this revealing passage in the *General History*. There has been a tendency to assume that Kidd sailed directly back from Madagascar to New York in accordance with his testimony, and that for many months Kidd and his depleted crew whiled away their time in Madagascar, waiting for the monsoon winds to change so that the ungainly and cumbersome *Queddah Merchant* could venture upon the voyage to the Cape, and the even longer voyage that lay ahead. The *General History* tells us otherwise, and if, as we suspect, Charles Atkins did co-author this work, then his word must prevail. He was in the region a few years after he reports Kidd as having visited Amboyna, and he was almost 300 years closer to the actual events than any writer in recent history. Dampier in his *Roebuck* was also in the Spice Islands in 1700, less than a year after Kidd's reported visit. For three months Dampier was stuck in Batavia Roads effecting repairs to his ship. He undoubtedly would have heard of any visit by Kidd into the region and this knowledge would have been relayed to others, especially to his friends.

This conclusion should not be interpreted to suggest that the authorship of the *General History* is correct on all matters of detail represented as fact within the text, even regarding the life of Captain Kidd, though there is consensus that the *General History* is a great deal more accurate than it was once considered. In Chapter 2 an excerpt was quoted from *The Flying Post* of May 9,

1701, to the effect that nine persons received sentence of death after Kidd and his crew were tried at the Old Bailey. If one did not know about the repeal of this sentence for most of these men, it would be a fair assumption that the death sentence had indeed been carried out as the *General History* implies. Notice of this stay of execution for most of those condemned was carried in a later issue of *The Flying Post* for May 13. It must be assumed that other newssheets carried similar announcements. The inconsistency of the *General History* regarding the actual numbers of Kidd's crew that were hanged merely suggests that the writer of this particular chapter did not scan his (or her) back issues of the newspapers with sufficient diligence, or did not possess them. After all, they were writing a quarter of a century after the event.

It is appreciated that the thesis advanced herein regarding the oft-speculated authorship of the *General History* flies in the face of general consensus. Another contentious issue is whether Jonathan Swift's *Gulliver's Travels* was based upon an archetype. Hitherto there has been an assumed link with Dampier. However, if a more positive connection can be made to Stella, and thereby an association with Swift, in the writing, or at least in the preparation, of the *General History*, it is not unlikely that there may indeed have been an "original" Gulliver, and that this man was one of the co-authors. There is scope in this literary puzzle for some interesting research.

Chapter 13

The Long Voyage Home

Ah! the pig tailed, quidding pirates
And the pretty pranks we played,
All have since been put a stop-to
By the naughty Board of Trade.
— "Ballad of John Silver" (Masefield)

There is nothing reliable on record that describes the long voyage of the *Queddah Merchant* (renamed the *Adventure Prize*) from the Indian Ocean to the shores of America, or if it is on record it is either not available to the public or has not yet been found. The lack of any detailed documentary evidence in this respect has prompted writers and biographers to assume the correctness of Kidd's testimony that he waited at St. Marie for several months for the contrary monsoon winds to change so he could make an easy run to the Cape before commencing the long northerly passage up the Atlantic.

There are some inconsistencies between the various statements and testimonies regarding what actually transpired when Kidd arrived at St. Marie to find Culliford already in harbour. Kidd's testimony should be viewed accordingly with some circumspection. What is clear, however, is that he arrived in the *Adventure Galley* on about April 1, 1698, and on about May 6 "the lesser prize was hauled into the careening island or key, the other prize not being arrived." Most testimonies seem to confirm these dates. Implicit in this is the inference that the *Adventure Galley* and the *Rupparell* (the lesser prize) both arrived about the same time at the beginning of April, but the *Queddah Merchant* (the other prize) had not made St. Marie until some five weeks later in May. The testimonies further relate that on about June 10 Culliford in the *Mocha* departed from St. Marie, after the *Rupparell* had been burned, leaving the *Adventure Galley* to sink in the harbour, Kidd and his remaining 13 crew taking up quarters aboard the *Queddah Merchant*. There was a good two months, therefore, for Kidd, Culliford, and the crews to carouse together, or fight and squabble with one another as the case may be, between Kidd's arrival and Culliford's departure. As stated in Chapter 6, sober argument suggests a pooling of resources, leading to the conclusion that much of Kidd's testimony can be considered a distortion, if not a web of lies. At the time Kidd made his testimony he knew he was in deep water, and though not yet charged with any specific crime, had good reason to be economical with the truth. He probably reasoned that his version of the events, not exactly truthful, might help him to wriggle out of the unpleasant predicament he had landed himself in.

The records indicate with some degree of certainty that Kidd remained at St. Marie until June 1698, and that his next appearance was in the West Indies in April 1699. This is a gap of 10 months, during which time he might have been anywhere, including Amboyna in the Dutch East Indies, according to that enigmatic personality Captain Charles Johnson.

It is a premise of this book that Kidd would not have lingered five months in Madagascar for the fickle monsoon to change. In fact there was great urgency on his part to take both himself and the *Queddah Merchant* as far away from St. Marie as fast as he could weigh anchor and put on sail. The *Queddah Merchant* was a prize laden with valuable merchandise, and any other pirate not so well disposed as Culliford would have found it easy picking. Kidd and the skeleton crew remaining loyal to him (if we believe the testimony) would have been very vulnerable on St. Marie with few weapons for their defence if they had indeed been deserted by Culliford. By mischance, they could have found themselves truly stranded in that tropical paradise with neither ship nor booty. It is, therefore, inconceivable that Kidd and his men would have spent an entire five months idling and frittering away their time, cavorting with native women, feuding with local chiefs, or carousing with other ne'er-do-wells that chanced their way. No! The *Queddah Merchant* had to get out to sea fast, and lose itself in the empty, lonely, but secure vastness of the Indian Ocean. Common sense suggests a voyage to Amboyna to rid themselves of some bulky but nevertheless valuable cargo. After all, a great deal of trade took place between India and the Dutch East Indies in cloth of all descriptions. What better place to go?

The transfer of the larger portion of Kidd's crew to Culliford's *Mocha*, together with cannon and small arms, is a highly suspicious act, one suggesting a joint enterprise between the two captains, especially as recent findings have proved the remains of the *Adventure Galley* to have been stripped bare. The enterprise that was in the offing was one which served the interests of both captains and crews. While Culliford, in his now well-armed and fully crewed *Mocha*, was free to roam the seas for further prey, Kidd could take his *Queddah Merchant* to a suitable rendezvous to await Culliford's arrival, hopefully with more booty, before sailing to Amboyna. For reasoning explained earlier, their rendezvous has been deduced as being in the Nicobar Islands, specifically at Car Nicobar.

We know that Culliford's *Mocha* took a French trader at Johanna on or about June 8, 1698, and that he later captured a rich Moorish merchantman, the *Great Mahomet,* off Surat on September 23.

It is highly likely that Kidd departed St. Marie in the *Queddah Merchant* either with Culliford or a short while later, as he was not in any hurry. With the southwest monsoon filling their sails, the two ships would have soon left the mountains of Madagascar far astern. Somewhere out in that barren, but secure, waste of water the two ships parted company, Kidd to sail eastwards to the Nicobars, Culliford to scour the trade routes.

Let us pause in this hypothesis to examine the daunting prospects Kidd faced if, in the 10 months that lay before him until he faced hostile inquisitors in New England, he could have sailed from Madagascar to the Nicobars, thence to Amboyna in the East Indies, before setting sail via the Cape of Good Hope to the West Indies. It is an immense circuitous voyage amounting to a total of some 18,000 to 19,000 sea miles. Could it have been done in those 10 months? Let us bear in mind, however, that when Kidd left

Madagascar in June 1698 he had little idea he was to end up in court in New England!

We know for a fact that Dampier in his tiny *Roebuck*, a cockleshell of only 96 feet long and 292 tons compared to Kidd's considerably larger *Queddah Merchant*, took exactly two months to sail from Batavia to the Cape. He took a further two months to cover the stretch from the Cape to Ascension Island, where his unfortunate vessel sprung one more leak, this time a final one. Only a few more weeks are necessary to extend such a voyage eastward to start at Amboyna, and westward to terminate in the West Indies. Five months, or six months at the very most, are all that would be required for Kidd to cover what would be the greatest leg of this monstrous roundabout voyage, one which stretched halfway around the globe, and which amounted to some 13,000 sea miles. But it was a voyage of constant sailing, one that only halted to take on water, fuel, and provisions.

We must also take into consideration in this comparison that the outward-bound voyage of the *Adventure Galley* from New York to Madagascar took five months, but their course took them further out into the Atlantic to avoid contrary winds and currents. The *Queddah Merchant*, though not a ship designed for speed, was a larger vessel and could press on more sail. On the open sea with favourable conditions, she was unlikely to be much slower than the *Adventure Galley*, but considerably faster than Dampier's dilapidated *Roebuck*.

We now have four or five months left out of the total postulated period for Kidd to travel from Madagascar to the Nicobars, wait for Culliford's arrival, and then sail to Amboyna through the Strait of Malacca. This is a mere 5,500 or so sea miles, but it would not have been continuous voyaging. There would have been an indeterminate period waiting for Culliford to show up at the rendezvous, and wrangling with the traders at Amboyna interested in purchasing stolen goods at knock-down prices. There might well have been attractions, or distractions, that caught the eye of his rambunctious crew along the way. Whichever way you look at it, the voyage, long and circuitous though it was, was perfectly feasible for Kidd, a skilled and proficient mariner and navigator. As we shall see, winds and currents would have favoured the *Queddah*

Merchant virtually throughout the duration of this voyage. Let us look more closely at the itinerary.

Whatever the particular circumstances of Kidd's departure from St. Marie, including the exact date, the winds were favourable. With the southwest monsoon behind him, a prevailing wind that would blow steadily for the next four months or so, handling his ponderous and relatively sluggish merchantman would have presented no difficulty. Even the currents would have favoured him if Kidd had any knowledge of Indian Ocean currents, and it must be supposed he did. North and south of the equator two bands of current stream steadily westwards, but between these two current streams there is a counter-current of equatorial water which flows east. This is of considerable benefit to the mariner intent on a rapid easterly passage if he is prepared to hug the equator and avail himself of this counterflow.

From the pirate base at St. Marie it is slightly in excess of 3,000 sea miles to the Nicobars. With favourable wind and current, and no need to engage with any enemy, a situation Kidd would have been keen to avoid at all cost, the overall sailing time would have been no more than four to six weeks to make his rendezvous. There would have been little urgency on this leg of his voyage anyway, as Culliford needed time to engage and take a suitable prize, and make the rendezvous with Kidd. We may safely assume that Kidd dropped anchor at the Nicobars sometime in late July or early August, after a leisurely and uneventful passage.

No sailor likes to lay off a lee shore where the prevailing wind can blow his vessel onto rocks if his anchor drags. It can be assured, therefore, that Kidd would have anchored in the security of what is now known as Sawi Bay, once he had identified Car Nicobar as the island where he was to meet up with Culliford. Though foul ground extends seawards from the extremities of the bay, Admiralty Sailing Directions for the island (quoted previously in Chapter 10) say this about Sawi Bay:

> Sawi Bay, on the northwestern side of the island,
> affords anchorage in a depth of 12 fathoms, over rock,

coral and a thin surface of sand, about three-quarters
of a mile northward of Sawi village, and in 7 fathoms
of water off Observation Point [a rocky headland
within the bay], where there is good landing for boats
at low water. A patch, with apparently a least depth of
5 1/2 fathoms, coral, over it, lies 6 cables [600 fathoms length] north-westward of Observation Point.

Kidd and mariners of his age did not have the benefit of
Admiralty Sailing Directions. They had, of course, to shift for
themselves. But an astute and shrewd sailor, as Kidd must have
been, would have had a keen eye to the dangers of any particular
anchorage. In this instance he is likely also to have had the benefit
of Culliford's knowledge and experience of the Nicobars.

Once the *Queddah Merchant* had attained the security of safe
anchorage there was time enough to spare. It can be expected that
the first priority for Kidd and his men was to replenish their water,
fuel, and food, garnering as much as they could from the island's
bounty, amongst which there was a great harvest of coconuts waiting to be reaped. Doubtless the opportunity was taken to explore
the island, which it is certain was virtually uninhabited at the time.
If there were a few native inhabitants, they would have shied away
from any contact with the strange white men, and would likely have
beaten a hasty retreat into the jungle undergrowth to view them
with primitive curiosity from a safe distance, especially if they had
had contact with white men before.

With the southwest monsoon holding steady, Sawi Bay is a secure
and safe place to anchor and lie close inshore, but under the influence
of the northeast monsoon such security vanishes. For good reason,
the fourth Kidd-Palmer chart denotes ominous wrecks at the extremities of the bay, where today beacons are positioned to enlighten
approaching mariners about the dangerous shoals in the vicinity. At
the change of the monsoon, Kémios Bay, on the south shore, is the
preferred anchorage where landing is good, despite a strong offshore
tidal current of about three knots. At the time of Kidd's visit to the
island it cannot be expected that he did much except hug his seclud-

ed anchorage while he waited for Culliford to appear. With only 13 men, it is unlikely that he would have ventured very far, apart from maybe cruising round the island, which he probably did anyway before he entered the secure haven of Sawi Bay there to bide his time. If there was anything on the minds of Kidd and his men, after they had satisfied their immediate needs, it was what to do with the booty they had on board in the form of gold, coin, and jewels.

Though the Kidd-Palmer charts have been studied in great detail, with probably as many different interpretations as people who have studied them (see chapters 9 and 10), one cannot be at all certain that the indications upon any of the charts reflect the actual location where Kidd buried his treasure. But bury it he must have done, or he would have been stupidly tempting fate by sailing through the Strait of Malacca on the next leg of his voyage, whether or not he was accompanied by Culliford.

Where in the vicinity of Sawi Bay would a commonsense man like Kidd bury booty with a view to its subsequent recovery? He would want a fairly obvious landmark, one that was clearly visible from an anchorage in the bay. Immediately to the southeast there is a ridge which juts out from the higher ground constituting the interior of the island. This ridge attains a height of 100 feet above sea level and has slopes of between 6 and 10 degrees to east and west respectively. Even against a heavily forested jungle backdrop, the profile of such a ridge would be prominent. The first knoll of high ground on this ridge is about 515 yards southeast of the nearby beach at the present native village of Passa. The reader will recognize the similarity of this distance with the directions on the third of the Kidd-Palmer charts. Did Kidd and his men bury their treasure at such a spot? No one is likely ever to know, but this is the spot the author would have chosen if he had been in Kidd's shoes, or rather seaboots, at the time. Whether a suitable cave might have existed on the slopes of this ridge is debatable, but since rock conditions on Car Nicobar consist of limestone, shale, and sandstone, with an overlay of coral, the existence of such a cave is highly possible.

What was in the treasure that Kidd and his men buried or concealed? Everyone has an image of pirate treasure, and it does not require a great deal of imagination to conjure up chests brimful of gold coins and jewels. And it must be supposed that at this relatively late period of over two years into his voyage, some material benefits had accrued. We learned in Chapter 6 that the cargo of the *Queddah Merchant* consisted of 1,200 bales of muslin, silk, and calico, with 1,400 bags of brown sugar, 84 bales of raw silk (it is not clear whether these were additional to those already listed), and 80 chests of opium, with iron and saltpetre. Kidd would not have buried any of these — they were bulky, tradeable commodities, commodities that could be exchanged for cash, and especially gold, whether in coin, dust, or bullion. Therefore he would have buried what everyone desires — gold, silver, and jewels that he currently had no need for, at least in the interim, and which were of considerably greater utility back home in North America. The records tell us that after he took the *Queddah Merchant* he sailed for Cochin, where he sold silk and opium to the value of £20,000 and received gold bars and dust in exchange. It can be safely assumed, therefore, that at the time Kidd and his men buried their treasure, the *Queddah Merchant* held a small ransom in such convertibles as bullion, gold dust, coin, and jewels. Kidd boasted of having lodged on that "island in the Indies," which he took pains not to name, treasure up to the value of £100,000. What he received for the silk and opium he traded at Cochin is 20 percent of this figure alone. Other "receivables" could have doubled or trebled this amount, even if Culliford did not make the rendezvous with even more booty. There is, therefore, some basis for Kidd's boastful claim.

When would Culliford have arrived at the rendezvous in his *Mocha?* We know that on September 23 he assisted Dirk Chivers in the taking of a major prize, the *Great Mahomet*, off Surat, and the value of the treasure taken from this trading vessel was reported as £130,000. Culliford and his crew, enhanced by the inclusion of some of Kidd's best fighting men, would have had a goodly share of these spoils when shared out in the best of pirate traditions. After the taking of the *Great Mahomet*, it would only have been a short voyage of two to three weeks to make the rendezvous with Kidd. With much booty on board the *Mocha*, Culliford would not have loitered upon the high seas putting himself at risk of being captured, either by other pirates or fleets sent out against him by an irate Mogul, or an equally irate East India Company. Thus the next encounter between Culliford and Kidd is likely to have been about the middle of October. Great would have been the encounter of pirate crews accompanied by much rejoicing and drunken revelling! We do not know whether Culliford himself buried any treasure on the island, or whether he had any knowledge that Kidd had done so. There is some degree of honesty among thieves, a degree that often astounds those holding public office today. Culliford, undoubtedly, was not a stupid individual, and if he didn't know or suspect it at the time he certainly learned it later when he and Kidd were on trial for their lives.

By the end of October the two vessels would have been set to continue their projected voyage to Amboyna to get rid of some of the cumbersome, but valuable, cargo that lay in the holds of the *Queddah Merchant*. On this leg of what was to be Kidd's furthest sailing east, the two vessels were to run the gauntlet of the Strait of Malacca, a stretch of ocean well known to Culliford. Some comment has been made already in Chapter 3 concerning the depredations of the native pirates that frequented this stretch of water, so suited for their evil and ugly purpose.

The Strait of Malacca is approximately 400 miles long, and narrows towards the southern entrance, where it diminishes in width to a mere 30 miles or so. The west side of the strait is typified by low-lying land infested with backwater swamps and creeks so favoured by the native Sumatran pirates, whereas to the east is the range of hills that flanks the length of the Malayan peninsula. At the southern end of the strait, in close proximity to modern-day Singapore, there are numerous islands, which from time immemorial have hosted their own piratical brethren. Here the channel available to the mariner becomes diverse and complicated with numerous shoals, which, if the wind changes or drops off suddenly, can lead to running aground. Many ships, both past and present, have had due cause to regret this stretch of water. The omnipresent pirates only gave cause for more caution on the part of the captains of vessels familiar with that part of the world. Neither wind nor current would have been of any particular benefit to Kidd in the dangerous waters of the strait. Though the prevailing wind would have been a following one, it would have been very changeable due to the land masses on either side, the wind being generally onshore during the day and offshore at night. The current running as it does from south to north would have retarded his progress, and passage through the strait is likely to have occupied several days. But once safely through into open sea, there would have been a strong wind from the north and he would have been blessed with the current that flows down from Indo-China. Whatever tedium, hard work, and vigilance had been imposed on his crew in working their way through the strait would have been rewarded by the time they were abreast of Borneo on their port side, and their passage relatively straightforward thereafter.

From the Nicobars to Amboyna is a distance of some 2,500 nautical miles, a distance which can be expected to have been covered in about four to five weeks. Thus, during the latter part of November, Kidd and Culliford would have reached their destination, the Dutch factory, hopefully to reap the financial reward of their joint enterprise. Amboyna had been a contentious issue between the Dutch and English East India Companies for many years. As described in Chapter 2, the Dutch had massacred the English outpost in 1623 and there was little love lost between the two organizations, despite the fact that the Dutch King William III now sat upon the throne of England.

Amboyna is a small island, with an area of almost 400 square miles, located off the southwestern tip of Ceram, a significantly larger island of the Moluccas. It is fairly mountainous, with its highest peak reaching 3,405 feet. At the time of Kidd's visit, Amboyna was a jealously guarded stronghold of the Dutch East India Company, being the centre of clove production, and all foreign vessels in the area were viewed with considerable suspicion. It was not until 1770 that the French broke the virtual stranglehold the Dutch had on the clove trade by stealing plants from Ceram and transporting them to Cayenne. Apart from the clove Amboyna supported other cash crops, such as sago, coconut, and a variety of tropical fruits.

Dampier, in his *Roebuck*, passed close to Amboyna in April 1700, but did not enter the port. His earlier experiences of Dutch hospitality in those waters was not likely conducive to such a visit. Earlier that same voyage, in the vicinity of Timor, he had encountered a Dutch sloop, and the master of the *Roebuck* records the following in the ship's log:

> Our captain [Dampier] hastened our boat to go on board her with my mate Mr Knight … when our boat came nigh them they stood on their guard and commanded our boat aboard. They had on board four small guns and sixteen hands with small arms, amongst whom was the Governor and his son. After the mate had discoursed [with] them they said they had very good water at the factory, but did not care we should come near them by the reason sometime since there was here a pirate which watered and being civilly used … fell foul of the natives and abused them grossly, which I believe is very false, only a false apology.

On another occasion when the *Roebuck* was in need of water, they could only get it from a Dutch ship by payment of cash in advance, and then only under the watchful eye of guns trained upon them. It is not surprising that when he could, Dampier sought out his own water and so refrained from entering Amboyna, even though it was one of the largest centres of trade in the region. But then, unlike Kidd, Dampier was not on a trading mission.

Some months later Dampier was to have another taste of Dutch hospitality when he was forced into Batavia to effect repairs to his now very leaky and increasingly unseaworthy ship. For three months he was stuck in the roads and the general dislike of the Dutch to their English rivals manifested itself in countless delays. Not only did the Dutch insist that all major repairs be carried out by their own tradespeople, but the work was slow, expensive, and shoddy. No doubt the Dutch hoped that the sooner their rivals' ships sank the better, leaving them undisputed masters of the region.

Kidd, when he sailed into Amboyna, is likely to have been met with as much suspicion as any other trader, though it cannot be expected that the sight of the strange merchantman in the harbour would have evoked much surprise, since Indian trading vessels visited Amboyna on a regular basis. There, however, a bombshell was awaiting the unsuspecting Kidd; he learned (according to Captain Charles Johnson) that a warrant was out for his apprehension. Though the British had issued a general pardon to pirates who voluntarily gave themselves up to authority, Kidd and another pirate named Avery were specifically excluded from such an amnesty. The Dutch, with whom he wished to trade some of his purloined goods, must be expected to have gleefully capitalized on this tasty tidbit of information, much to their financial satisfaction.

How much of the merchandise within the holds of the *Queddah Merchant* did Kidd manage to get rid of at Amboyna? A statement of the goods carried on board the ship when it was captured gives the quantity of muslin, silk, and calico as amounting to 1,200 bales, a weight of about 300 tons depending on which trading standard is adopted (an Indian bale being between 500 and 600 pounds weight, others being either more or less). When Kidd was finally apprehended, only 190 bales could be accounted for. Thus, allowing for the fact that Kidd must have managed to cash in some of his goods along the way, for we know that he sold silk and opium at Cochin shortly after he captured the *Queddah Merchant*, and rid himself of more on arrival in the West Indies, there is still a significant quantity of goods, in the form of "stuffs" of one sort or another, for which there is no account. He must have managed to relieve himself of at least 700 to 800 bales at Amboyna, and probably some of the other commodities he possessed. What did he receive in return? We don't know, but certainly it would have been in a more easily portable form than the bales he sold.

Kidd was now in a quandary. What was he to do next? He could return to the Nicobars, recover his treasure and sail away to seek further fortune as a pirate; he could recover the treasure and give himself up to the authorities and plead clemency, and in the process run the risk of losing both booty and his neck; he could render himself up to the authorities without the treasure, thereby gambling upon the lure of the cached treasure to save his neck, and possibly the necks of some of his crew; possibly the goods and treasure he would carry back to North America direct from Amboyna would "buy off" authority and he would be free to return to recover the treasure cached in the Nicobars. No doubt the issue, and the various alternatives that presented themselves, were vigorously debated by all in a most laudable and thoroughly democratic manner. His crew, and possibly that of Culliford, would have had some share of the booty cached in the Nicobars, but Kidd would have been able to buy out any shares belonging to his men from the proceeds he received from his own share of the merchandise offloaded at Amboyna, which is likely to have been considerable. It is more than likely that the younger, more adventurous members of his crew would have opted to stay in the Indian Ocean, either to serve with Culliford, or to seek berths on other pirate vessels, such as that of Shivers, who may well have tagged along. The older members of the crew, more anxious to return to families ashore, or sick of a wandering life afloat, would probably have voted for a return to North America, which offered the prospect of a quick disappearance into the vastness of the continent. There, numerous communities existed that were not too particular about observing the niceties of English law, and where gold of any hue was made welcome, with no questions asked.

Having cast their lots, there must have been a general shuffling about of crews, and it may be expected that many of Kidd's crew of Dutch origin preferred to remain in the Dutch East Indies, rather than return to an uncertain fate handed out by British justice. Some of Culliford's men might have opted to go aboard the *Queddah Merchant*. Kidd's strategy, rather foolish perhaps but perfectly understandable, must have been to leave his treasure where he had cached it. This was a card up his sleeve. Not taking the treasure with him back to America, he doubtless felt that he could bargain with the authorities when confronted by that particular hurdle, under the impression that his friends in high places would come to his rescue and help save his skin, if only at a price. Without the knowledge of the whereabouts of his treasure, which amounted to a veritable fortune, they could not lay their fingers upon it. Or could they? Kidd must have felt very confident that he could wriggle out of the predicament in which he found himself. After all, he had French passes in his possession, which proved beyond any doubt that he had taken only French vessels, and Britain had been at war with France at the time. He had no knowledge, or any understanding, of the murky political games that were played by men of high position intent on safeguarding their own skins, their own interests, and their own fortunes.

It is a long way from Amboyna to North America, half a world away in fact, a voyage of some 13,000 sea miles. Water, fuel, and provisions would be needed at intervals. From where would these be obtained? Obviously Kidd would not feel inclined to tempt providence by an early arrest, so he would have avoided the Cape of Good Hope and islands such as St. Helena, which were regular ports of call for British naval vessels and ships belonging to the East India Company. It can be expected that the captains of all such vessels would have been warned to keep a careful lookout for that new curse on the high seas — Captain William Kidd! Madagascar would have provided a suitable first stop along the way, as later would Ascension Island, or any of the Cape Verde Islands, already well known to Kidd. It is possible that Culliford would have accompanied Kidd to Madagascar on this return voyage, giving time for further sober reflection on the part of themselves and their crews before they separated one from the other, until they were to meet again in London two years later — this time in jail.

Relieved of a great deal of weighty and bulky cargo, the *Queddah Merchant* would have drawn less water than before, and with the steady southeast trades blowing, and under the influence of the south equatorial current, passage from the Dutch East Indies back across the Indian Ocean to Madagascar would have proved a rapid transit. It took two months for Dampier to make the Cape from Batavia in his leaky *Roebuck*. The *Queddah Merchant* would have made Madagascar in a much shorter length of time. Thus Kidd could have returned to the old familiar pirate haunt after an absence of five months or so, the same period he later testified he spent waiting on the island for the change of the monsoon. In that period he would have voyaged approximately 10,000 sea miles, not an impossibility with good winds to carry him over those boundless limits of ocean. However, it would appear that Kidd did not select the old pirate base at St. Marie as a staging point on his return to North America. Instead he opted to revictual and take on fresh water at Fort Dauphin, a settlement at the southeast tip of Madagascar. We know that Culliford returned to St. Marie on December 12 in the company of Chivers in his *Soldadoes*. On board Culliford's ship was Abel Owen, previously cook aboard the *Adventure Galley*, and he returned with Kidd on the *Queddah Merchant* from Fort Dauphin. How did he get from St. Marie to Fort Dauphin to connect with Kidd? Apparently Giles Shelley was at St. Marie in his ship the *Nassau*, and although he was to deny ever meeting Kidd at Madagascar when put on oath at Kidd's trial, there is a limit to credulity. One simply cannot accept Shelley's statement. What is more believable is that Owen transferred from Shelley's *Nassau* to Kidd's *Queddah Merchant*, either at Fort Dauphin or later, if, as is probable, Shelley accompanied Kidd around the Cape and up the Atlantic. This evidence suggests that Kidd did not depart from Madagascar until the middle of December, a month later than he testified. We have a period of four months for him to make landfall in the West Indies, a perfectly feasible accomplishment.

Kidd must have thought long and hard about his future prospects. After Madagascar there was scarcely any opportunity to turn back, unless to remain a pirate and a wanted man. With a wife and children in New York, and his own overwhelming belief that he had not actually committed any really reprehensible act of piracy with which he could be connected, he made what for him would be a fatal decision. Doubtless he was under the impression that his friends in high places would look after the best interests of all of them. When all was said and done, he had the French passes taken from the French vessels he had captured, and if they weren't actually Frenchmen then they shouldn't have been flying French flags! Who can blame Kidd for his misplaced confidence? What he didn't know was that his former Whig friends who held high office, and in whom he trusted, were under attack by a virulent Tory opposition in the British House of Commons, and that those Tories smelt blood! Kidd's friends were to prove of little support in the end — they were to bend like feeble reeds under the political whirlwind.

Once the *Queddah Merchant* had safely rounded the Cape, beating her way westwards against the blustery winds and keeping her hull well down over the horizon, the Benguela Current would have steadily swept them north into the Atlantic. With the constant southeast trades astern, there would have been little hindrance to their northward flight. Contrary to the outward-bound voyage in the *Adventure Galley*, where they were more often closer to the Brazilian coast than to any African shore, the northerly passage of the *Queddah Merchant* would most likely have taken Kidd close to St. Helena, Ascension Island, and the islands in the Cape Verde group. Certainly Kidd would not have replenished at St. Helena; in fact he would have avoided it at all costs. For the same reason he would have avoided the Cape, but he would have to have watered somewhere in that wasteland of ocean. The likelihood is that it was at Ascension Island.

Ascension Island, a mere speck in the Atlantic, lies midway between the continents, the result of geologic volcanic activity. The jagged black cliffs are stiff with guano and the island's beaches are pristine. There on the beaches giant turtles lay their eggs, swimming the 1,500 miles from the Brazilian shore in some annual fertility rite that has gone on since before mankind set foot on earth. These turtles often attain lengths of over six feet, and weigh over 1,000 pounds. Since sailors first discovered the island, the breeding season was viewed as an opportunity to vary shipboard fare. And the breeding season begins in December! It can be surmised, therefore, that Kidd and his men would have been unable to resist feasting on such a delicacy. A sparkling sandy beach, the gaunt cliffs, the scream of gulls, all dominated by the sombre peak of the old volcano, would have left a memorable impression on all those participants at that pirate banquet.

There is a peculiarity of life about present day Ascension Island which is worth mentioning. The island boasts no permanent resident population, the 200 or so inhabitants being transients employed by the British Government, or various cable and wireless companies. Every now and then a birth takes place, but due to some strange bureaucratic reasoning, all such births are registered under the London Borough of Wapping, the same place where Kidd and so many other pirates of his age were summarily dispatched by the hangman's noose!

Off the bulge of Africa, the Benguela Current sweeps westwards and is known as the South Equatorial Current. As in the Indian Ocean, there are two streams of westward-flowing water with a narrow band of eastward flowing counter-current between. Kidd, the experienced navigator that he was, and familiar with Atlantic currents, and with easterly winds in his favour, would soon have struck that more northerly flow, a current that would have brought him rapidly into the Antilles, a chain of islands he had frequented in the past. His testimony taken in Boston some months later states that he arrived at the island of Anguilla at the beginning of April, approximately five months after his stated departure from St. Marie.

Anguilla is a small island, no more than 20 miles long, located at the northern extremity of the Leeward Island chain. Kidd claims that he "sent his boat on shore where his men heard the news that he [Kidd] and his people [crew] were proclaimed pirates which put them into such a consternation that they sought all opportunity to run the ship on shore upon some reefs or shoal fearing he would carry them into some English port."

We will discuss in the next chapter aspects of various testimonies, made presumably when Kidd and his crew were under oath. The above extract describes his landfall in the West Indies, and it is easy to imagine that he was at pains to colour his words to his own best advantage. Kidd and his crew knew full well they had been declared pirates long before they got anywhere near Anguilla, but Kidd is trying to convey the impression that his men were scared he would turn them in, thereby suggesting to his interrogators that he wasn't such a bad chap after all!

The *Queddah Merchant* stayed no more than a few hours at Anguilla, sufficient time for Kidd to revictual the ship, and for the unwelcome news first heard the other side of the world to be reaffirmed. By now a sense of unease prevailed among the crew, and Kidd might well be questioning his own decision to bring the ship back. During the voyage from Madagascar, Kidd would have had ample time to dwell on his predicament. His brother-in-law, Samuel Bradley, urged him to set sail for Jamaica and give himself up to the authorities there. Kidd might have listened to his relative, who had sailed with him throughout his many voyages even before he first beheld the *Adventure Galley*, but he did not follow his words of advice. Instead he set sail for the Danish held island of St. Thomas, and thereafter began a game of hide and seek with the British over the following few months as he slowly progressed northward up the east coast of North America.

The story of Kidd's return to North America has been told many times, with considerable dramatic and literary licence. It has formed the basis of many books, films, and television documentaries. Romantic tales have been spun of secret visits at dead of night to creeks and backwaters, there to land men and booty ashore, the men to vanish into the hinterland as if they had never been, with their share of the plunder won through their daring in the Indies. The truth of many of these tales can never be affirmed. Some of Kidd's men stayed with him to the bitter end, an end which was to take them to London, prison, and a brush with the hangman's noose. The majority escaped that fate.

The best factual account of what happened to Kidd and his crew after their landing at Anguilla is probably that by Robert Ritchie in his book *Captain Kidd and the War Against the Pirates*. The author sees no point in repeating these acknowledged facts, but for the sake of completeness feels compelled to summarize the final episode of Kidd's fatal voyage. The basis of this summary is the account rendered by Ritchie, and the reader is encouraged to make reference to *Captain Kidd and the War Against the Pirates* for fuller information.

At the urging of the East India Company, the British Government had despatched notices to all the territories under their jurisdiction, or wherever they had some representation, to the effect that Kidd was "wanted." This order for his arrest had now been in effect for over a year. Kidd was truly on the run. Where could he seek refuge? His immediate move was to sail west to the small island of St. Thomas, now part of the U.S. Virgin Islands, doubtless, in his opinion, more neutral territory than Jamaica, as advocated by Bradley. There he attempted to bargain with the Danish governor for protection, presumably with the offer of a substantial bribe in mind, with the object of initiating some communication with Lord Bellomont, now firmly established in his post as governor of New York. It was a good ploy, but the governor of the island was not prepared to become inveigled into British politics. He refused point blank to permit Kidd and the *Queddah Merchant* to remain within his jurisdiction. Kidd was forced to move on. However, he managed to land five of his men on a secluded beach, one being his brother-in-law, who was very sick, and had been so for most of the voyaging in the Indian Ocean. Kidd then steered further west, following the southern coastline of Puerto Rico, until he struck the Mona Passage that separates Puerto Rico from Hispaniola. There on the small island of Mona, unclaimed by any of the European nations, a certain amount of security was afforded to Kidd and his *Queddah Merchant*, but they would not be able to stay there long. The unusual outline and rigging of the merchantman would soon attract a great deal of interest, and some of that interest could prove hostile.

On his way to Mona, Kidd chanced upon a sloop belonging to Henry Bolton, a trader from Antigua. Bolton had a somewhat unsavoury reputation, but he had on board a cargo of hogs, some of which he was quite ready to sell to Kidd. Bolton was also prepared to go further. At Kidd's request, he would sail to Curaçao with some of the bales of muslin and calico that remained on board the *Queddah Merchant* and, amongst other things, buy Kidd a small ship with the proceeds. It is obvious that at this time Kidd had plans of mooring the *Queddah Merchant* safely out of sight somewhere and sailing off to New York, in an attempt to make peace with Lord Bellomont, and more likely offer a goodly bribe! He had no intention of abandoning the *Queddah Merchant*, his stated intention being to return in August.

While he was moored at Mona, a couple of other traders appeared in sloops, one Dutch, the other French, and a few more bales of cloth changed hands. However, the anchors dragged during a storm, and after they had managed to regain control of the *Queddah Merchant*, Kidd decided to seek the security of a safer anchorage in the vicinity. They entered the Bay of Savona at the eastern extremity of Hispaniola, sailed a short distance up the Higuey River and tied up to the river bank. It was here that Bolton found Kidd on his return from Curaçao, where, true to his word, he had purchased a small sloop for Kidd, the *Saint Antonio*. Other traders appeared and Kidd was engaged in ridding himself of more of his merchandise, making the most of this undoubtedly welcome opportunity.

In his later testimony, Kidd claimed that the total amount of trade he conducted in Hispaniola amounted to 11,200 pieces-of-eight. He received the sloop *Saint Antonio*, valued at 3,000 pieces-of-eight, 4,200 pieces-of-eight in bills of exchange drawn upon merchants in Curaçao, and 4,000 pieces-of-eight in gold dust and gold bar. The truth in reality may be far different. Whatever the actual extent of his trade, he had now got himself a vessel which he could sail to New York in his attempt to bargain with the man who was to become his nemesis, Lord Bellomont. Shifting some of his goods onto the *Saint Antonio*, Kidd prepared to journey on leaving the *Queddah Merchant* under the watchful eyes of Bolton, some of his newfound friends, and those members of the crew that decided to stay with the ship.

The records suggest that Bolton, being the unscrupulous man that he was, had little intention of staying on as watchman of the *Queddah Merchant*. The vessel was soon stripped bare of its remaining cargo, the men disappeared into the blue of the Caribbean, and subsequently the ship was burned. The *Queddah Merchant*, a vessel that had played a not insignificant role in the annals of piracy, had found its resting place in the mud of an estuary thousands of miles from home. A sad end to a sad ship! Bolton was later found, arrested, and sent to England for trial and punishment.

In the meantime Kidd, in the *Saint Antonio*, set course for Florida and hopped his way up the coast. Rumours began to fly about, now that he was known to be in the region, and rife was the speculation of the size of the wealth he had on board his small vessel. Some went as far as to claim, with no justification whatsoever, that he carried with him up to half a million pounds sterling! One can imagine that the estimates of this portable wealth grew even greater as time progressed, and popular rumour overcame common sense. By the time Kidd reached Long Island, the coast was ablaze with passions and emotions of one sort or another, because Bellomont for some time now had taken a great personal interest in stamping out piracy, and had been very vocal and obvious about it. Intent on establishing a squeaky-clean image for himself, he had unleashed the entire arsenal at his command, in the form of officers of one sort or another, to hunt down these predators of the sea, as he saw them. Kidd could not have arrived at a worse time to try to make his peace with Bellomont and talk reason into him. Even bribes were not going to work!

It has been suggested that Kidd first landed at Oyster Bay, Long Island, where he was greeted by his wife, children, and staunch friends, but there is also evidence that he took the precaution of landing at other places around the island for the purpose of smuggling ashore some of the goods he had brought with him in the *Saint Antonio*. Gardiners Island, off the east tip of Long Island, features strongly in these accounts. From these accounts, as well as Kidd's own statement to the fact that he buried some of this treasure, has emerged countless speculation and rumour of where this treasure might lie buried. Long Island and its immediate environment has seen a great number of hopeful treasure-seekers as a result.

When Kidd arrived in New York in early June, Bellomont happened to be in Boston. Kidd's friend, James Emott, a true and trusty one (for a change), offered to travel to Boston on Kidd's behalf and make overtures to his lordship. This he did on June 13. His reception by Bellomont was distinctly icy. Bellomont cunningly avoided mentioning the most important fact that Kidd was specifically exempted by name from any consideration of a pardon, a fact that does not seem to have been very well broadcast by the British authorities. Furthermore, Bellomont had not heard of the loss of the *Adventure*

Galley, but knowing the *Queddah Merchant* was in the general vicinity, he was anxious to determine its whereabouts, especially when he was told that goods to the value of more than £3,000 still lay aboard. For the rest of the month, a game of cat and mouse went on between the various parties with poor James Emott, being the emissary for Kidd, shuttling back and forth between Boston and New York. To prove beyond any doubt that he was not a pirate, and that he had only attacked and taken French vessels, Kidd agreed to render up the passes he had in his possession to Bellomont, the same passes he had taken from the French vessels captured in the Indian Ocean. This was to prove a fatal mistake, and the cause of his undoing.

In conference with his own council, Bellomont invited Kidd to Boston, assuring Kidd on his word and honour that he had no doubt that Kidd would be granted the king's pardon, and that in Boston arrangements could be made to bring the *Queddah Merchant* safely to New England. Little did either Kidd or Bellomont know that by this time the *Queddah Merchant* lay a burnt-out hulk resting upon the mud that was to entomb her. As a small token of his appreciation Kidd sent some gifts, one of which was an enamelled box with some jewels in it which was intended for Lady Bellomont. A further gift was to follow, this time a small gold bar. In fact Kidd was generous to many people after he arrived back in New England — with some of the loot he had brought back!

Private meetings were conducted by the two men, and various promises were made, the true substance of which we will never know. Bellomont was keen to maintain his squeaky-clean image, make a strong stand against piracy, and show the public at home in England that he was a man of integrity and honour. But he was just as keen to put money into his own pockets, if he could do so without fear of compromising his position as governor. Too many governors in the past had had sticky fingers and itchy palms, but Bellomont was intent on being different from his predecessors. The outcome was that Kidd was called before Bellomont's council on Monday, July 3, 1699, and this is the date of the first of the various testimonies that Kidd made before they hanged him at Execution Dock 21 months later. Three days after that first meeting he was seized and thrust into jail.

In February 1700, HMS *Advice* arrived in Boston, and the prisoner Kidd and 30 or so other prisoners found themselves incarcerated below decks. It was an uncomfortable crossing with storms and heavy weather, but the *Advice* eventually made the safety of The Downs in early April. A list of Admiralty prisoners discloses that Kidd was transferred to the security of Newgate immediately, and that 14 of his crew were removed to the Marshalsea, the usual place of confinement for Admiralty prisoners awaiting trial. Of these 14 men, 6 had signed articles drawn up in New York on September 10, 1696 before the *Adventure Galley* set out on its historic voyage.

The trial of Kidd was a shabby affair; in fact it was little better than the vigilante justice so often meted out in the era when gun-slinging hoodlums ran the Wild West of America. It serves no purpose for us to retell here this sordid trial, except to declare it was a travesty of justice held in the name of that lady who, blindfolded, carries in her hand the scales of life and liberty!

Chapter 14

Testimonies and Letters

> *Sometimes truth is so precious,*
> *it must be attended by a body guard of lies.*
> — Winston Churchill (1943)

It is timely to take a look at selected passages from Kidd's testimonies. The various testimonies he made will not be reproduced in their entirety, as space forbids that. But it is of value to scrutinize some of his statements, with an eye to discerning the various discrepancies in the statements he made, not so much to imply some moral censure by sitting in judgement on a man from the comfort of one's own fireside, but to place ourselves in the same predicament in which he found himself — that is, on trial for our lives! Would we have testified any differently? The original depositions to which we have access are in the hand of Isaiah Addington, secretary to the Vice-Admiralty Court at Boston, Massachusetts. Addington's writing is difficult to decipher accurately, but the gist of the text is intelligible.

The first examination of Kidd took place at six o'clock in the evening on Monday, July 3, 1699, at Lord Bellomont's house, when Kidd was requested to "give an account of his proceedings in his late voyage to Madagascar and parts adjacent and other places." Kidd responded by stating that his journal had been destroyed by his crew, but he would prepare an alternative record if granted the time. He was then asked to give details of the lading of his hoys presently in port, and the lading left on board the *Queddah Merchant*, which was still at Hispaniola. The council examining Kidd appear to have given greater immediate concern to the value of the goods Kidd still had in his possession, or that could be easily recovered, than any other consideration regarding the piratical actions for which he had been arrested! Kidd supplied the following details:

(a) In port:
Forty bales of calico, silk and muslin, both striped and plain.
Five or six tons of refined sugar in bags.
About forty pounds (weight) in gold, both in dust and bar.
About eighty pounds (weight) in bar silver.

All these were stated to have been purchased at Madagascar from the powder, small arms, and other furniture originally belonging to the *Adventure Galley*.

(b) On board the *Queddah Merchant*:
About one hundred and fifty bales of stuffs.
Seventy or eighty tons of sugar.
About ten tons of iron in short parcels
About fourteen or fifteen anchors.
Forty tons of saltpetre.
About twenty guns in the hold.
Thirty guns mounted, lately belonging to the *Adventure Galley*.

As has been pointed out earlier, there is a huge discrepancy between the number of bales of calico, silk, and muslin captured with the *Queddah Merchant* when compared with the sum of bales admitted by Kidd to be in his possession at the time of his formal examination by the Court. The council were unaware of this fact, as the cargo manifest for the *Queddah Merchant* at the time of its capture only became fully known two years after Kidd had been tried, sentenced, and executed. The discrepancy amounted to about 1,000 bales, and William Bolton, trader from Antigua, and his unscrupulous friends could not have relieved Kidd of this fantastic amount in the short time he lay at Mona and Hispaniola. This is even allowing for the fact that Kidd had managed to get rid of some cargo at Cochin after he captured his prize.

Kidd's written narrative of his voyage, prepared shortly after this first interview with the council, gives some very full details of his outward-bound journey, and this has already been covered. Kidd carefully avoids making any statement to the effect that he was in the Red Sea, whether or not he was intent on committing piracy, merely stating that after careening the *Adventure Galley* in the Comoros Islands, he set sail for the coast of India on April 25, 1697, and "came upon the coast of Malabar at the beginning of September." That is a period of four months, a fair length of time to get into some mischief, but the council in their subsequent examinations of Kidd do not seem to have queried how this time was spent. Kidd then describes in some detail how the *Adventure Galley* had a brush with two Portuguese men-o'-war, and then chanced upon the *Loyal Captain*, which carried an English pass, and which he (naturally) did not attempt to restrain. Kidd enlarged upon this incident by stressing that his crew learned there were some rich Greeks and Armenians on board in possession of valuable goods, and would have taken the vessel if he (Kidd) had not kept them under restraint.

Kidd then comes to the time when they took the *Rupparell*, and writes this:

> … that about the 18th or 19th day of the said month of November met up with a Moors ship of about 200 tuns coming from Surat bound for the Coast of Mallabar loaded with two horses, sugar and cotton to trade, there having about 40 Moors on board with a Dutch pylot, boatswain and gunner, which ship [he] hailed and commanded on board, and with him came 8 or 9 Moors and these three Dutchmen, who declared it was a Moors ship, and demanding their passes from Surat, which they showed, and the same was a French pass which he believed was showed by

a mistake for their pylot said … she was a prize, and
staid on board the Gally and would not return again
on board the Moors ship but went with the Gally to
the port of St. Marie.

Depositions taken from five of Kidd's crew at the same time support this version of events given by Kidd. The men were Abel Owen
(mariner of full age and cook), Samuel Arry (mariner and late steward), English Smith, Humphrey Clay, and Hugh Parrott (all mariners
of full age). The only other information that can be gathered is that
the five men attested that the lading of the *Rupparell* consisted of
linens, perfumes, silks, and other dry goods, with some horses, and
that the three Dutchmen afterwards took up arms on board the
Adventure Galley. The five men say nothing about the burning of the
Rupparell at St. Marie. They say that of the two vessels (the
Adventure Galley and the *Rupparell*) one of them sank, although they
do not say which one, and that the deserters attempted to sink the
other. Only Kidd mentions the burning of the *Rupparell* after it had
been hauled into the careening yard. There is some difference of opinion, therefore, as to what actually transpired. Furthermore, although
the five men all returned with Kidd on the *Queddah Merchant*, it
appears that Abel Owen, whose joint deposition with Samuel Arry is
the longest (bar that of Kidd), was one of those who fought with
Culliford on the *Mocha*. He returned to St. Marie after the capture of
the *Great Mahomet*, when Culliford returned to the pirate base on
December 12, 1698. How did Owen, and others like him, rejoin Kidd
on the *Queddah Merchant*? Kidd says he sailed from St. Marie in
November, at least three to four weeks earlier. Other depositions indicate that Giles Shelley, in his ship the *Nassau*, was in St. Marie at the
time of Culliford's return and that Owen, amongst others, took passage on the *Nassau* to Fort Dauphin on the southeast tip of
Madagascar. We cannot surmise whether they rejoined the *Queddah
Merchant* there, or somewhere else. The conclusion is that Owen and
the others were not at St. Marie when the *Rupparell* was burned, as
Kidd claimed. They had joined Culliford's crew, so they would not
necessarily have known of the true fate of the *Rupparell* if the *Mocha*

had sailed out of St. Marie ahead of Kidd. The burning of a ship, even one that sank in the process, would surely have made a visual impression more worthy of retelling!

Kidd claimed in his testimony that those men who had deserted him at St. Marie took his journal, the logbook of the *Adventure Galley*, when they plundered his belongings. His words are:

> … their wickedness was so great after they had plundered and ransacked sufficiently went four miles off to one Edward Welche's house where his the Narrator's chest was lodged, and broke it open and took out of it money, gold, forty pounds of plate, 370 pieces-of-eight, my journal and a great number of papers that belonged to me and the people of New Yorke that fitted us out.

Either the information in this testimony is true or it is false, there is no middle ground. If it is true, it was a very fortunate incident, as without the logbook, the whereabouts of the *Adventure Galley* during her wanderings in the Indian Ocean would never be known with any certainty, and Kidd's piratical actions would be duly masked. If it is false, then what really happened to the journal of the *Adventure Galley*? Was it destroyed? And if so, by whom? Was it returned to North America? These questions on their own are not terribly important, but they lead on to the immeasurably greater question, and one that is of vital importance — what happened to the logbook of the *Queddah Merchant*? This is a question no one appears to have asked.

It is inconceivable that an experienced seaman and navigator such as Kidd would have sailed the *Queddah Merchant* back to America without using navigational instruments. He would have had to keep a daily record of his latitude and departure, or longitude. Without a well-maintained logbook, updated on a daily basis, he would never have been able to find his way home using common navigational practice. One suggestion that immediately comes to mind is that the logbook eventually found its way into the archives, otherwise how would the forger that prepared the fourth Kidd-Palmer chart, the one that resembles Robert Louis Stevenson's *Treasure Island* in all but name, know that the island upon which Kidd cached his treasure was at latitude 9°16'N and longitude 43°30'E from the pirate haven of St. Marie? The conclusion must be that the logbook of the *Queddah Merchant* fell victim to the "laundering" process during which the Kidd-Palmer charts were prepared. It is to be sincerely hoped that this exciting piece of history has not been destroyed, and that one day it will resurface from the confines of some dusty basement.

Several of Kidd's and Culliford's crews returned to North America with Shelley, being landed at Cape May, New Jersey on Delaware Bay. Shelley arrived there May 27, 1699, about the same time as Kidd in the *Saint Antonio* was cautiously inching his way up the East Coast. In fact there could not have been more than a few days' sail between them. Amongst the men who took passage with Shelley were Robert Bradinham and Joseph Palmer, both of whom were to testify against Kidd at his trial. Also on board the *Nassau* were James Howe and Nicholas Churchill, who later were rumoured to have dug up gold in the wilds of Pennsylvania. Since all these pirates had sailed with either Kidd or Culliford, or both, and arrived at about the same time at the same place, there is more than a hint of collusion between the various parties concerned. Shelley gave testimony six weeks before Kidd's trial and the records state:

> The Nassau was owned by New York merchants, Stephen Delancy, John Barberio, Caleb Heathcote, Joseph Brigno and Shelley himself. He made a third voyage to Madagascar in 1698, with powder, and small armes, rum, beades and toyes. He did not see Kidd at Madagascar, in his stay, but bought muslins and callicoes, spoilt by salt water, from one Edward Welsh, who hath lived for seven years in that island. The stuffs came from a wrecked ship, cast away at that place. Shelley said that Kidd was not look't upon as a pirate, but as one that had the King's Commission.

If the cargo of muslin and calico brought back to New York by Shelley did not come from the *Queddah Merchant*, then it must have come from the "wrecked" ship as stated. However, bearing in mind that Shelley was a neighbour of Kidd when at home in New York, and the coincidental timing of their return from Madagascar, the suspicion arises that not only did they sail together, but Shelley also carried with him some of the surplus goods from the *Queddah Merchant*. In his testimony, Shelley would understandably have cast as good a light as possible on Kidd, as he was on trial himself, being under the suspicion of piracy.

Another interesting testimony is that of Edward Davis, who was not an original member of Kidd's crew, but one who returned with him on the *Queddah Merchant*. Davis was apprehended at the same time as Kidd and his men, and sent to England to stand trial. In his testimony Davis states that he joined the *Fidelia*, under Captain Tempest Rogers, as bosun. The ship was bound for the East Indies to establish a factory. On its return voyage, the *Fidelia* entered the pirate harbour at St. Marie to take on water and supplies, which is an interesting act for an honest merchantman. The suspicion arises that Rogers was on the lookout for some useful merchandise at a discount. There is some substance to this suggestion, as the *Fidelia* was later seized by Bellomont on its return to Boston and some East India goods, suspected to be Kidd's, were recovered from it. Davis's testimony regarding how he came to be on the *Queddah Merchant* is as follows:

> … they left for Madagasco, where they stayed till the end of July 1698. They took on board some water for the shipps provision, and there mett Captain Kidd, who came from England in an English shipp called the *Adventure Galley*, which had been sunck, and then Captain Kidd had a Moorish ship. Capt. Tempest Rogers went on board Capt. Kidd at St Marys, after having been on board for half an hour, Captain Rogers sent a boy with a message to Davis, who went on board Capt. Kidd carrying nailes or

spikes. Rogers said nothing to Davis on the ship, and about foure houres later, Rogers went back to the Fidelia, and when Davis offered to go with him, he said: "It's no matter. I shall send my boate for you before I saile." But he did not, and left Davis on board Kidd. Some time after, Davis went to a place ashore called the Hill, about four miles from where Kidd's ship lay, and here he was told that Rogers had left a message that if Davis had a mind to come on board the Fidelia, he was to fire a gun as signal. Davis, being told that the Fidelia was lying behind a point on that very day, fired one of the greate guns that lay upon the hill. But Rogers did not come in and the next day when Davis went to the hill, the Fidelia appeared in sight under sail. Davis thereupon fired another gunn, but the shipp sent no boat in. After Davis had been on the hill for 19 or 20 days, finding that the Fidelia did not return, he, fearing if he continued there longer, he might be in great danger of falling into ye handes of some white men that dwell there, he chose to return to Capt. Kidd and get a passage home. He was on Kidd's ship for 15 days before he sailed, and had the Fidelia returned, would have gone on her againe.

Edward Davis thus became an involuntary member of Kidd's crew, having been marooned at St. Marie as a result of some deal struck between Kidd and Rogers. Kidd must have needed a few more hands to crew the *Queddah Merchant* before the ship set sail, but of interest from this testimony is the date given by Davis. He states that they were at St. Marie at the end of July 1698 and that he was on Kidd's ship for 15 days before it sailed. Even allowing for the time spent on the island while Davis waited on the hill, one cannot make Kidd's sailing from the pirate base any later than about the end of August. Certainly not as late as November as Kidd affirms in his narrative. In actual fact Davis was a notorious pirate, and once

Captain Rogers realized this, he might have taken the first opportunity to get him off his ship before it was taken from under him.

Davis's piratical career had begun in 1683, and he was familiar to Dampier, as both men had served under one named Cook when they took the Danish ship off the coast of West Africa. This they renamed the *Batchelor's Delight* and set sail for the Pacific coast of South America in search of fortune. As has been recounted in Chapter 11, Dampier served under Davis after Cook died, but parted from him to venture further west to the Philippines in the *Cygnet* under Captain Swan. Davis eventually returned to the West Indies with much booty, and is reported to have accepted a pardon from King James II. His presence in the Indian Ocean in 1698 demonstrates that he is unlikely to have turned his hand to a more honest pursuit after accepting the earlier royal pardon.

Another equally notorious pirate who returned with Kidd on the *Queddah Merchant* was James Kelly (or Kelley), otherwise known as Sampson Marshall or James Gillam. Kelly was an associate of both Davis and Dampier and had also sailed on the *Batchelor's Delight*. Later on he sailed with Culliford on the *Mocha*, and was the man responsible for killing the captain when they took the ship. After he was caught at Charleston, near Boston, in 1699, he was described by the Governor of Massachusetts as "the most impudent, hardened villain I ever saw." Further evidence states that he "had entered the service of the Mogul, turned Mohammedan, and been circumcised. To settle this last point, the prisoner was examined by a surgeon and a Jew, who both declared on oath that it was so."

Both Davis and Kelly were returned to England on the *Advice*, along with Kidd and the rest of his crew. They were incarcerated in the Marshalsea, with Kelly later being transferred to Newgate. Kelly was tried separately, found guilty, and executed on July 12, 1700. Kelly's wife later delivered her husband's autobiography to a printer for publication, entitled *A Full and True Discovery of all the Robberies, Pyracies and other Notorious Actions of that Famous English Pyrate, Captain James Kelley, who was executed on Friday 12 July 1700*. Davis was found not guilty of engaging in piracy, which is rather strange bearing in mind his earlier history. It is understood he languished in jail for some time before his final release, but this release was not too long coming, as by July 1702, he was in Jamaica going "on account" once more, this time on board the *Blessing*, a ship of 20 guns and 79 men.

A man is generally judged by the company he keeps, and with two rascals such as Davis and Kelly on board the *Queddah Merchant*, Kidd's character can only be judged harshly. However, though we know how Davis came to be aboard, if we can believe his testimony, which appears a little fanciful and over dramatic, no explanation has been offered as to how Kelly found his way onto the ship. Kelly was one of Culliford's crew on the *Mocha*, and the *Mocha* had supposedly left Kidd and the *Queddah Merchant* at St. Marie. This supports the argument that the two ships did not separate either permanently, as has been testified, or indeed for any great length of time, at least until the end of 1698, when the *Queddah Merchant* finally sailed for North America.

The testimonies given by Kidd and the men who sailed with him are invaluable and interesting in themselves, but, because of the inconsistencies they contain, must of necessity be treated with caution. They lack the mark of veracity that should be expected in official accounts conducted by men of high office engaged in the exercise of the law and anxious to determine "the truth, the whole truth, and nothing but the truth." There may be other testimonies that are not within the public domain, and to which we have no access, and these may tell a more truthful story. But in the meantime, the only conclusion that can be reached by studying and comparing those testimonies available is that every man that was brought before the authorities was telling a story to save his own skin, to the best of his ability. Each man was fearful of authority, and perhaps deserving of some sympathy, standing before the imposing might of bewigged justices for interrogation; but just as each felon had his own agenda, so did those holding court. Determining truth was not the object of the court. That object appears to have been to find Kidd guilty, to condemn him and see him hanged. Kidd's execution was a political necessity to calm the anger of the Mogul of India, to cast oil upon the troubled waters of Anglo-Indian commerce, and restore profitability to the East India Company. In this sense the men in the long robes and furred gowns were no better that the miscreants standing in the dock.

Let us divert our attention to look at some correspondence. There is a letter dated June 8, 1698, from Bellomont to Kidd informing the latter that he (Bellomont) had arrived in New York on April 2 to take up his official post and "being informed by the ship lately come from Madagascar that you were on a further cruise and did not doubt of your making a good voyage." On the same date a letter was also dispatched from New York by Livingston to Kidd, ensuring Kidd of Lord Bellomont's "trust and pleasure." One must ask the question — why were these letters sent to Madagascar? Which ship did they go on — Shelley's *Nassau*? Why were they sent to a known pirate base? If it was necessary for any communication to be sent to Kidd in the Indian Ocean, and Kidd's proposed voyage was to live up to its stated intention of "seeking out and destroying pirates," then surely the post box should have been one of the East India Company's factories, or another more acceptable address, but certainly not the pirate rat's nest of St. Marie.

On June 19, 1699, James Emott, a trusted friend and confidant of Kidd, had informed Bellomont that:

> Kidd had left in the sloop [that he had brought from Hispaniola] goods and treasure about the value of £10,000, and that the said Kidd had left a ship somewhere off the coast of Hispaniola, in safe hands, goods and treasure to the value of about £30,000 …

Following his return to New York, Kidd received a letter from Bellomont written the same day and carrying a decidedly specious undertone. It read:

> Captain Kidd,
> I make no manner of doubt but to obtain the King's pardon for you, and those few men you have

left, who, I understand, have been faithful and refuse as well as you to dishonour the Commission you have from England. I assure on my word of honour, I will perform honestly what I have now promised, tho' I declare beforehand that whatever treasure or goods you bring hither, I will not meddle with the least bit of them, but they shall be left with such trusted persons as the Council shall advise, until I receive orders from England, how they shall be disposed of. Mr Campbell will satisfy you that this that I have now written is the sense of the Council and of your humble servant.

Kidd accepted this letter at face value. He travelled to Boston and within a few days found himself locked up in jail! One would suspect that under the circumstances, the letter Bellomont wrote to Kidd was prompted by his learning from Emott that Kidd had brought back to North America a considerable amount of goods and treasure, and he was certainly quick to respond to this tidbit of information.

Bellomont was later to write to James Vernon, the Secretary of State in England, as follows:

> I owne I writ to Kidd to come to New Yorke, and if it be rightly considered I did therein what became of me … Tis plain, menacing him had not been the way to invite him hither, but rather wheedling … and after that manner I got him at last into Boston …

After Kidd and his crew had been apprehended by Bellomont, during which process of law Bellomont acted impeccably at all times, the prisoners in Boston were brought overland to New York, from whence the *Advice* sailed for England with its cargo of jail-birds. Bellomont was to write to Sir Paul Stanley from Boston on March 5, 1700, in the following terms:

> I send home every script that was taken with Kidd, or
> any of the pirates. The gold and jewels, some pounds
> weight, Kidd had nothing to do with; they belonged
> to James Gillam, who is now also sent home … I am
> told that, as Vice-Admiral of these seas, I have a right
> to a third part of them; if the rest of the lords come
> in for snacks, I shall be satisfied, but that Sir Edmund
> Harrison should pretend to a share of what was not
> taken by Kidd, is very unreasonable.

Sir Edmund Harrison had become a sponsor of Kidd's voyage after Bellomont had pulled out because of his inability to obtain the required funding for a full share in the venture.

On the same date, (March 5, 1700), Bellomont wrote to the Duke of Shrewsbury, another sponsor of Kidd's voyage, and along with the letter he sent a wedding present for the Duke. This seems a little strange as the Duke did not marry until August 25, 1705. Perhaps he was contemplating marriage to someone else at the time! Bellomont included the following in his letter:

> I am heartily vexed to understand that some angry
> gentlemen in the House of Commons have raised a
> clamour about Kidd, and have brought your Grace's
> name and other of your friends, on the stage … I
> hope the East India goods and treasure that is sent
> will amount to £20,000, which will reimburse every-
> body, if the King will consent it shall be so; for I doubt
> Kidd will be proved a pirate.

Presumably Bellomont was hopeful that the Duke, because of his influence on the King, might manage to effect a distribution of the "East India goods and treasure" among the sponsors of the voyage. However, there was little hope of such a happy outcome.

The *Advice* arrived at the Downs on April 2, 1700, and Kidd was not long in writing to Lord Russell, who was the only navy man among his sponsors. Kidd may have seen him as a valuable ally who understood maritime matters better than any of the others. Also, it will be recalled that at the outset of the voyage of the *Adventure Galley*, when Kidd had been delayed at Sheerness, it was to Russell that he scurried in order to unravel the tangled mess that he found himself in as a result of not observing naval etiquette. There is also the probability that Russell had taken a great personal interest in formulating the objectives of the voyage. Now Kidd was to write to him, from imprisonment on the *Advice*, in the following terms:

Advice Downs, April 11th, 1700

My Lord,
The inclosed is copy of a protest drawn up at Boston in New England, the truth whereof those of my men are prisoners with me are ready to attest upon oath, but it was not permitted to be done there. If your Lordship will be pleased to give yourselfe the trouble of reading it, you will find a plain and faithfull narrative of my whole voyage in the Adventure Galley wherein there is nothing of moment omitted that was transacted in the said voyage. I know not what is generally thought of me, nor what is alleged against me, but I do assure your Lordship I have done nothing but what is punctually declared in the said protest, wherein if anything be accounted a crime twas so far contrary to my sentiments, that I should have thought myselfe wanting in my duty had I not done the same. I am in hope your Lordship and the rest of the Honourable gentlemen my owners will so far vindicate me that I may have no injusticies, and I fear not at all but upon an equitable and impartial tryal, my innocence will justifie me to your Lordship and the world.

I doubt not but your Lordship is allready informed of what effects were seized in the sloop Antonio in New England, but this I must needs declare in justice that there were severall things of considerable value, whereof they have given no account, so far as I can learn. Besides what was contained in the sloop there is in the Adventure Prize [the *Queddah Merchant*] mentioned in the protest (as near as I can compute) to the value of ninety thousand pounds, which is left in very secure hands and I doubt not when I am clear of this trouble but to bring the same for England without any diminution.

The inclosed list is the names of those men that left me at Madagascar and went on board the Mocha Frigot.

Whatever may be omitted here is more particularly contained in the protest to which I beg leave to refer your Lordship being My Lord

Your Lordship's Most Humble servant
Wm Kidd

What is likely to have been Russell's reaction on receiving this letter? Lord Macaulay in his *History of England* describes Edward Russell, Earl of Orford, in a most unflattering manner, and since Macaulay lived much closer to his age than the present, we must attribute some authority to his character assessment. Russell's character will be considered in greater detail in the next chapter and Appendix III, but from the *History of England* we note the following:

… people in general were quick to discern his faults; and his faults were too discernible … His arrogant, insolent and quarrelsome temper, made him an object of hatred. His vast and growing wealth made him an object of envy … One set of writers described him as the most ravenous of all the plunderers of the poor overtaxed nation … Orford was covetous and unprincipled; but he had great professional skill and knowledge, great industry, and a strong will. He was therefore an useful servant to the state when the interests of the state were not opposed to his own … When Orford had nothing to gain by doing what was wrong, he did what was right, and he did it ably and diligently.

This does not sound like a man that one would entrust with the knowledge that one had goods and treasure to the value of £90,000, even if it was "left in very secure hands." One can imagine Russell staring long and hard at Kidd's letter and the information it contained. It should be noted that this sum greatly exceeds the £30,000 mentioned by Kidd to Bellomont as being the value of goods left in the *Queddah Merchant* "in safe hands" off the coast of Hispaniola. A difference of £60,000 is a big difference indeed, and Russell would most certainly have thought long and hard. This was payback time for himself and the other members of the consortium who had financed the voyage of the *Adventure Galley*!

Kidd was transferred to Newgate, while the rest of his crew were incarcerated in the Marshalsea. One wonders why they were separated, as Admiralty prisoners were invariably imprisoned in the Marshalsea. Was the separation a consequence of any direct intervention by Russell himself? If so, it would give time to interrogate the crew well away from Kidd's influence, and to adopt the wise policy so often used by modern-day interrogators to play one party off against the other in an attempt to get at the truth. One can imagine Russell, and those he may have drawn into any plot he had in mind, travelling to and fro between the two prisons, cajoling, wheedling, and making promises, to Kidd on the one hand and the crew on the other, of life, liberty, and wealth as a reward for their collaboration. Only Darby Mullins, perhaps, could see through it all, and was obdurate that he would have no part in a plan to see his captain hanged, even if others might be willing to sell the knowledge of the whereabouts of the treasure for a few pieces of silver and a guarantee of freedom.

The unenviable circumstances in which Kidd found himself while in prison have been described in Chapter 1, but before his well-publicized trial on May 8 and 9 he wrote the following letter:

Before I make any answer to the indictment read against me, I crave leave to acquaint your Lordship that I took no ships but such as had French passes for my justification.

In confidence that they would and ought to be allowed for my defense, I surrendered my selfe to my Lord Bellomont when I could have secured my selfe in severall parts of the world.

But my Lord Bellomont having sold his share in my ship, and in the adventure, thought it his interest to make me a pirate, whereby he could claim a share of my cargo, and in order to it stript me of the French passes, frightened and wheedled some of my men to misrepresent me, and by his letters to his friends have advised them to admit me a pyrate, and to obtaine a new grant of my cargo from the king.

The more effectually to work my ruine, he has sent all over papers that would either doe me little service, or as he thought, would make against me, but has detained the French passes and some other papers which he knew would acquit me, and baffle his designe of making me a pyrate, and my cargo forfeited.

If the design I was sent upon, be illegall, or of ill consequence to the trade of the nation, my owners who knew the laws, ought to suffer for it, and not I, whom they made the tool of their covetousness.

Some great men would have me dye for salving their honour, and others to pacify the Mogull for injurys done by other men, and not my selfe, and to further their trade; but my Lord! whatsoever my fate may be, I shall not contribute to my own destruction by pleading to this indictment till my passes are restored to me. It is not my fault that I have them not here, but it will be my fault if I admit my selfe a pyrate as I must doo if I plead without having those passes to produce.

Let me have my passes, I will plead presently, but without them I will not plead. I am not afraid to dye, but will not be my own murderer, and if an English Court of Judicature will take away my life for not pleading under my circumstances, I think my death will tend very little to the credit of their Justices.

Three days after the trial had ended with the pronouncement of the death sentence, Kidd was to make a final desperate plea for his life, but his plea was in vain. He addressed his letter to Robert Harley, Speaker of the House of Commons, under whose auspices the trial had been held. Whether Kidd had had a previous encounter with Harley we do not know, but obviously he hoped for a more favourable reception than he may have expected from any of the other luminaries of the land. The letter dated May 12, 1701 reads:

My Lord,

The sense of my present condition (being under condemnation) and the thoughts of haveing bene imposed on by such as seek't my destruction therby to fulfill their ambitious desieres makes me incapable of expressing myselfe in those terms as I ought, therefore doo most humbly pray that you will be pleased to represent to the Honorable house of Commons, that in my late proceedings in the Indies I have lodged goods and treasure to the value of one hundred thousand pounds, which I desiere the government may have the benfitt of, in order thereto I shall desiere no manner of liberty but to be kept prisonner on board such shipp as may be appointed for that purpose, and only give the necessary directions and in case I faile therein I desiere no favour but to be forthwith executed according to my sentence, if

your Honourable House will please to order a comit-
tee to come to me I doubt not but to give such satisfaction as may obtaine mercy, most humbly submit-
ting to the wisdom of your great assembly I am

Sir Your unfortunate humble Servant
Wm Kidd

The treasure that Kidd claims in his earlier letter to Russell amounted to £90,000 as near as he could compute, but he gave no indication of where that treasure was located except that it is (or was) in the *Queddah Merchant* (or *Adventure Prize*). It appears that there might be some deliberate ambiguity in the letter to Russell, as in his later letter to Harley, the value of his treasure increases to £100,000 and it is "lodged in the Indies." Which Indies — East or West? Even on the eve of his hanging, Kidd is not going to tell everything, for why should he? He had nothing to lose. But that does not mean that others did not know the exact location and may have already made their deal with authority. In that case Kidd was, in effect, making an empty gesture of defiance. The authorities were intent on hanging Kidd for all the world to see, especially the Mogul. By that time Kidd must have become painfully aware that he had no cards left to play in the desperate gamble for his life. His letter to Harley is quite pathet-ic in itself, but that does not mean that Kidd was going to go to the gallows willingly, peacefully, contrite, or with a humble and penitent heart. Kidd's last words were an exhortation to all seamen to beware of those in high places, and he was speaking from bitter experience. It is good advice, not only to seamen!

From the letters to Russell and Harley one is left wondering whether the estimated values of £90,000 and £100,000 relate to the same treasure. As we have noted, the estimate that Kidd gave to Bellomont regarding the value of goods on board the *Queddah Merchant* left in Hispaniola was a mere £30,000. If, as we surmise, Russell had aided and abetted piracy by financing and planning Kidd's voyage in the *Adventure Galley*, then Kidd's letter, written as soon as he arrived back in England, would have been perfectly natural. What Kidd is telling Russell in effect is "you got me into this mess; you get me out; and when I'm out I'll bring the £90,000 of loot back to England." Russell didn't take the bait because he had made other plans in which he would wheedle the information he required out of Kidd's crew! In the letter to Harley, Kidd rounds up his estimate to a neat £100,000 — it is the same treasure, but for obvious reasons it is not in the *Queddah Merchant* in Hispaniola, because that is only worth £30,000, or thereabouts.

What sort of man was Harley? His character will be dealt with in greater detail in the next chapter and Appendix III, but for the present we will confine ourselves to the following extracts taken from the *Dictionary of National Biography*:

> A shrewd and unscrupulous politician, he made a skilful party leader, but owing to his deficiency in most of the higher qualifications of statesmanship he proved a weak and incapable minister … He was insincere, dilatory and irresolute … His want of political honesty, his indifference to truth and his talent for intrigue were alike remarkable.

In his search for friends in high places, Kidd had unwittingly stuck his hand into a barrel full of snakes, and plucked out a couple of the most venomous!

Chapter 15

Recovering the Treasure

Through tatter'd clothes small vices do appear,
Robes and furr'd gowns hide all.
— Lear in *King Lear* (Shakespeare)

In the Foreword to this book, mention was made that this is a detective story, but unlike its fictional counterpart it has no neat ending. In many of the classical works of detection it is customary for the sleuth to assemble all the leading characters together, often in an oak panelled library or drawing-room of some great house, and then make a suitable exposition culminating in the unmasking of the felon who committed the crime. Let us in our imagination do the same, but our task is great, as the crime was committed 300 years ago, the trail is cold, and this is not fiction. Furthermore, all the evidence cannot be presented, so at best our reconstruction is speculative. However, truth has a habit of eventually emerging from the dim and distant past to brush away the cobwebs of time, and the layers of dust that have shrouded it. We will find some eminent persons among our hypothetical gathering, in our quest to determine the answer to the question — who recovered Kidd's treasure? A brief biography of each of these persons is included in Appendix III.

Some will argue that no crime has been committed by this act — but there has. A man who steals someone else's property is a thief, and anyone who steals this property, knowing the goods to be stolen, is likewise culpable in the eyes of the law. Kidd stole treasure and goods that rightfully belonged to the Mogul of India by piracy on the high seas, a crime for which he was hanged.

Anyone who recovered those same goods from Kidd's hiding place is no less guilty of the same crime, or of being an accessory after the fact, or at best being the recipient of stolen goods. By the norms of the age in which these crimes were perpetrated, some of those found guilty would have been given the death penalty, though it is difficult to imagine that any of the illustrious gentlemen gathered together in our imagination would have been transported to Execution Dock. Perhaps to the Tower of London, but not to Execution Dock. Privilege does have its advantages!

As stated, we do not have the full evidence to set before you, the reader, in order for this examination to carry any force. Perhaps, one day, through the tenacity of researchers and historians, the missing evidence will be found to justify the accusations made herein, or to support the hypothesis to be presented. That evidence will take the form of sea-stained ships' logs, letters, diaries, and correspondence between the conspirators, as conspiracy it surely was. It will be found buried amidst dusty archives, or in boxes and crates stuffed full of papers from long ago and probably marked "never to be opened." Let us look at the known facts and assemble a thesis.

Lord Bellomont is approached by Livingston with a plan designed to enrich himself, and any others that he could attract to the venture, by confiscating pirated goods. Once these goods were properly condemned by law, a percentage would fall to those enterprising individuals who had participated in this worthy act, whether in its financing or in its execution. Bellomont then approaches Lord Somers, his political neighbour from Worcestershire and a very influential person. Together they make various approaches to others of Whig persuasion and before long we have the formation of a consortium eager to discuss Livingston's scheme and benefit accordingly. Only Edward Russell has any knowledge of the sea and he views the project from a slightly different perspective than that of Bellomont and Livingston. Russell's good friend, Henry Sidney, well practiced in the art of intrigue, colludes with him, and before long there is a different agenda being discussed à trois (Russell, Sidney, and Kidd) than amongst the rest of the group, the trio seeing the merits of conducting a little piracy on the sideline. Ensuring that all captured vessels have French passes in their possession is one necessary precaution to keep the *Adventure Galley* and her crew on the right side of the fine dividing line between piracy and privateering. Somers-Shrewsbury-Bellomont probably know nothing of this alternate agenda, but Bellomont is suspicious and decides to opt out. Possibly he didn't have the ready cash, but even though he was as eager as anyone to secure riches with minimum effort, he did not compromise himself. In everything he did afterwards, he acted with foresight, and prudently covered himself in the official records.

The *Adventure Galley* sets sail from London, and promptly runs into trouble with the navy through lack of observing some trifling etiquette. To whom does Kidd scurry? Why to Russell, of course! Russell extricates him from the mess as only admirals know how, and soon Kidd resumes his voyage, not direct to Madagascar as originally intended, but to New York in order to bring his now depleted crew up to full strength. Finally he reaches Madagascar as planned and, without troubling to poke his nose into the pirate haven of St. Marie, promptly sets sail as soon as he can for the Red Sea in order to waylay the Muslim fleet on its annual sailing back to India. As Russell asked Dampier — how long to sail from London to Madagascar and thence to the Red Sea? This is a dead giveaway! Russell is as good as admitting that he is aiding and abetting piracy. His other question — how long to sail from the Red Sea to Cape Comorin? — confirms this admission. Cape Comorin was where the *Adventure Galley* captured the *Queddah Merchant*, and Russell was well aware of this fact when he asked the question.

With his piratical actions behind him and his ship now sinking beneath him, Kidd eventually sails to the pirate base on St. Marie, hardly a secure haven for an unseaworthy vessel intent on combatting piracy in the Indian Ocean. There Kidd meets up with his old companion from buccaneering days of long ago, Robert Culliford. Perhaps he knew Culliford would be there from his chance encounter with William Mason at Carrawar. Kidd is in a predicament, and so is Culliford. The former has three vessels, two of which are of doubtful value in any engagement with an enemy, the third an ungainly merchantman, laden with a rich cargo that would be a liability in any sea fight. Culliford, on the other hand, needs men to bring his ship, the *Mocha*, up to full strength. What is more natural than they should pool their resources? Kidd lends Culliford his best fighting men, his cannon and other materials, and the rigging stripped from the now useless *Adventure Galley*, and makes plans to voyage to Amboyna to rid himself of the merchandise in the holds of the *Queddah Merchant*. However, the Dutch East Indies are infested with native pirates, and it would be foolish to attempt to sail through those waters with a clumsy vessel and a vastly depleted crew. Culliford and Kidd arrange to rendezvous in the Nicobars in the hope that in the meantime Culliford will make a good voyage and bring in more booty.

Culliford meets up with Dirk Chivers and together they take the *Great Mahomet* and rendezvous with Kidd as arranged. Since the Strait of Malacca is highly dangerous, and encounters with hostile natives are virtually certain, the booty, or a large part of it, is cached on the island for future recovery. In Amboyna, Kidd learns of the warrant out for his arrest and is now in a quandary — should he return to the island to recover the treasure, or sail back to North America without it, in the hope that his lordly backers will be able to get him off the hook? He decides on the latter and the first leg of his return voyage takes him back to Madagascar, but probably not to St. Marie. Instead he calls in at Fort Dauphin. Some of his men, who previously sailed with Culliford, decide in the interim that they would like to return to North America on the *Queddah Merchant*. Giles Shelley in his *Nassau* is at St. Marie and he catches up with Kidd at Fort Dauphin, where a transfer of men takes place. The *Queddah Merchant* begins her return voyage with the *Nassau* in attendance. We can only speculate as to whether Kidd encountered any other ships on the return voyage that might have caused him to alter course and, instead of sailing direct to North America, made him veer off westwards to Anguilla. Kidd's old friend Dampier, in his *Roebuck*, would have been sailing south while Kidd was sailing north. When their paths crossed in mid-Atlantic, only a few sea-miles would have separated them. Had they managed to meet and exchange gossip, Kidd would soon have learned about the hornet's nest his actions had stirred up back home in England. That might have been the incentive to sail further west to seek refuge at St. Thomas. The rest is history.

Meanwhile, in London, frenzied assaults are being made upon the Whig lords that funded the voyage. The names of Russell, Sidney, Somers, and the Duke of Shrewsbury are being dragged through the mire by jubilant Tories. The king is angry, since no attempt has been made to follow the explicit terms laid down in his commission. Bentinck, his chief advisor, would have been equally irate, having been the man whose advice William relied on most prior to having given his sanction to Kidd's projected voyage. Only Robert Harley, leader of the exultant Tories, would have gleefully welcomed the dreadful scandal that broke, and the sleaze that was being daily stripped away. He can be expected to have taken every opportunity to maximize his political gains.

In New York, Bellomont is eager to distance himself from the incident, if only to protect his reputation. Zealously he carries out his enquiries, arrests Kidd and those members of his crew that he can lay his hands upon, and seizes all goods, treasure, papers, and anything else that could be incriminating to ensure Kidd's conviction. He is likely to have been little concerned about the fate of the four nobles who actually funded the voyage. Bellomont must have been aware of the hidden agenda to the voyage of the *Adventure Galley* before it sailed off down the Thames. He adroitly distanced himself from it, but whether by good luck or good management is not known. Secure in his post in New York, he was well out of harm's way when the scandal finally broke, as he probably knew that one day it must.

It has often been speculated that King William was a secret backer of Kidd. However, this rumour has little or no foundation; in fact, quite the reverse is true. William's Dutch background may not have endeared him to the populace at large, for he was viewed as an alien monarch, and the English have always viewed foreigners with some suspicion, especially foreign kings. William's personal qualities, however, were such as to engender admiration, even if that admiration was tainted with envy. On the battlefield, where he had fought in many campaigns against Louis of France, he is said to have exposed himself to danger like a man seeking death, being foremost in the charge with sword in hand and last in retreat. In the thickest of the fighting, even with a musket ball in his arm and blood streaming from his wounds, he would manfully stand his ground. He was neither a timorous nor irresolute person. Unfortunately he had a phlegmatic disposition, which gave rise in many quarters to the belief that he was cold-blooded; he rarely exhibited anger, but when his passions were roused he could be terrible indeed. In society, on the other hand, he was kind, cordial, frank and, when occasion demanded, convivial and jocose.

In 1695 a financial scandal was unearthed, which at first some believed may have involved William. Subsequent investigations at the highest level were to prove that William derived no benefit at all, and in fact he and his closest adviser had acquitted themselves honourably from the very beginning. Highly suspicious entries had been discovered in the accounts of the East India Company under the heading of "special service," and in 1693 alone, the expenditure on this item exceeded £80,000. But what was this "special service," if not bribes in all but name? Accounting practices of the age were just as creative as today, if not quite as sophisticated. The impartial enquiry that followed disclosed the fact that though many honourable men had been offered bribes, and had accepted them, neither the king nor any of his close advisers were among them. It transpired that the East India Company had attempted to buy favours from the Crown with an offer of £50,000, but this had been rejected outright. Undeterred, the agents of the Company had pestered and persisted, eventually leaving the money in a special account ready for payment, should William have a change of heart. With his patience finally exhausted, William had let it be known that if the Company did not desist from these overtures, they would make him their enemy. For some years, ever since his accession to the throne, William had declined the customary gift (of a smaller amount) that the East India Company had annually tendered to the sovereign during previous reigns. The man at William's side throughout this turmoil was Hans Willem Bentinck, a loyal and devoted servant for

30 years, and one who was his most trusted confidant. On his accession, William had created him Earl of Portland.

Kidd's financial backers were well known to both William and Bentinck, as all had proved loyal to William's cause, in helping to remove James II from the throne of England. Most of them had actively participated in the invasion of November 5, 1688, when troops landed at Torbay and commenced their march on London. Although the scheme had been projected by Livingston to Bellomont in the first instance, and Bellomont had attracted the interest of others, Russell, being the only one with any experience of maritime affairs, would have played the leading role in defining and planning the details of Kidd's voyage. He must be considered, therefore, to be the senior member of the "junta," as they have been collectively termed, or perhaps a more apt description would be "cabal" since Kidd's voyage had a greater element of intrigue associated with it than that declared in his privateering commission. In terms of seniority, as this relates to the influence wielded within this cabal, one can list the following members irrespective of either age, position, lordly title, or amount invested:

> Edward Russell, Earl of Orford (1653–1727)
> Henry Sidney, Earl of Romney (1641–1704)
> Lord John Somers (1651–1716)
> Charles Talbot, Duke of Shrewsbury (1660–1718)
> Richard Coote, Earl of Bellomont (1636–1702)

In addition there was Edmund Harrison, a leading merchant in London, who was later to be knighted and to assume a directorship on the board of the New East India Company, the main rival of the East India Company. There was also a Dr. Cox, about whom we know nothing. According to Kidd, it had been necessary for Bellomont to sell his interest in the venture because he could not raise the required funds, and Harrison and Cox had assumed his stake in the voyage.

Out of Kidd's four main backers, only Russell would have been likely to have appreciated the importance of the logbook of the *Queddah Merchant*. When Kidd wrote to him while in chains on board the *Advice*, after being brought back to England, Russell is likely to have moved heaven and earth to obtain that logbook. Kidd had volunteered the fact that he had £90,000 in goods and treasure and that logbook would have been vital in determining where the treasure might have been hidden, whether it was still on board the vessel or on some desert island. It is probable that Russell eventually retrieved it since it would have been in the papers and other effects that Bellomont confiscated from Kidd and dispatched to Sir Paul Stanley, as we have seen in the last chapter.

Kidd was separated from the rest of his men by being incarcerated in Newgate and deliberately kept incommunicado, whereas the others were locked up in the Marshalsea. This gave Russell, or his agents, the opportunity to interrogate the crew well away from the influence of their hapless captain, who was totally ignorant of the goings-on behind his back. When Culliford was returned to England, he too was committed to the Marshalsea, and although first allowed bail, was soon re-arrested. He was later transferred to Newgate, presumably after Kidd's trial, and there he was to remain on one pretext or another until he was granted his pardon by Queen Anne in April 1702. During this period, some of the pirates were set free, some were acquitted, but only one of the crew, Darby Mullins, was to suffer the same fate as Kidd. They were released in dribs and drabs, and where they went we do not know, but it must be suspected that those who might be useful in any attempt to recover the treasure were kept in secure and useful employment.

Once Russell had foreknowledge of what might have happened to the treasure Kidd had accumulated during his voyaging in the Indian Ocean, he would have gone to Bentinck. Russell's name had been tarnished like all the other investors in the voyage of the *Adventure Galley*, and one way of regaining royal favour was to make the king party to what had been discovered regarding the whereabouts of the treasure. Any other action would have been considered treasonable. King William is unlikely to have distanced himself from a project which now would be fully controlled and operated by the navy, and it must be presumed that plans were set in motion to recover the fortune. This planning certainly would have taken place well before Kidd's execution. Kidd's letter to Harley, pleading for his life and disclosing the fact he had cached £100,000 of treasure, would have only served to reinforce the conclusions drawn by Russell, and fuel determination for its recovery.

In whom would Russell have first confided the knowledge he had gained, apart from Bentinck? Obviously Lord Henry Sidney, Earl of Romney, because he is the one most likely to have collaborated with Russell in formulating the pirate agenda for the voyage of the *Adventure Galley* in the first place. Harley would have entered the conspiracy, but likely only after he had received his letter from Kidd on the eve of the latter's execution. Harley, like Russell, was eager to earn royal accolades, and after receiving Kidd's letter he too would have gone straight to Bentinck. There he would have learned that King William was already aware of the matter, and that plans were afoot to recover the treasure cached upon that distant island. Harley had little to contribute to a naval operation that was going to be tightly controlled, but being one of the most skilful politicians of the day, he would soon have inveigled himself into the clandestine activities of the group that had been formed. If whispers broke out in the House of Commons regarding the new intrigue that was afoot, Harley, as Leader of the House, could be relied upon to quell such rumours.

Somers and Shrewsbury are likely to have been excluded from any new consortium, as they had little, if anything, to contribute to the execution of the enterprise, and their money was of even less importance. In any event, Somers was still licking his political wounds, and Shrewsbury was away on the continent, where he was to remain for several years. The conspirators, therefore, are likely to have consisted of Bentinck, Russell, Sidney, and Harley, with King William taking a keen interest in the whole strategy. One other important participant who is believed to have been drawn into the planning of this recovery operation was Dr. Hans Sloane.

Sloane had participated in a previous conspiracy, involving the recovery of treasure in 1687–88, and was thoroughly familiar with the intrigue that surrounds such ventures. He was personal physician to the Duke of Albermarle, who had been a major stakeholder in William Phips's famous exploit of recovering a fortune in silver from the wreck of a Spanish galleon off the coast of Hispaniola during a previous voyage a year earlier. The story of how the sunken vessel, the *Concepción*, was found, has been told in thrilling detail by Peter Earle in *The Treasure of the Concepción*. Albermarle had cunningly arranged to be appointed governor of Jamaica, at the same time that a second expedition, led jointly by Sir William Phips (his previous achievement had earned him a knighthood) and Sir John Narbrough, was to revisit the wrecksite. The conspiracy, whereby the more valuable cargo of gold and jewels remaining in the hull of the wreck was to be retrieved for William, Prince of Orange, and thereby aid in the overthrow of James II, has been described in *Oak Island and its Lost Treasure*, by Graham Harris and Les MacPhie. The fact that the treasure was subsequently lost on a fog-shrouded island off the coast of Nova Scotia has led to one of the most enduring attempts to recover buried treasure in the history of treasure seeking.

Sloane's vast collections of manuscripts, books, maps, engravings, and numerous specimens of botanical, zoological, and mineralogical interest, acquired over his lifetime, were later to form the nucleus of the British Museum. In 1904, Edward J. Scott, the Keeper of the Department of Manuscripts, produced his *Index to the Sloane Manuscripts in the British Museum*, a document totalling 583 pages, further additions being placed in an *Index to Additional Manuscripts*. The entries classified under "East India" are worthy of close inspection. Apart from some interesting volumes, some of which are written in Dutch, relating to the early history of India, there are a number of journals of sea voyages undertaken between 1648 and 1705. One of them carries the title "Instructions for Sailing from Pointe de Galle [SW tip of Ceylon] to the Bay of Bengal, 17th Century." It seems strange that Sloane's interest in navigation to and around the Indian Ocean should terminate in 1705, almost 50 years before his death. The fact that a number of ship's logbooks from a distinct period are included in his collection is suggestive that he was engaged in doing some "homework." By 1705, there was no longer any need to continue with that "homework."

Sloane's involvement in any conspiracy to recover the treasure is likely to have been one in which he contributed only his professional and scientific knowledge, a man whom today we would call a consultant. Perhaps Dampier might have been consulted if he had been in London, and possibly he might have been entrusted to help in the recovery of the treasure. However at the time when Kidd was in jail, Dampier was sailing in southern waters, and following his return to England he was charged with ineptitude in the handling of the *Roebuck*. Therefore, it was from Sloane that advice was sought. This would explain why, amid the Sloane Collection, we find many extant ships' logs and navigational data from the period immediately prior to the date the recovery expedition is likely to have been mounted, but none from a later period. Unfortunately, in the British Library we find neither the log of the *Queddah Merchant*, nor that of the ship that was engaged in the recovery operation. Should either of these be there, then they are not accessible to the public.

As secretary to the Royal Society, Sloane would have attended most of their regular meetings. Inspection of the minutes of the Society between 1699 and 1706 indicates 22 meetings being held, of which Sloane attended 18. The greatest length of absence between his attendances was about six months during the first half of 1705. This record demonstrates that he was not out of the country for any great length of time, at least not long enough to journey to the Indian Ocean to recover buried treasure.

Russell may have managed to lay his hands on various papers, including the priceless log of the *Queddah Merchant,* that enabled him to reconstruct the voyage of the ship in the Indian Ocean. Sloane may have carried out his equally valuable studies, but there was nothing so essential to the success of the proposed new voyage as men who had actually set foot on the island where the treasure lay buried. Culliford, therefore, would have been an invaluable member of any expedition. Various members of the crews, such as Nicholas Churchill, James Howe, Robert Hickman, and others, may have been able to recognize the island, but they most certainly would never have been able to find it as easily as Culliford could in that vast expanse of ocean. Most assuredly, therefore, there must have been a good number of ex-pirates that eventually found their way aboard the navy ship appointed to sail to the Indian Ocean, and the most important of these was Culliford. It has often been rumoured that following his release from Newgate jail, after receiving his royal pardon, Culliford sailed in a navy ship, undoubtedly the recovery vessel, but the name of that vessel remains obscure.

We know nothing of the provenance of the Kidd-Palmer charts, except that they appear to be forgeries, if only on the most recent expert opinion given by the Maps Department of the British Library. But there is more than a hint of suspicion that a member of the same department was responsible for their preparation in the first instance, sometime during the 1920s. It is probable that the originals of these documents were found amidst the vast collections of papers constituting the Harley and Sloane manuscripts, and came to light during the mammoth cataloguing process completed in 1922. Of the four Kidd-Palmer charts, it is the third one, referred to previously as KP3, that is the most useful, and most likely bears the closest resemblance to any map drawn 300 years ago. It could also possibly be a replica of an original. It does not carry any longitude or latitude, unlike KP4, and the view is hereby expressed that KP3, or its original, was drawn by Robert Culliford, in crude form, to represent the real island. KP4 is a twentieth-century reproduction of KP3, on which has been included the basic longitude and latitude, enabling the island to be eventually located.

King William died on March 8, 1702, as a result of a fall from his horse, and was therefore not fortunate enough to see the recovery expedition set sail. The treasure from the *Concepción* had eluded his grasp, and now this! Easy riches were not destined for William. It is doubted whether the new monarch, Queen Anne, was fully aware of the things going on in her name on her accession to the throne. The recovery vessel probably sailed in May or June 1702, after Culliford received his pardon from the queen. The voyage to the Nicobars and back would have occupied a period of 12 to 18 months, and it may be assumed that the ship returned with its mission accomplished by the end of 1703 or early 1704. All the participants were to become wealthy, or certainly wealthier than prior to the venture. The Crown would have received its due, amounting to at least 10 percent of the value of the recovered treasure, and possibly more, depending on how the project had been structured and financed.

In 1705, Harley began to expend large sums of money on acquiring a collection of rare books and manuscripts. Within 10 years he acquired 2,500 manuscripts, and by 1721 the manuscript section of his personal library consisted of 6,000 volumes, together with 14,000 charters and 500 rolls. He spent considerable sums of money in the bindings of these volumes, using Moroccan, Turkish, and Russian leather, doeskin, and velvet. His library was to be later incorporated into the section of the British Library that carries his name, the Harley Collection, which has attained world fame. Sloane also spent lavishly improving the quantity and quality of his own collections, and no doubt both Russell and Bentinck would have also spent the largesse due to them both wisely and well. Since Sidney died in April 1704, it is likely that any benefit accrued from his financial involvement in any expedition would have passed to his heirs, namely his three nephews.

We hear little about any of the pirate crews after this date, either of those who sailed with Kidd on the *Adventure Galley* and the *Queddah Merchant*, or of those who sailed with Culliford on the *Mocha*. Jonathan Swift relates how he made a surprise visit to Robert Harley's house one night to find Harley and William Penn, the Quaker, engrossed in conversation over a flagon of wine. This harmless incident on its own is no evidence, but rumours were circulating at the time, and probably with some credibility, that Pennsylvania was fast becoming a safe haven for pirates who forsook the sea, and it is rumoured that five pirates-turned-planters were in Penn's government there. The suggestion is made that those members of the pirate crews that collaborated with the Crown in the recovery of the various treasures cached in the Nicobars were given the chance to start a new life in the American colonies, where their past would not cause any embarrassment to those in authority. Doubtless a "golden handshake" accompanied this gesture.

Some interesting intermarriages subsequently took place. One of Sloane's daughters married into the Stanley family, and it may be recalled from the previous chapter that Bellomont corresponded with Sir Paul Stanley after Kidd's arrest in Boston. This letter accompanied all the "script that was taken with Kidd," as well as the various testimonies. Thus the logbook of the *Queddah Merchant* may well have been included among this parcel of papers. Robert Harley's granddaughter was to marry into the Bentinck family and become Duchess of Portland. The rest of the known participants in the treasure recovery project, including Queen Anne, were to die without heirs, legitimate or otherwise.

Queen Anne had some disagreeable experiences during her frequent audiences with Robert Harley, and it must be concluded that, because he had been one of the instruments whereby the Queen had been enriched, he felt he could take liberties with his monarch. Though he had an aversion to gambling, which was very much in vogue at the time, he had an addiction to drink, a vice which the Queen found troublesome in one of her senior ministers. When she fired him a few weeks before her own death, she is reputed to have said this of him: that he neglected all business; that he was seldom to be understood; that when he did explain himself she could not depend upon the truth of what he said; that he never came to her at the time she appointed; that he often came drunk; and to crown it all, he behaved himself with bad manners, indecency, and disrespect.

One is left wondering why the Queen put up with him at all, and didn't just dispatch him to the Tower of London to sober up!

It is obvious why Kidd had to die. It was not because he had committed piracy and murder, though being guilty of such crimes is a sufficient justification to mete out the death penalty, but because he had cached an immense wealth in stolen goods and treasure — goods and treasure that other men coveted! Whether these men could be termed pirates, as equally culpable in the eyes of the law as those periodically hanged at Execution Dock, or patriots serving the best interests of the nation is left for the reader to ponder.

After he had been found guilty of murder and piracy, Kidd had written the last plea for his life to Robert Harley, Speaker of the House of Commons. Obviously Kidd thought he recognized in Harley a man who was approachable, sympathetic, compassionate, and hopefully a "square dealer" with whom he could do business and keep a bargain. We don't know how Kidd viewed Harley from his position in the dock at the hearings that preceded the trial or during the trial itself. We might ask ourselves what traits of character we would look for in a judge, if placed in the same predicament where a ruling of guilty carried the sentence of an ignominious and painful death. We must look to the written record for an assessment of Harley's character. Among the Harley Papers in the British Library is an unsigned paper, and in view of its unflattering nature, one wonders why Harley would have kept it. It carries the date Friday, January 9, 1702, and reads:

> I happened to be at The Lamb in Albchurch Lane about 3 or 4 a clock in company with Mr Joyce and 2 other gentlemen, where in discourse I inquired how the King of Sweden did and what truth there was in the discourses that had been lately spread abroad of his being missing; the answer was made by Mr Joyce, that there was a Dutch mail come in this day that brought news that he was safe and well.
>
> Whilst we were talking a gentleman brought word into the house that he heard that the Parliament had voted 20,000 men to be raised, another person in the room made answer, he heard that it was 30,000, at which a person in the company said it was good news, and that he did not doubt but that Parliament would take the effectuall case to oppose the power of France. Mr Joyce replied By what means? For the raising of 20,000 or 30,000 men would do nothing, for that was but shaming the King as the Parliament did by disbanding the army, which was more than a million of money prejudiciall to the nation; and that it was a trick of Harley's, for Robin Harley, the Speaker, is the King's enemy; he is a rascall and has imposed on the nation in severall things, and particularly by demanding 6 shillings a day for the votes, a tax greater than was given to any

Speaker. His father was an old knave, and a rogue, and had ten thousand pounds, for bringing in of King Charles. Robin is a knave and a rogue. I hope to see him hanged for he is the nation's enemy, and the king knows it, and has put out several persons for being concerned with him, particularly Secretary Hedges and Sir George Rook and others of his party. You may believe him to be what you will, but I know him to be a knave, and so does my Lord Somers and Lord Halifax, and I care not if you tell him.

When the political furor concerning the Kidd Affair was at its height in the House of Commons, Harley thundered the following words on December 2, 1699:

Yesterday, in a Committee of the Trade was started a complaint that one Captain Kidd was commander under the Great Seal of England to go against pyrats at Madagascar … That severall great men were to have shares with him, amongst whom the pyrates' goods were to be divided, whereas by law, *they should be returned to the owners* [the author's italics]. This Kidd turned pyrate as he had been before. It is said the Great Seal [Somers] and others are concerned in it.

Kidd was under arrest at Boston at the time Harley took this virtuous position, but it could be expected that he was prepared to compromise his stand by the reality of actually acquiring a portion of the same wealth. Harley's portrait hangs outside the Department of Manuscripts in the British Library. Go — look into his eyes! Is this a man you would trust with your life? Especially if you had a fortune tucked away somewhere!

The reader with a knowledge of the law can probably suggest a number of charges that might be brought against the notable person-ages that we have brought together in our imagination during the course of our detective work. They include piracy, aiding and abetting piracy, fraud, conspiracy, accessory before and after the fact, receipt of stolen goods, and goodness knows what other charges the legal gymnast might derive from the vast array of statutes that the law has at its command. Members of the British Government and its agents in the twentieth century would not be excluded from such legal considerations. However, there does exist a statute of limitations and, since the crime was committed 300 years ago, there is now little need to observe the sensitivities of any Indian government today regarding the theft of the Mogul's treasure. The recovery of the treasure that Kidd cached upon that island in the Indian Ocean would make a great story, and one well worth the retelling. Let us hope that historians and archivists, eager to penetrate the intrigue that shrouds the Kidd treasure, will continue to seek the ultimate truth, and it is hoped that this volume will be of assistance in this search.

As a guide for any further investigations, listings to the whereabouts of some of the papers of the notables who appear to have played a part in the conspiracy may be obtained from the Historical Manuscripts Commission, Chancery Lane, London, an invaluable starting point for such research. In addition, there are the archives of the Public Record Office which, on occasion, yield surprising finds for the tenacious researcher, for it was as late as 1920 that the French passes, so besought by Kidd at the time of his trial, were discovered there. They might have even helped him escape the hangman's noose, to the chagrin of those who had their own selfish reasons for wanting him hanged!

There is no doubt that Kidd committed acts of piracy in the Indian Ocean. Equally, there can be no doubt that he never made a single attempt to live up to the terms of the commission he had been granted by King William to combat piracy in the region. However, the research indicates that he was induced into these reprehensible acts by lords of the realm, men who should have known better than to break the laws of their own nation. By their honeyed words, their cajoling and their wheedles, temptations were created in Kidd's mind that his simple trusting character was unable to dispel. With false assurances from their lordships he was like putty in their hands, and, to their everlasting discredit, they permitted him to be hanged for a crime that was totally alien to his otherwise blameless character. As the Pirate King sings in Gilbert and Sullivan's *Pirates of Penzance* — "Away to the cheating world go you, where all the pirates are well-to-do."

Appendix I

Articles of Agreement Signed at New York for the Voyage of the Adventure Galley

ARTICLES OF AGREEMENT made and concluded upon this tenth day of September Anno Domini 1696 between Captain William Kidd, Commander of the good ship the Adventure Galley, on the one part, and John Walker, Quarter-master to the said ship's company, on the other part, as followeth:

Imprimus   That the above said Capt William Kidd shall receive for the above said ship (Hee finding the said ship in wear and tear) thirtie five shares; as also five full shares for himselfe, & his commission, of such treasure, wares and merchandises as shall from time to time be taken by the said ship & company by sea or land.

2ndly   That the master for his care shall receive two shares of all such treasures, and the Capt shall allow all the other officers a gratification above their owne shares out of the said ships shares as the said Capt or other in his place shall deem reasonable.

3rdly   That the above ships company do oblige themselves to pay out of the first money or merchandise taken for all such provisions as were received on board the said ship in the River of Thames according to the tradesmens bills, and for what provisions the said Wm Kidd shall from time to time purchase for victualling the said shipp and company in America or elsewhere, the said ships company do oblige themselves to pay for the said provisions such advance as shall be demanded by the inhabitants of the places where the said provisions shall be purchased.

4thly   That the said ships company shall out of the first purchase taken after the victualling of the said ship is paid, pay for the surgeon's chest and all ships debts by the said voyage contracted.

5thly   That if any man shall loose an eye, legg or arm or the use thereof in the ship or company service, shall receive as a recompense for the loss thereof six hundred pieces of eight or six able slaves to be paid out of the whole stock before any dividend be made.

6thly   That if any man shall receive a flesh wound or loose a finger or toe in the said ship or company service, he shall receive for smart money one hundred pieces of eight out of the whole stock before any dividend be made.

7thly   That if any man loose his life in time of engagement or by any accident in the ship, or companys service, his share shall be paid to his attorney for the use of his family or friend. And if no purchase twenty pounds out of the stock.

8thly   That man who shall first see a sayle, if she prove to be a prize, shall receive one hundred pieces of eight to be paid out of the whole stock before any dividend be made.

9thly   That whosoever shall disobey command shall loose his share or receive such corporall punishment as the Capt and major part of the company shall think fit.

10thly   That man that is proved a coward in time of engage-
          ment shall loose his share.

11thly   That man that shall be drunk in time of engage-
          ment before the prisoners then taken be secured,
          shall loose his share.

12thly   That man that shall breed a mutiny or ryot on
          board the ship or prize taken shall loose his share,
          and receive such corporall punishment as the Capt
          and major part of the company shall think fitt.

13thly   That if any man shall defraude the Capt or compa-
          ny of any treasure, as money, goods, ware, mer-
          chandise or any other thing whatsoever to the value
          of one piece of eight either on board the man of
          war, prize or prizes taken shall loose his share and
          be put on shore upon the first inhabited island or
          other place that the said ship shall touch at.

14thly   That such men as go on board of any prize taken by
          the said ship, if such prizes should be retaken the
          men notwithstanding shall receive their share of
          what stock is left in the man of war or elsewhere.

15thly   That what money or treasure shall be taken by the
          said ship and company shall be put on board of the
          man of war, and there be shared immediately, and
          all wares and merchandise when legally condemned,
          to be equally divided amongst the ships company
          according to articles.

16thly   That what prizes shall happen to be taken by the
          said ship and company, that shall be found on board
          the said prize that may be convenient for the man
          of warr as anchors, cables, sayles or riggen or other

things needfull and necessary that the man of warr shall be supplyed therewith for the better fitting of her to proceed her voyage.

17thly   That all those that have taken up arms of Capt Wm Kidd as gunns, pistells, cartouche [cartridge] boxes, and cutlasses, shall pay for one gun, one pistell, one cartouche box and one cutlass six pounds, to be paid out of the first money that shall be shared, And the said Capt to find ammunition convenient for the said voyage.

18thly   That the said Capt doth oblige himself to use all proper meanes and take all diligent care to proceed from place to place where he shall think convenient for making himselfe and ships company a voyage, and not to return, want of provisions and other absolute necessities excepted before the said ... be made.

Signed
Wm Kidd

Appendix II

Biographical Details of Kidd's and Culliford's Crews

The brief details given below have been drawn from a variety of sources, some of which are conflicting. They should not therefore be considered conclusive. Many of Kidd's men died on the voyage, many absconded to other vessels, but some remained surprisingly loyal.

JAMES ALGER (or Algeo) — Signed on with Kidd at New York. Was witness to the will of Jan Cornelius whereby Kidd was granted a half of Cornelius's share of the voyage (Sept. 27, 1697).

SAMUEL (or John) **AYERS** (or Arris or Aires) — Steward on the *Adventure Galley*. Signed on with Kidd at London. Remained with Kidd on the *Queddah Merchant* after St. Marie. Arrested in New York and sent to England for trial. Committed to the Marshalsea April 15, 1700. Died in jail.

RICHARD BARLEYCORN — Signed on with Kidd at New York as an apprentice. Served as cabin boy to Kidd. Stayed with Kidd on the *Queddah Merchant* after St. Marie. Arrested in New York and sent for trial in England. Committed to the Marshalsea. At the time of his arrest he was 18 years of age. Testified on behalf of Kidd with regard to the circumstances of Moore's death. Acquitted.

WILLIAM BECK (or Berk/Burke) — An Irishman. Signed on with Kidd at New York. Left the *Queddah Merchant* at St. Thomas.

GEORGE BOLLEN — Signed on with Kidd at New York. Chief mate on the *Adventure Galley*. Took over command of the *Queddah Merchant* after its capture and sailed it to St. Marie.

ROBERT BRADENHAM (or Bradinham) — Signed on with Kidd at New York. In charge of the starboard watch on the *Adventure Galley*. Also ship's surgeon — attended to Moore after Kidd's assault. Joined Culliford's crew at St. Marie. Returned to New York with Giles Shelley in the *Nassau*, landing at Cape May. Was arrested in Pennsylvania and sent for trial in England. Committed to the Marshalsea for piracy on July 12, 1700. Testified against Kidd at his trial.

SAMUEL BRADLEY — Brother-in-law of Kidd. Sailed with Kidd to London on Kidd's ship the *Antigua*. Was with Kidd continuously from 1695 until he was put ashore in St. Thomas, West Indies, in April 1699. Became sick while in the Indian Ocean and never recovered. His will bequeathed everything to Kidd. Believed to have returned to New York and died 1702 or 1703. Some reports suggest he may have died at St. Thomas.

JAMES BROWNE (or John Browne) — Previously sailed with Kidd. Signed on at New York. Joined with Culliford at St. Marie. Returned with Shelley on the *Nassau,* landing at Cape May. Arrested in New York and sent for trial in England. Committed to the Marshalsea July 12, 1700 and granted bail August 19.

EDWARD BUCKMASTER — An ex-mariner who kept a tavern in New York. Signed on with Kidd at New York.

Remained with Kidd on the *Queddah Merchant* after St. Marie, but returned with Shelley in the *Nassau*, landing at Cape May. Was described as being "one of Culliford's men" and reported, during examination following his arrest, that Kidd had not made a good voyage.

JOHN BURDING — One of Culliford's crew. Brought from the East Indies to stand trial for suspicion of piracy. Committed to the Marshalsea August 6, 1700 and granted bail August 19.

MICHAEL CHURCHILL — One of Culliford's crew. Tried for piracy in the taking of the *Great Mahomet*. Found guilty — fate unknown.

NICHOLAS CHURCHILL — Described as being from Lissot, Dorset. Joined Kidd at the Comoro Islands after being marooned by the *East India Merchant*. Sailed with Culliford after St. Marie. Returned with Shelley in the *Nassau*, landing at Cape May. Arrested and sent for trial in England. Committed to the Marshalsea July 12, 1700 and convicted of piracy May 8, 1701. Pardoned on June 20. Rumoured that money was paid to effect his release, and that later he appeared in Pennsylvania with a small fortune in gold. Some years later he was re-arrested in the West Indies and returned to England. Aged 26 years at the time of his trial.

HUMPHREY CLAY — Signed on with Kidd in New York. Returned on the *Queddah Merchant*. Arrested at Boston, managed to escape, but was recaptured.

JAN CORNELIUS — Signed on with Kidd at New York. Bequeathed Kidd a half-share of his proceeds from the voyage in a will dated Sept 27, 1697, witnessed by John Wier (or Wies) and James Alger (or Algeo). Died at sea.

EDWARD DAVIS — A notorious pirate with a long history of buccaneering. His piratical career began in 1683 in the West Indies. Dampier served under him in the Pacific. Returned with Kidd on the *Queddah Merchant* having joined the crew under unusual circumstances, reputedly having been marooned on Madagascar by the master of the *Fidelia*. Was arrested in New York and sent for trial in England, being committed to the Marshalsea on April 15, 1700. Found guilty of piracy but reprieved. Went to Jamaica and resorted to more piracy.

DUNDEE — A black slave. Taken with Kidd and sent to England for trial on suspicion of piracy. Committed to the Marshalsea April 27, 1700. Died in prison.

JOHN ELDRIDGE (or Aldridge) — One of Culliford's crew. Arrested in New York after returning with either Kidd or Shelley. Sent for trial in England and committed to the Marshalsea July 12, 1700 on suspicion of piracy. Granted bail August 19. Found guilty but reprieved.

MICHAEL GALLOWAY (or Calloway) — Signed on with Kidd at New York. Returned on the *Queddah Merchant*.

BENJAMIN FRANKS — Born in 1650. At 46 years of age, the oldest member of Kidd's crew. Came from a Jewish family with interests in the jewellery trade in North America, West Indies, and India. Had operated the family's outlet at Port Royal when the earthquake struck in 1692, reducing him to penury. Signed on with Kidd at New York as far as Surat where his family had trade interests. There is some disagreement whether Franks had to jump ship when the *Adventure Galley* arrived in India, or whether his parting from Kidd was amicable. Later sent to England to give evidence at Kidd's trial.

JOHN HARRIS — Returned with Kidd on the *Queddah Merchant*. Arrested at Boston, escaped, but later recaptured at New York.

ROBERT HICKMAN — One of Culliford's crew. Arrested in New England and sent for trial in England. Committed to the Marshalsea on suspicion of piracy July 12,1700. Granted bail August 14. Later re-arrested and charged with several piracies and robberies while on the *Mocha*. Convicted of piracy on May 8 and pardoned June 20. Released at the same time as Nicholas Churchill and James Howe, and it is rumoured that monies were paid for their release.

JAMES HOWE (or How) — Joined Kidd in London. Signed articles in New York. Sailed with Culliford after St. Marie and returned with Shelley in the *Nassau*. Arrested in New England and sent to England for trial. Committed to the Marshalsea July 12, 1700 for piracy. Convicted of piracy May 8, 1701 but pardoned June 20. Evidence suggests money was paid for his release. Later rumoured to have returned to Pennsylvania (with Nicholas Churchill) with a small fortune in gold.

WILLIAM JENKINS — Apprentice to George Bollen, chief mate on the *Adventure Galley*. Originated from Bow, London, and likely signed on with Kidd at London. Returned on the *Queddah Merchant* and was arrested with Kidd and sent for trial in England. Committed to the Marshalsea April 15, 1700. Aged 18 years at the time of his arrest. Acquitted.

JAMES KELLEY (or Kelly, alias Sampson Marshall, alias James Gillam) — A notorious pirate. Born in Hartlepool, Durham. Commenced his career on West Coast of Africa 1680. Voyaged to Virginia where Dampier joined the crew, took the *Batchelor's Delight* off the Guinea Coast, sailed in the Pacific. Joined with Culliford in the Indian Ocean on the *Mocha*. Returned with Kidd on the *Queddah Merchant*. Captured in Charleston, near Boston, in 1699. Hanged July 12, 1700. Autobiography later published by his widow (see Chapter 14).

ROBERT LANGLEY (or Lamley) — Joined Kidd at London at 12 years of age. Apprentice to Abel Owen, cook. Returned with Kidd on the *Queddah Merchant*. Arrested in New York and sent to England for trial. Committed to the Marshalsea April 15, 1700 for piracy. Acquitted.

GABRIEL LOFF (or Lane) — Signed on with Kidd in New York. Returned with Kidd on the *Queddah Merchant*. Arrested in New York and sent to England for trial. Committed to the Marshalsea April 15, 1700 for piracy. Found guilty but pardoned June 21, 1701. Thirty years of age at time of trial.

JOHN MARTIN — Signed on with Kidd at New York. Returned on the *Queddah Merchant*. Was arrested but escaped by slipping overboard from the warship holding him, HMS *Greyhound*, and stealing the pilot's boat moored alongside. He was not recaptured.

HENRY MEADE — Signed on with Kidd at New York. In charge of larboard (port) watch of *Adventure Galley*. Believed to have died at sea.

WILLIAM MOORE — Gunner. Signed on with Kidd at New York. Died as a result of Kidd's assault of October 30, 1697. Had been ill for some weeks prior to the quarrel.

DARBY MULLINS — Irishman from Londonderry (born 1661). Kidnapped as a young boy and sold into slavery in Jamaica. Regained his freedom and opened a tavern in Port Royal. Subsequently moved to New York. Made several voyages in trading vessels. Wife died while he was at sea. Signed on with Kidd at New York. Transferred to Culliford's crew after St. Marie. Arrested in New York and sent to England for trial. Committed to the Marshalsea July 12, 1700 for piracy. Found guilty of piracy including piracy on the *Great Mahomet*. Hanged at Execution Dock along-side Kidd, May 23, 1701.

JOHN NICHOLAS — Aged 28 years.

ABEL OWEN — Cook on the *Adventure Galley*. Signed on with Kidd at London. Transferred to Culliford's crew after St. Marie. Took part in the attack on the *Great Mahomet*. Returned to St. Marie with Culliford in the *Mocha* (December 12, 1698) then sailed with Shelley in the *Nassau* to Fort Dauphin, Madagascar, where he rejoined Kidd for return voyage on the *Queddah Merchant*. Arrested at Boston, escaped, but was recaptured. Sent to England for trial, but acquitted and pardoned June 21, 1701.

RALPH PADDISON (or Pattison) — Member of Culliford's crew. Brought back from the Indian Ocean with Culliford on board the *Sidney*. Committed to the Marshalsea August 6, 1700, on suspicion of piracy. Granted bail August 19.

JOSEPH PALMER — From Westchester, New York. Originally served on HMS *Duchess*, but was transferred to the *Adventure Galley* after Kidd's non-compliance with naval etiquette on sailing from London. Signed articles with Kidd at New York. Sailed with Culliford after St. Marie. Returned with Shelley on the *Nassau*. Arrested in New York and sent for trial in England. Committed to the Marshalsea April 15, 1700. Testified against Kidd. Aged 32 years at time of arrest. Acquitted.

HUGH PARROTT — From Devon, England. Returned with Kidd on the *Queddah Merchant*. Arrested at New York and sent for trial in England. Committed to the Marshalsea on charges of piracy. Found guilty but pardoned June 23, 1701.

RICHARD ROPER — Arrested in 1699 on board Samuel Burgess's *Margaret* at the Cape of Good Hope. Had previously sailed with Kidd. In possession of £400 at time of his arrest. Believed to have been sent to trial in England alongside Kidd. Found guilty of piracy but reprieved.

VENTURA ROSAIR — A black slave. Taken with Kidd and sent to trial in England. Committed to the Marshalsea April 27, 1700, for piracy. Died in prison.

MARTIN SHRINK — Returned with Kidd on the *Queddah Merchant*. Arrested at Boston, escaped, but recaptured.

JOHN SMITH — Signed on with Kidd at New York. Arrested in 1699 on board Samuel Burgess's *Margaret* at the Cape of Good Hope. In possession of £400 at time of his arrest. Found guilty of piracy but reprieved.

ENGLISH SMITH — Returned with Kidd on the *Queddah Merchant*. Arrested at Boston, escaped, but recaptured. Said to have had a taxable estate worth £5.

STEPHEN SMITH — Arrested 1699 at the Cape of Good Hope on board Samuel Burgess's *Margaret*. Previously sailed with Kidd. In possession of £500 at time of his arrest.

NICHOLAS TURNER — Sailed with Culliford. Participated in the taking of the *Great Mahomet*. Deposition made to the effect that the booty amounted to £130,000.

THEOPHILUS TURNER — Sailed with Culliford. Claimed he saw Kidd's *Adventure Galley* bottom up in the pirate harbour of St. Marie. At the trial of Kidd and the rest of the pirates, he testified against Eldridge. Later pardoned.

HUMPHREY VIELE — Sailed with Kidd. Arrested on board Samuel Burgess's *Margaret* at Cape of Good Hope with £1,100 in his possession. Found guilty of piracy but reprieved.

JOHN WALKER — Quartermaster. Signed on with Kidd in New York.

JOHN WARE (or Wier) — Signed on with Kidd at New York. Returned with Kidd on the *Queddah Merchant*. Arrested and sent for trial in England. Committed to the Marshalsea June 23, 1701.

WILLIAM WHATTLEY (or Weatherly) — Returned with Kidd on the *Queddah Merchant*. Sent to trial in England.

RICHARD WOOD — Returned with Kidd on the *Queddah Merchant*.

Appendix III

Kidd's Backers and Others

HANS WILLEM BENTINCK (1649–1709) — EARL OF PORTLAND

Bentinck was the third son of Count Bernard Bentinck, a Dutch nobleman. He was a year older than William, Prince of Orange, and his service to the prince was unswerving up to his master's death in 1702. He is reported to have been rather handsome with reddish-blond hair, and to have shared William's fondness for field sports and works of art. When William was stricken with smallpox, a virtual death sentence, Bentinck remained at his bedside for 16 days and nights, and it was from his hands alone that William took food and medicine during this period. Bentinck also succumbed to the dreadful disease, but as soon as the peril was over, he joined William on further campaigning. It was in the sickroom that the strongest bonds of friendship were forged between the two men, and it was in the sickroom that their friendship was to end when Bentinck attended the dying William in 1702. After the birth of Bentinck's first son, William was to write: "He will live, I hope, to be as good a fellow as you are; and if I should have a son, our children will love each other, I hope, as we have done."

Such a happy circumstance was never to arise as William had no heir of which he could be justly proud, and to whom he could pass the Crown of England, but he was kind, protective, and devoted to the Bentinck children. The son, Henry, was to succeed his father as Earl of Portland, and later to be created Duke of Portland in 1716. Welbeck Abbey was to become the seat of the Portland family, being acquired in 1734. It is situated a few miles from Worksop, Nottinghamshire, and stands in a vast park which includes some of the old Sherwood Forest.

Bentinck was a man of strict probity when it came to matters of state, especially those involving money. He liked money, of course (who doesn't?), but he never stooped to demean himself by accepting bribes, and many were proffered. His personal friendship with William ensured that he was granted everything that was due to him and, since he was one of the king's most trusted companions, this was in good measure. Patriotism, friendship, and loyalty were prominent in all Bentinck's actions. He was unskilled in the art of flattery, and is said to have created many enemies through his bluntness. As a diplomat he was successful by his personal intercourse with Europeans, without any hint of obsequiousness. He was a brave soldier. Because he was trusted by William, he may have been respected by the English population at large, but he was never liked. It might be said that he was the most hated man in England because of his close attachment to William and his intolerance of cant.

RICHARD COOTE (1636–1702) — EARL OF BELLOMONT

Richard Coote was the only son of Lord Coloony of Ireland, and inherited the title on the death of his father in 1683. He married an heiress from Worcestershire, and in 1688, the year of the revolution against King James, was elected a member of parliament for Droitwich. Later that same year he departed for the continent, where he associated himself with William, Prince of Orange, returning to England with the invasion force. His career thereafter shows he was a vigorous supporter of the new king during the ensuing military campaigns in Ireland. For this he was rewarded by William with the appointment as the governor of County Leitrim and, on November 2, 1689, was created Lord Bellomont. He continued to sit in the House of Commons until 1695, when he was appointed governor of New York.

Richard Coote was not a wealthy individual. His estates in Ireland yielded little revenue, and it must be supposed that, like many of the day, he had an inclination to live beyond his means. His appointment as governor of New York would have ensured him a much-needed additional source of income. He sailed for New York, arriving on April 2, 1698, and was immediately beset with the many problems of colonial government. One of these was the covert support given by the merchants and population at large to piratical adventurism, both at home and overseas. Since Bellomont had attached himself to the cause of combatting piracy on the high seas, he expended a great deal of effort in trying to create order out of what had become a nightmare of illegal activity. To his everlasting credit, Bellomont did make an impact. His greatest accomplishment was to apprehend Kidd on his return to New York, and during the whole of the proceedings thereafter he conducted himself in an exemplary manner.

Lord Bellomont's government in New York was short-lived, as he died on March 5, 1702, less than a year after Kidd had been hanged. He was honoured by a public funeral, and it was said of him that he was "an Irish peer with a kind heart, and honourable sympathies for popular freedom."

ROBERT HARLEY (1661–1724) — EARL OF OXFORD

Harley was born on December 5, 1661, in Bow Street, London. His family held estates in Herefordshire, which included two castles, one at Brampton Bryan and the other at Wigmore. The former had been burned down during the Civil War, some 20 years earlier, under singular circumstances. Harley's grandfather had sided with the Parliamentary forces, and during one of his absences from Brampton Bryan, the king's men attacked and laid siege to the castle. Robert Harley's grandmother valiantly mobilized all the resources available and successfully repelled the besiegers for six weeks, from July to September 1643. The king's men returned six months later and this time they were successful. During the siege, the entire body of defenders were captured, numbering about 70 in all, and a vast number of arms and barrels of gunpowder was seized, along with provisions, which included 500 deer that were slaughtered. The castle was burned and all laid waste. Despite this huge setback to the Harley fortunes, the family flourished during the ensuing Parliamentary period.

Robert Harley was, by nature, a Whig and a Dissenter; i.e., one inclined towards Presbyterianism rather than the established church. He was educated in a number of private schools and he entered into law, but was never called to the bar. During the revolution of 1688, he assisted his father in raising a troop of horse, and entered Worcester in the name of King William III. From this time on, Harley was inextricably entangled in affairs of state. He soon showed an aptitude for politics, in the conduct of which he made friends and enemies on both sides of the House of Commons. His inclinations began to change and he finally broke with his Whig friends and entered fully into Parliamentary debate as the leader of the Tory party. On February 10, 1701, Harley was elected Speaker of the House of Commons, a position for which he was extremely well qualified, having become fully conversant with the minutiae of Parliamentary procedure and an expert practitioner of it.

In 1704 Harley became a member of Queen Anne's privy council and other high appointments followed, including that of Earl of Oxford in 1711. In 1705 he began to indulge himself freely in his passion for collecting rare books. The vast library that he began was enlarged by his son Edward, the second Earl of Oxford, whose daughter married into the Portland family. In 1753 this immense collection of books, antiquarian texts, manuscripts, and letters was sold to Parliament by the second countess and her daughter, the Duchess of Portland, for the very small sum of £10,000. Lady Harley is reputed to have expressed the opinion that she thought the collection to be worth at least £20,000, but when half that figure was tendered, she generously refrained from bargaining for a higher amount.

In 1715 Harley was imprisoned in the Tower of London on accusations of treason in the wrangling related to the succession to the throne. He languished there for almost two years before his name was cleared. Though he re-entered politics he never regained his previous powerful position in affairs of state. He died at his home in Albemarle Street on May 24, 1724, and was buried at Brampton Bryan, in the shadow of the ruined castle so valiantly defended by his grandmother 80 years earlier.

Both Pope and Swift sang his praises, the latter declaring that he was "the most virtuous minister, and the most able, that I ever remember to have read of." But Swift was of the same political persuasion and, furthermore, was a man who knew upon which side his bread was buttered. Others who held him in high esteem considered his greatest fault to be mere vanity, allowing that "his friendship was never to be relied upon, if it interfered with his other designs."

EDWARD RUSSELL (1653–1727) — EARL OF ORFORD

Edward Russell's uncle was the Earl of Bedford (later created Duke). In 1671, at the age of 18, Russell was given a commission and went to sea, being appointed lieutenant on the *Advice*, the same ship that was sent to New England 30 years later to repatriate Kidd to London to face his indictment for piracy and murder. He fought at the Battle of Sole Bay in 1672 on board the *Rupert*, being later promoted to the captaincy of the *Phoenix*. In the Anglo-Dutch Conflict of 1673 he commanded the *Swallow*, of 560 tons and 48 guns, and thus participated in the same actions as Kidd and Dampier, though in a more senior capacity. After these successes he continued in the navy, serving under Sir John Narbrough in the Mediterranean War against the Moors. Other naval appointments followed and he held a succession of commands. However, he quit active service in 1683 after the execution of his cousin, William Russell, on July 21, 1683, following allegations of treason to Charles II, which seem to have had little foundation or merit.

With good reason to be hostile to the Stuart dynasty, Edward Russell became an active agent in plotting its downfall, and he passed many times into Holland engaged in this pursuit. When the revolution finally broke, he accompanied William to England with the invasion force. In April 1689 he was appointed treasurer to the navy, and later that year was promoted to Admiral of the Fleet under Torrington, with whom he seems to have had an uneasy relationship. When Torrington was found guilty of failing to come to grips with the French during the Battle of Beachy Head in July 1690, Russell was again promoted.

By May 1692 the combined English and Dutch fleets held an overwhelming supremacy over the French in the English Channel. In using information as soon as it became available, and deploying his ships expeditiously, Russell managed to bring the French to account, firstly at Barfleur, and then a week later at La Hogue. The French were hopelessly outmanned and outgunned by the Allied fleet, on a scale of more than two to one, and the outcome was predictable.

Notwithstanding the impressive victories at Barfleur and La Hogue, there was a feeling within the British government that more could have been done to remove the French menace from the high seas. Though Russell had "behaved with courage, fidelity, and conduct," he was censured and dismissed from his command, but after the disaster of Lagos (1693) he was reinstated, and in May 1694 he was appointed First Lord of the Admiralty. In 1695 he was in the Mediterranean attempting to combat perceptions of French hostility, but in the autumn returned and was to see no further service at sea. Until his death in 1727 Russell was involved in politics, representing various constituencies: Launceston (1689), Portsmouth (1690), and Cambridgeshire (1695). In May 1697 he was created Earl of Orford. In 1691 he married a cousin, but left no issue.

Russell is described as "of sanguine complexion, inclining to be fat; of a middle stature." This description belittles somewhat a man who during his career had seen a great deal of active service with commensurate responsibilities. His preparedness to face dangers of political antagonism to the former King James, and his readiness to face shot and shell in battle with the enemy, are suggestive that in Russell we have a man unafraid of accepting personal responsibility.

His character is summed up by Macaulay in his *History of England*. Macaulay writes:

The name of Russell acted as a spell on all who loved English freedom. The name of La Hogue acted as a spell on all who were proud of the glory of the English arms … but the fame of his exploits had lost their gloss; people in general were quick to discern his faults: and his faults were but too discernible … His arrogant, insolent and quarrelsome temper, made him an object of hatred. His vast and growing wealth made him an object of envy. What his official merits and demerits really were it is not easy to discover through the mist made up of factious abuse and factious panegyric. One set of writers described him as the most ravenous of all the plunderers of the poor overtaxed nation. Another set asserted that under him the ships were better built and rigged, the crews were better disciplined and better tempered, the biscuit was better, the beer was better, the slops were better than under any of his predecessors; and yet that the charge to the public was less than it had been when the vessels were unseaworthy, when the sailors were riotous, when the food was alive with vermin, when the drink tasted like tanpickle, and when the clothes and hammocks were rotten. It may, however, be observed that these two representations are not inconsistent with each other: and there is strong reason to believe that both are, to a great extent, true. Orford was covetous and unprincipled; but he had great professional skill and knowledge, great industry, and a strong will. He was therefore an useful servant to the state when the interests of the state were not opposed to his own: and this was more than could be said of some who preceded him. …When Orford had nothing to gain by doing what was wrong, he did what was right, and did it ably and diligently.

HENRY SIDNEY (1641–1704) —
EARL OF ROMNEY

Henry Sidney was the fourth and youngest son of the Earl of Leicester. He was 19 years younger than his elder brother, the well-known Algernon Sidney, who held Henry in low esteem. Inter-sibling rivalries are commonplace, but such feelings from an older brother towards a younger, across a span of 19 years, suggests a lack of moral fibre in the younger as perceived through the eyes of the older.

Henry Sidney was his mother's favourite, as youngest children often are, and after her death in 1659, when he was 18 years of age, he inherited a small estate. The next few years saw him travelling on the continent, but following his return in 1664, he was favoured by James, then Duke of York. He became involved in a number of romantic intrigues, and took some personal satisfaction in cuckolding men in their own homes. One of these men is likely to have been the Duke of York himself! Scandal was never far removed from Sidney and in later years he was beset by continuous claims from his numerous illegitimate offspring.

King Charles bore no ill-will towards Sidney for the romantic assaults upon his brother's wife, and might have shown sympathy towards him, but nevertheless he took the precaution of removing him from England for a period. Sidney spent the next few years on the continent, either as an emissary or in the army, where he rose to the rank of colonel of a regiment of foot. In 1679 he returned to England, entered politics, and represented Bramber in Sussex.

Sidney may have been obtuse in many respects, but he was to become a wily political animal. While in Holland, he had come to the conclusion that the odds were very much in favour of William, Prince of Orange succeeding to the English throne. He gained William's confidence and discreetly associated himself with those partisan to the prince's cause. The more obtuse Charles appointed him to serve as general in charge of certain British regiments then in the service of Holland. Sidney held this post from 1681 until a few weeks after the accession to the throne by James II, the new king obviously not having forgotten, or forgiven, Sidney for the invasion of his own bedroom. For a couple of years Sidney kept himself well out of harm's way, once again on the continent and only returning in early 1688, the year of the revolution. We have no knowledge of Sidney's romantic conquests while in Holland, but immediately after his return to England he took a shine to his nephew's wife!

Sidney vigorously allied himself with the revolutionary cause, and possessed as he was with a zeal for intrigue, no doubt honed to a rare degree by his fascination with other men's wives, committed himself to the advancement of William's cause. Unknown to those more loyal to King James, he was instrumental in gathering together some of the greatest men in England as secret allies of William. One of the most prominent of these was Edward Russell. Also associating himself with this treasonable group was Charles Talbot, Duke of Shrewsbury.

It was Sidney who went to The Hague in July 1688, vowing loyalty to William and bearing the invitation for him to assume the Crown of England signed by many of the English notables of the day. The signatures to this traitorous document included those of Edward Russell and the Duke of Shrewsbury, as well as his own. Sidney, Russell, and Shrewsbury were to return with the invasion force the following November. As a consequence of his part in the revolution, Sidney was created Earl of Romney.

There is some disagreement among historians as to the importance that Sidney played in the revolution against King James. One commentator has declared that he was "the great wheel upon which the revolution turned." Jonathan Swift stated that "he had not a wheel to turn a mouse and, as for his character, he had none at all." There were many that denigrated Sidney, and their motives are likely to have been various, and for some, deeply personal. After all, a man who targets other men's wives for personal satisfaction, and possesses the skill to evade being called to account in a duel, is likely to attract many enemies. However, he appears to have been a tactful diplomat, and one who loved intrigue in whatever form it manifested itself. The *Dictionary of National Biography* sums up his character in the following words:

... pleasure-loving though he was, he had an exceptionally square head where his own interests were concerned, and a decided gift for conciliating people who were irritated against him. He had no scruples about taking advantage of his good looks.

Until William's death he was favoured with high appointments, but following the accession of Queen Anne, he relinquished his positions. He died, unmarried, on April 8, 1704, after contracting smallpox.

HANS SLOANE (1660–1753) — PHYSICIAN

Hans Sloane was born at Killileagh, Co. Down, the seventh son of a receiver-general of taxes. At the age of 16 he suffered from haemoptysis, and as a result of this illness he refrained from drinking alcohol and adopted temperate habits for the rest of his life. He studied medicine in France and was elected Fellow of the Royal Society in 1685, being admitted to the College of Physicians two years later. That same year (1687) he sailed with Christopher Monck, Duke of Albemarle, to Jamaica as personal physician to the duke and duchess, and it was here that the duke died of jaundice, either as a result of disease or as a consequence of his excessive drinking. His death on October 16, 1688 was just a few weeks before William, Prince of Orange, landed at Torbay.

Sloane remained in Jamaica with the duchess, engaged on various botanical and related studies, which were later published in a monumental work known as *The Natural History of Jamaica*. Together with the duchess, he returned to London in May 1689, bringing with him over 800 species of plants. Under the duchess's patronage Sloane acquired many wealthy and influential clients, and by 1695 had established a permanent practice in Bloomsbury, the most expensive and fashionable area at the time.

Honours were deservedly showered upon Hans Sloane, and in 1693 he was appointed secretary of the Royal Society, later being elected as president in 1727, following the death of Sir Isaac Newton. He wrote many papers, mostly concerning his professional opinions on aspects of medicine, botany, and allied topics relating to natural history. He became an avid collector, gathering together anything that one might describe as collectible. His library was almost as extensive as his other collections and, after its donation to the British Museum on his death in 1753, it was many years before an intensive effort was made to catalogue all the items. His vast number of manuscripts, books, maps, engravings, and other precious artifacts thus became the responsibility of the various departments of the museum.

Queen Anne first consulted Sloane in 1701, and thereafter he attended Prince George of Denmark, the consort of the queen. In 1716 he was appointed a baronet, and in 1727 he was made King's Physician in Ordinary to George II. Sloane was to die a very rich man, with his collections considered to be the largest in the world, being listed in 38 volumes, the total inventory amounting to 200,000 items. His will, bequeathing his collections to the nation for a meagre £20,000 to be paid to his family, represents a handsome gift, of which English-speaking nations, through the British Museum, can be justly proud.

JOHN SOMERS (1651–1716) — LORD HIGH CHANCELLOR

John Somers came from a family of small landed gentry in Worcestershire. He was well educated in various schools, including the school of Worcester Cathedral, and subsequently went to Oxford where, though he did not graduate, he became accomplished in languages, and was later admitted to the bar in 1676. Thereafter he devoted himself to civil and constitutional law with a view to entering politics. Somers' role in the revolution of 1688 has often been downplayed, but during the much-publicized trial of the seven bishops, his skill in their defence was adroit and led to their acquittal. The publicity and rancour surrounding this trial led to the departure of Sidney to the Hague to deliver the invitation for William to undertake his invasion of England.

Following the revolution Somers entered the House of Commons, being returned as the member for Worcester. It should be noted that Bellomont, being the member for the neighbouring constituency of Droitwich, thus sat in the House of Commons at the same time, and being neighbours they likely shared a lot of common interests and concerns. On October 31, 1689, Somers was knighted by King William, and from then on, through his devotion to the king's interests, he rose to the position of Lord High Chancellor in April 1697, and was finally elevated to the peerage the following December. Thus, at the time he became involved as a backer of Kidd's venture to the Indian Ocean, Somers was a bright and aspiring lawyer and statesman who held the confidence of many, including the king himself.

When the Kidd affair broke it proved to be a great embarrassment to Somers, and the Tory opposition agitated for his impeachment and removal. Though he resisted these motions, his health was shattered by the long and tedious battles he had fought in politics and law, and he did eventually retire. On the accession of Queen Anne, he was excluded from those positions he had managed to regain, proving to be totally unacceptable to the new monarch. She preferred to follow advice in such matters as tendered by that consummate of all politicians of the age, Robert Harley. Somers died of paralysis at his Hertfordshire home in April 1716. He was unmarried.

The *Dictionary of National Biography* says this about his character:

> Courtly and reserved by nature or habit, Somers carried into the relations of ordinary life a certain formality of demeanour, but in his hours of relaxation could be an agreeable companion. It does not appear that he was a brilliant talker, but his vast erudition and knowledge of affairs placed him at ease with men of the most diverse interests and occupations. ... His domestic life did not escape the breath of scandal ... On the other hand his sagacity, indus-

try, and disinterestedness are undeniable; his motto, "Prodesse quam conspici," was no idle boast, and only once towards the close of his career … did he dally with faction.

CHARLES TALBOT (1660–1718) — DUKE OF SHREWSBURY

Charles Talbot had the unique honour of having King Charles II as his godfather and being named after the king, following the restoration of the monarchy. His father had married a second time and his mother had a paramour, George Villiers, Duke of Buckingham. This romantic attachment led to a duel being fought between Charles's father and the duke, a contest of honour which cost the father his life. It is alleged that Charles's mother was present at this fatal scene, attired as a page holding her lover's horse. Thereafter she continued her relationship with Buckingham before going on to marry someone else. Charles Talbot was only eight years old at the time, and the violent circumstances of his father's death, and the fact that his younger brother was later killed in a duel (1686), is considered by many to have affected his character. Throughout his life he was plagued with health problems, being also psychologically affected to some degree because of a blemish in one eye, which some considered "offensive to look upon." Nevertheless, he carried himself with grace and dignity.

Though Talbot was a strong supporter of the Stuart dynasty, he became increasingly concerned about James II and his designs to subvert English law. In 1687 he boldly attached himself to the cause of William, Prince of Orange, and permitted his house to be used as a rendezvous for those plotting against the king. He crossed to Holland with Edward Russell to join the army that William was gathering to invade England. To show his zeal for William's cause he mortgaged his estates for the sum of £40,000, lodging £12,000 cash in Amsterdam.

After the revolution, at only 28 years of age, Talbot was awarded high office, becoming Privy Councillor, Secretary of State, and Bearer of the Royal Seals. In 1694 he was created a Knight of the

Garter, and the earldom he had inherited from his father was exchanged for a dukedom. In the absence of the king he was generally regarded as head of the administration. High political office was not without its problems, and various controversies made Talbot's life difficult. Eventually he resigned on grounds of ill health. At the time when Bellomont was touting his scheme to combat pirates in the Indian Ocean, Talbot was a man of great influence in the affairs of state, and obviously would have had the ready ear of King William himself.

After retirement in 1700, made at the time the Kidd affair was breaking, Talbot left for the continent where he remained for many years. There is an extract from a much-quoted letter that he wrote to Somers in June 1701, which best sums up politics from his own cynical experience. He writes: "How any man who has bread in England will be concerned with business of state. Had I a son, I would sooner bind him a cobbler than a courtier, and a hangman than a statesman."

After marrying the daughter of the Marquis of Bologna, who has been described as ignorant, flighty, and ill-bred, he returned to England in 1707 and was persuaded by the wily Robert Harley to enter the Tory administration. He died at Isleworth, Middlesex in February 1718. His wife survived him another eight years. Although a man of grace and dignity, whom Jonathan Swift described as "the favourite of the nation," he often lacked resolve and was easily led along paths that were not necessarily to his own advantage.

References

Anon. *The Andaman and Nicobar Islands*. Calcutta: Superintendent of Government Printing, 1908.

Abbott, John S.C. *Captain William Kidd, and others of the pirates or buccaneers who ravaged the seas, and the continents of America two hundred years ago*. London: Ward Lock & Co, 1880.

Atkins, John. *A Voyage to Guinea, Brazil and the West Indies*. London: Frank Cass & Co, 1970. First published 1735.

Bonner, William H. *Pirate Laureate: The Life and Legends of Captain Kidd*. Rutgers University Press, 1947.

Botting, Douglas. *The Pirates*. Virginia: Time-Life Books, 1978.

Brooks, Graham, ed. *The Trial of Captain Kidd*. London: William Hedges, 1930.

Bryant, Arthur. *Samuel Pepys: The Years of Peril*. London: The Reprint Society, 1952. First published 1935.

Cordingley, David. *Under the Black Flag*. Florida: Harcourt Brace & Co, 1996.

Dalton, Cornelius N. *The Real Captain Kidd*. London: William Heinemann, 1911.

Dampier, William. *Dampier's Voyages*. Ed. by John Masefield. London: E.Grant Richards, 1906.

Dampier, William. *A New Voyage Around the World*. Ed. by Sir Albert Gray. London: Argonaut Press, 1927.

Earle, Peter. *The Treasure of the Concepción*. New York: Viking Press, 1980. First published as *The Wreck of the Almiranta*. London: 1979.

Edmunds, George. *Kidd — The Search for His Treasure*. Bishop Auckland, Durham: Pentland Press, 1996.

Ellms, Charles. *The Pirates*. New York: Gramercy Books, 1996. First published as *The Pirates' Own Book*. Boston: 1937.

Esquemeling, John. *The Buccaneers of America*. New York: Dover Publications, 1967. First published as *De Americaeneche Zee Roovers*. Amsterdam: 1678.

Furneaux, Rupert. *Money Pit: The Mystery of Oak Island*. London and Toronto: Fontana Books, 1976. First published as *The Money Pit Mystery: The Costliest Treasure Hunt Ever*. London: Tom Stacey, 1972.

Gosse, Philip. *The Pirates' Who's Who*. New York: Burt Franklin, 1968.

Harris, Graham, and Les MacPhie. *Oak Island and its Lost Treasure*. Halifax: Formac Publishing, 1999.

Harris, John, ed. *A Compleat Collection of Voyages and Travels: Consisting of above Four Hundred of the Most Authentick Writers*. (2 vols). Private publication, 1705.

Harris, Peter R. *A History of the British Museum Library 1753–1973*. The British Library, 1998.

Hinrichs, Dunbar M. *The Fateful Voyage of Captain Kidd*. New York: Bookman Associates, 1955.

Howlett, Anthony D. "The Mystery of Captain Kidd's Treasure." *Wide World Magazine*, October 1958.

Johnson, Capt. Charles. *A General History of the Robberies and Murders of the Most Notorious Pirates*. London: Conway Maritime Press, 1998. First printed 1724.

Leslie, Sir Stephen, and Sir Sidney Lee, ed. *Dictionary of National Biography* (22 vols). London: Oxford University Press, 1885–1901.

Macaulay, Thomas B. *The History of England* (5 vols). Boston: Aldine Publishing.

Montagu, Ewen. *The Man Who Never Was*. Philadelphia: J.B.Lippincott, 1954.

Montgomerie, H.S. "The Nicobar Islands," *The Geographical Journal*, Royal Geographical Society, London, 1922.

Ritchie, Robert C. *Captain Kidd and the War Against the Pirates.* Cambridge, Massachusetts: Harvard University Press, 1986.

Seitz, Don C., ed. *The Tryal of Captain William Kidd for Murther and Piracy.* New York: R.R.Wilson, 1936.

Swift, Jonathan. *Gulliver's Travels.* Ware, Hertfordshire: Wordsworth Editions, 1992. First published 1726.

Wild, Antony. *The East India Company: Trade and Conquest from 1600.* London: HarperCollins, 1999.

Wilkins, Harold T. *Captain Kidd and His Skeleton Island.* London: Cassell and Co, 1935.

Woodhall, Edwin T. *Captain Kidd — Old Time Pirate.* London: 1938.

Index